PRAISE FOR *DOCUMENTING COMMUNISM*

"Charles Palm did the world a tremendous service by having the vision to seize the moment after the collapse of the Soviet Union to secure a truly unique archive about how the Communist Party ruled the Soviet Union. Scholars, including perhaps most importantly scholars from Russia, will be using these materials for many decades. Reading at times like an action thriller, *Documenting Communism* tells the incredible story of how Charles did it. It's a fantastic story."

—Michael McFaul, *director, Freeman Spogli Institute for International Studies, professor of political science, and Peter and Helen Bing Senior Fellow, Hoover Institution, Stanford University; and former US ambassador to Russia*

"For twelve years, Charles Palm led the Hoover Institution's Soviet archives project, a major effort to microfilm and make accessible the records of the Gulag, of the secret police, and of other repressive institutions. His memoir records what it took to pull off this archival feat, transmitting the excitement of an international collaboration that profoundly affected scholarship and helped render history's judgment on a dangerous, pathological ideology."

—Anne Applebaum, *author of numerous works on Soviet and Russian history, including Pulitzer Prize winner* Gulag: A History; *senior fellow, Johns Hopkins School of Advanced International Studies; and staff writer for* The Atlantic

"This well-written, informative book provides a fascinating account of how the Hoover Institution negotiated and carried out an immense project to microfilm Soviet-era records at formerly closed archives in Moscow. Despite all the vexing obstacles and disruptions that arose amid the turbulence in Russia in the 1990s, Hoover managed to bring the project to fruition. The success of the venture is due in large part to Charles Palm, who conceived of and led the project for Hoover. His memoir of that period will be of great interest to scholars who have done research in the Russian archives and also to anyone who wants a better understanding of Russian politics and archival affairs during the first decade after the disintegration of the Soviet Union."

—Mark Kramer, *director of Cold War studies, Harvard University*

"In the turbulent 1990s, as Russians stumbled into life after Communism, the secret archives of Communist rule were opened. Charles Palm led a mission to copy and preserve them for both Russia and the world. The achievement was literally historic. This book tells the fascinating, at times gripping, story."

—Mark Harrison, *emeritus professor of economics, University of Warwick*

"Charles Palm provides a rare firsthand account of the opening of the Soviet Union's archives, previously hidden behind an Iron Curtain that was supposed to last. Against considerable odds, Palm pulled off one of the most complex and successful coups in modern national-archives history. In all, some ten million pages were microfilmed and made available to researchers. The documents include such holy grails as the archives of the Central Committee, the Gulag administration, and the Party Control Commission; and Fond 89, containing records prepared for a trial of the Communist Party. The archives describe a cruel system, heavily reliant on repression, violence, and propaganda, and a justice system that pitted the state against the individual. They extol the principle of a supreme individual or a politburo whose orders, irrational or wise, are to be followed, no questions asked. Most of all, we learn from the archives that the Soviet social, political, and economic system could not compete with Western democracies."

—Paul R. Gregory, *research fellow, Hoover Institution, and Cullen Professor Emeritus, University of Houston*

DOCUMENTING COMMUNISM

DOCUMENTING COMMUNISM

THE HOOVER PROJECT TO MICROFILM AND PUBLISH THE SOVIET ARCHIVES

Charles G. Palm

HOOVER INSTITUTION PRESS
STANFORD UNIVERSITY | STANFORD, CALIFORNIA

With its eminent scholars and world-renowned library and archives, the Hoover Institution seeks to improve the human condition by advancing ideas that promote economic opportunity and prosperity while securing and safeguarding peace for America and all mankind. The views expressed in its publications are entirely those of the authors and do not necessarily reflect the views of the staff, officers, or Board of Overseers of the Hoover Institution.

hoover.org

Hoover Institution Press Publication No. 729

Hoover Institution at Leland Stanford Junior University, Stanford, California 94305-6003

Cover art: (*top*) "Eshche vyshe znamia leninizma - znamia mezhdunarodnoi proletarskoi revoliutsii," N. Kochergin, 1932, Poster RU/SU 2309, Poster Collection, Hoover Institution Library & Archives; (*bottom*) photo of document folders in archives storage cabinets by Charles Chadwyck-Healey; (*background*) photo of archival documents by Charles Chadwyck-Healey

First printing 2024
30 29 28 27 26 25 24   7 6 5 4 3 2 1

Manufactured in the United States of America
Printed on acid-free, archival-quality paper

Library of Congress Cataloging-in-Publication Data
Names: Palm, Charles G., author. | Rice, Condoleezza, 1954- writer of foreword.
Title: Documenting communism : the Hoover project to microfilm and publish the Soviet archives / Charles G. Palm.
Other titles: Hoover project to microfilm and publish the Soviet archives | Hoover Institution Press publication ; 729.
Description: Stanford, California : Hoover Institution Press, [2024] | Series: Hoover Institution Press publication ; no. 729 | Includes bibliographical references and index. | Summary: "A memoir of the project to microfilm and publish ten million pages of Soviet Archives, bringing worldwide access to a Russian history that had been closed for nearly a century"—Provided by publisher.
Identifiers: LCCN 2023058825 (print) | LCCN 2023058826 (ebook) | ISBN 9780817925550 (paperback) | ISBN 9780817925567 (epub) | ISBN 9780817925581 (pdf)
Subjects: LCSH: Federal'noe arkhivnoe agentstvo (Russia) | Hoover Institution on War, Revolution, and Peace. | Archival materials—Soviet Union—Reproduction. | Documents on microfilm—International cooperation. | Communism—Soviet Union—History—Sources. | Soviet Union—Politics and government—Sources.
Classification: LCC CD1713 .P35 2024 (print) | LCC CD1713 (ebook) | DDC 320.53/2209—dc23/eng/20240131
LC record available at https://lccn.loc.gov/2023058825
LC ebook record available at https://lccn.loc.gov/2023058826

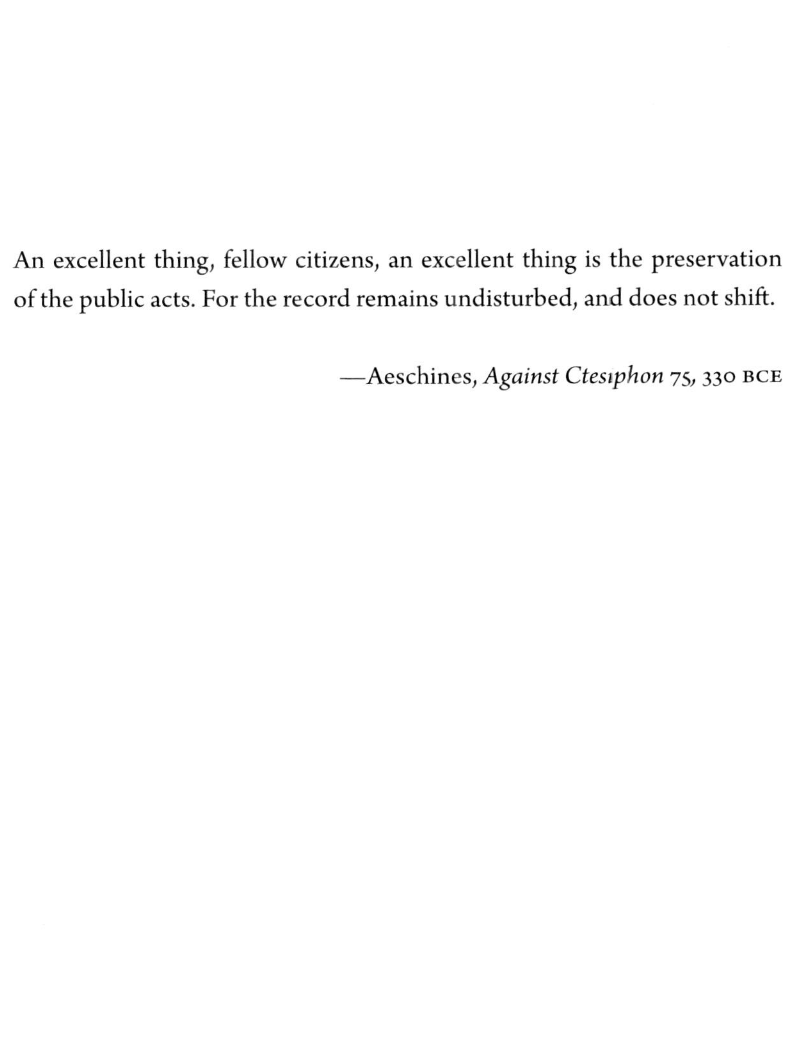

An excellent thing, fellow citizens, an excellent thing is the preservation of the public acts. For the record remains undisturbed, and does not shift.

—Aeschines, *Against Ctesiphon* 75, 330 BCE

CONTENTS

FOREWORD

Charles Palm's memoir detailing his leadership and determination to gain access to materials of the Soviet Archives is also the story of the enduring mission of the Hoover Institution's Library & Archives, and it reminds us of the value of preserving the past to guide us to a better future.

In the winter of 1914–15, while steaming across the English Channel on his way to bring humanitarian relief to war-torn Europe, Herbert Hoover read the autobiography of historian Andrew D. White. In his book, White noted the importance of primary-source materials for his study of the French Revolution. Hoover realized that he himself was witness to another fateful historical event—the Great War then raging across Europe—and was in a unique position to collect the documents and fugitive literature it generated. By studying such material, he reasoned, mankind might come to a better understanding of the causes of war and thus find ways to promote peace. With this insight, Herbert Hoover founded the institution that bears his name.

Since its beginning in 1919, the Hoover Institution and its Library have remained faithful to the vision of its founder. Incorporating coverage of new historical periods and responding to new opportunities, the Hoover Library evolved from a small collection of documentation on World War I to a comprehensive research repository covering the history of war, revolution, and peace from the beginning of the twentieth century to the present time. Today, the Hoover Institution Library & Archives is widely recognized as one of the world's great collections, serving not only the students and faculty at Stanford University, of which it is a part, but the entire global community of scholars.

Hoover's core collections have been built with a singular focus on primary-source materials—internal records of organizations and governments, manuscripts and papers of individuals, underground and dissident literature, issuances of political parties and political action groups, posters, pamphlets, leaflets, and other fugitive materials. These are the kinds of materials that, if not collected promptly when they appear, can disappear forever. Such collections do not walk in the front door. Their acquisition requires special methods—frequent trips abroad; networks of collecting agents; cash purchases from street vendors; direct contacts with individuals and organizations involved in political, social, or economic change; and, most importantly, enterprising archival collectors.

Throughout the Hoover Institution's history, its curators, archivists, and librarians have taken up positions on the front lines of wartime upheaval and in the back alleys of revolutionary change, gathering up materials during brief windows of opportunity and saving them from oblivion. Notable examples of enterprising collecting efforts abound. In 1919, Stanford professor Ephraim D. Adams assembled a team of young scholars in Paris from General Pershing's American Expeditionary Forces; by 1921 they had collected eighty thousand items of material. In 1921, Hoover curator Frank Golder went to Soviet Russia and gathered up the records of the last days of tsarist Russia and the early revolutionary years. In 1939, as war once again approached, Hoover director Ralph Lutz carried from Berlin the last shipment of anti-Nazi materials, including the papers of German Communist Party leader Rosa Luxemburg. Between 1945 and 1947, Stanford professor Hubert Schenck assembled three hundred boxes of material in occupied Japan. After the fall of the Berlin Wall in 1989, Hoover curator Maciej Siekierski spent two years in Warsaw collecting two and a half tons of material on the end of communism and the transition to democracy in Eastern Europe.

No collecting initiative has better exemplified the mission of the Hoover Institution Library & Archives than its project to microfilm the archives of the Soviet Communist Party and Soviet State. Charles Palm's memoir, *Documenting Communism*, tells the story of this historic enterprise, when, from 1991 to 2002, as Hoover's deputy director, he initiated and led efforts to produce microfilm of ten million pages of documents from the Soviet Archives, then newly opened.

The mission required gaining the trust of Russian archivists, putting together a winning bid against worldwide competition, raising the necessary financial support, and assuming a responsible role in opening up a century of secret archives. Palm assembled a team to make it work, and he managed technical and communication difficulties among three partners across three continents. Facing down suspicious critics, struggling against the political setbacks of the Russian partner, and riding the wave of hurt national pride in a country with a tragic history were all part of a challenge successfully met.

Palm's story is manifold in its significance: It records an important episode in the history of the Hoover Institution. It shows how the Russians opened their secret archives and confronted their past, and how they reacted to the values and practices cascading in on them from the West. It reveals the challenges of undertaking an international partnership in a difficult environment. It points to future opportunities for scholarly research on Soviet Communism and the system it created. And it offers inspiration to future archivists at the Hoover Institution and elsewhere to save historical records endangered by war and revolution and, in the process, enable historians who may, in the words of Herbert Hoover, "recall the voice of experience against the making of war . . . and man's endeavors to make and preserve peace."

Condoleezza Rice
Tad and Dianne Taube Director
Hoover Institution

ACKNOWLEDGMENTS

The project to microfilm the Soviet Archives described in this book involved the work of dozens of donors, administrators, archivists, librarians, historians, lawyers, technicians, and others in three countries. I attribute the success of the project largely to their talents, skills, and perseverance. I identify all of them in the book and acknowledge them here with my warm thanks.

The publication of this book was made possible by the Hoover Institution, beginning with its director, Condoleezza Rice. Her support for the project as Stanford's provost during the 1990s and for the publication of this book now as director is greatly appreciated and reflects her continuing devotion to the Hoover Institution Library & Archives, which has thrived under her direction. I give special thanks to Eric Wakin, deputy director of the Hoover Institution and director of its Library & Archives, and Christopher S. Dauer, Hoover's chief external relations officer. It was their encouragement that led me to transform a memoir for the record into a book they thought worthy of publication.

Stephen Kotkin was among the very first to see the value of writing an account of the Hoover project. His inducement, first given some years ago, kept returning to my mind until finally I followed his advice and put it all down on paper. As an enthusiastic user and supporter of the Library & Archives over several decades and a distinguished historian of Russian history, Professor Kotkin was the ideal person to write the book's introduction. His insights are a valuable guide to the reader. For all these contributions I give my appreciation and thanks.

This book is best read alongside another account of the project written by Charles Chadwyck-Healey, entitled "Red Archives" and included in the appendix. I thank him for his permission to include it. While our experiences and views were similar, his unique perspective as a publisher and project partner helps to complete the story. I also thank him for granting permission to publish several of his photographs. How fortunate we were that he always carried with him a camera or two, which he used with such skill.

Several colleagues and friends generously took the time to read my memoir and offered valuable advice, which led to many improvements. They are Charles Chadwyck-Healey, John F. Cogan, Christopher S. Dauer, Terence Emmons, Judith Fortson, Paul R. Gregory, Jana Howlett, Stephen Kotkin, Mark Kramer, George H. Nash, Bertrand M. Patenaude, Dena Schoen, and Eric Wakin. I am grateful to all of them for their help and support.

Others helped me in specific ways. They include Roger Mertz and Bruce Sanford for professional advice on publication questions; Elena Danielson, Hoover archivist emerita, who gave support to my efforts and made her institutional records available to me; Anatol Shmelev, Hoover's Robert Conquest Curator for the Russia and Eurasia Collections, who helped me select the illustrative documents and answered numerous questions from Russian sources; Lora Soroka, archival specialist at Hoover, now retired, who helped clarify issues relating to the "Checklist of Microfilmed Records" and whose guides describe the records; Michael S. Bernstam, Hoover research fellow, who tracked down information on Russian salaries and exchange rates; Carol A. Leadenham, assistant archivist for the Hoover Archives, now retired, for her list of publications based on the microfilm collection; and Sarah Patton and her team, who assisted me with access to the project records and verified the reel count for every record group and series of the microfilm collection. I thank them all.

The staff at the Hoover Institution Press were immensely helpful in bringing my manuscript to publication. I am grateful especially to Barbara M. Arellano, head of the press, Danica Michels Hodge for her patient and expert editorial management, Barbara Egbert and Mike Iveson for editorial assistance, and Alison Law for her stewardship of the manuscript through design and publication.

Finally, I wish to record here my thanks to Miriam Palm, my spouse, who kept the printer and laptop working, scanned numerous documents, used her library reference skills to find answers to countless questions, and gave encouragement and valued advice throughout.

INTRODUCTION

Charles Palm performed a public service on behalf of scholars and researchers by fulfilling one of Herbert Hoover's loftiest hopes for the institution he founded. This book tells that story—engagingly, judiciously, and resolutely.

The achievements of America's then future president in founding and funding what began as the Hoover War Library at Stanford, and is now the Hoover Institution, have been well told by biographers and chroniclers—most importantly by George Nash in *Herbert Hoover and Stanford University*. In a nutshell, Herbert Hoover succeeded in realizing much more than his original idea in 1919 of a "documentary history bearing on the war" to make and preserve peace. He set in motion arguably the greatest private repository in the world for the study of military conflict, revolution, tyranny, and freedom. Current holdings include hundreds of thousands of rare books, nearly full runs of scarce periodicals, hundreds of thousands of rare photographs, exceptional posters, and more than six thousand archival collections, in sixty-nine languages from more than one hundred fifty countries. The surpassing quality of the collections renders them singular. Mr. Palm inherited and, through ingenuity and guile, enhanced this extraordinary legacy, administering the Library & Archives variously for eighteen years, the last twelve as the Hoover Institution's deputy director.

Mr. Palm took over from John Dunlop, a veteran user of the Library & Archives and prescient scholar who plumbed the obscure depths of Russian nationalism under the Soviet regime long before other scholars understood that it existed. On Mr. Palm's watch, the Berlin Wall and then the Soviet imperium fell, a disorienting moment that he transformed into a propitious one. Instead of celebrating Herbert Hoover's vindication, for which he had every right, Mr. Palm moved to reenergize Hoover's archival enterprise. Indeed, even before the momentous events transpired, he had perceived a historic opportunity and had begun to make inroads and map out a vision. This quintessential "uncommon man"—to use a favorite turn of phrase from Mr. Hoover—found fortune in a partner on the other side of the Iron Curtain: Rudolf G. Pikhoia, the accomplished historian of eighteenth-century Russia and a member of Russian leader Boris Yeltsin's entourage that came to Moscow from the Urals in the mid-1980s. Dr. Pikhoia headed up the archives of the Russian Soviet Federative Socialist Republic (RSFSR), one of the fifteen constituent republics of the Union of Soviet Socialist Republics (USSR), and soon he became the newly appointed head of the archival administration of independent Russia. Russia's government laid claim to Soviet state property in the capital of Moscow, including the archives of the Soviet Communist Party. Forging and sustaining a relationship of mutual trust with Dr. Pikhoia set apart Mr. Palm's approach from that of many other US actors during the archival gold rush.

Mr. Palm's account makes incontrovertibly clear that the collaboration was two-way. The Hoover Institution never sought, nor did it receive, originals, only copies (in the then reigning technology of microfilm), and its investments enabled the Russian side to achieve many of its own goals of preservation. The word *daunting* would barely begin to describe the latter task.

Readers should know that the Soviet Union had a dualist party-state structure. The system, effectively, had no legal private sector, so everything was "statized" (a very convenient circumstance for researchers, once the state imploded in 1991). At the same time, the Communist Party shadowed all (state) institutions and was more important, given that the Communist Party general secretary and Politburo served as the decision makers. The result was separate party archives and state archives. To make matters even more complicated, part of the party archives were never made available even to favored Soviet researchers: these were the working archives of the Politburo, which were inherited by Mikhail Gorbachev's newly created presidency (hence their designation as the Presidential Archive, parts of which, such as Joseph Stalin's personal files, were eventually declassified into the regular party archives). Additionally, the Soviet foreign ministry, the ministry of defense, and the KGB (security police) retained their own documents, never turning them over to the state archives. That said, matters of foreign affairs, defense, and state security are illuminated in the Central Party Archive. The key point is that because the regime left behind both party and state archives, Hoover's acquisition strategy needed to encompass this dualist structure—and it did.

When the Wall came down and the Soviet State dissolved, there would be countless discoveries, beginning with the circumstance that the Communist Party archives were not only preserved, for the most part, rather than destroyed, but they were also properly cataloged and orderly. The newfound openness might have suggested that it would lead to an enduring breakthrough to a permanently open society. But those with a historical sensibility could have pointed out that after the downfall of the tsarist state in 1917 and the onset of dizzying freedoms, a new autocracy under the Communists soon arose. How long might the astonishing window of opportunity of 1991 last? What values should balance any opportunism of the moment? In other words, regardless of what might happen next in this part of the world, how could we best ensure that present and future generations would obtain and maintain unfettered access to the secrets hidden inside the Soviet Communist Party's vast internal documentation? The answers would become obvious only in retrospect. In prospect, the Hoover Institution was readier than most to seize the day.

It all began in 1919 when Stanford historian Ephraim D. Adams went to Europe, where he met Herbert Hoover and began collecting materials testifying to the horrors of the Great War in France, Belgium, and Germany for the future Hoover Institution, with the aim of maintaining the peace. Just as Mr. Palm would later do, Mr. Adams enlisted helpmates, such as Ralph G. Lutz (a Stanford graduate), who ventured to Poland, the former Habsburg empire (Czechia, Austria, Hungary), Serbia, Bulgaria, Italy, and Switzerland. Mr. Adams and Mr. Lutz assumed joint directorship of what was christened the Hoover War Collection. Soon, another perspicacious collector, the Russian-born Frank Golder, became a director, too. Their titles evolved, but this threesome produced the nonpareil foundations that Mr. Palm would expand. Mr. Lutz outlasted the others and saw the dedication of a special building to house the now enormous collection devoted to fostering peace, the Hoover Tower, on June 20, 1941, two days before the Nazi invasion of the Soviet Union. By the time Mr. Lutz stepped down two years later, during World War II, Hoover had expanded its collecting ambitions from Russia and Eastern Europe to the entire globe. Even researchers who have worked at the Hoover Library & Archives for decades can make new discoveries (as this writer knows firsthand).

The history of the Hoover Institution is, in some ways, a match for the history that has been, and still can be, written as a result of its collections. That story lies beyond the scope of this introduction. But consider the acquisition of the tsarist secret police's overseas archives (a story told so well in Bert Patenaude's *A Wealth of Ideas* [Stanford University Press, 2006]), which forms a telling counterpoint to the acquisition of the Communist Party archives narrated by Mr. Palm. Vasily Maklakoff was the ambassador to Paris of Russia's short-lived Provisional Government of 1917, which took over from the tsar in February but was thrust aside by Vladimir Lenin and the Bolsheviks in October. He had to act expeditiously when the French government belatedly recognized the Soviet State in 1924. Mr. Maklakoff, now an émigré, became legally bound to turn over tsarist property to the revolutionary regime in Moscow. Instead, he arranged for the wondrous archives of the Paris branch (the overseas arm) of the imperial secret police to be shipped to the Hoover Library on the Stanford campus—scores of thousands of files, clandestinely packed and transported across the ocean. Because so many revolutionaries were living in European exile, the holdings of the Paris branch in some ways surpassed those of the secret police archives in the old tsarist capital of St. Petersburg. One can safely bet that the Soviet regime would not have made available documents detailing the earlier crimes and machinations of the revolutionaries then in power. Few other nearly complete records of a national intelligence service operating abroad are available to researchers.

Mr. Maklakoff signed a document falsely testifying to his destruction of the materials, which remained under seal. Hoover announced the survival of the invaluable materials on October 28, 1957, not long after Mr. Maklakoff had passed away. In his deception, he had acted against what he deemed an illegitimate regime in his homeland and, arguably, in the best interests of humanity. Mr. Palm enjoyed the luxury of being able to act scrupulously within the law of the Russian state in his acquisition—crucially, he decided to do just that. His book matter-of-factly presents examples that are contemporaneous with his own, when distinguished individuals chose, shall we say, otherwise. The behavior of the then librarian of Congress particularly stands out, an essential aspect to understanding the wider story that Mr. Palm relates with his notable blend of elegance and resoluteness.

For all the advantages Hoover's history presented to an archival entrepreneur in the late 1980s, potential hindrances existed as well. In the decades after the formidable W. Glenn Campbell assumed the mantle of Hoover director on January 1, 1960, a position he would hold until 1989, a course was set for the establishment of a public policy center alongside the Library & Archives. Dr. Campbell, an economist, established a secure funding basis for the Library & Archives, but in the bargain its assignment expanded from an exclusive focus on primary materials to a general focus on basic collections (often general trade books), which diverted attention and resources from the special collecting that constituted the founding mission of the Library & Archives. He also assembled a stellar constellation of scholars and scholar-practitioners, such as Milton Friedman and George P. Shultz, who raised the Hoover Institution's profile immeasurably. Director Campbell's success opened up something of a divide in the institution between the burgeoning think tank and its foundation as a library and an archive. This split could have pushed to the side Mr. Palm's efforts to acquire the Soviet Communist archives.

To be sure, a handful of the scholars at Hoover continued to work in the archives and overcame the division, such as the aforementioned John Dunlop. And one person bridged the divide with special luster: the poet, public intellectual, former Foreign Office official of the United Kingdom, and Sovietologist Robert Conquest, who arrived in 1981 as senior research fellow and scholar-curator of the Russian Collection. During Dr. Conquest's publishing heyday, the Soviet Communist Party archives were closed to scholars of independent mind, but he took full advantage of Hoover's Soviet periodical collections and the voluminous holdings of émigré materials to produce masterworks that have stood the test of time (not to mention the opening of the fallen regime's archives). No one did more to convey to a mass audience the horrors and squalor of Communism during the Cold War struggle. (Dr. Conquest would go on to earn the Presidential Medal of Freedom.) But fellows immersed in archival materials and history such as Dr. Conquest were far outnumbered by those working on contemporary and domestic policies of the United States, meaning that no internal scholarly lobby group existed to support Mr. Palm. By the same token, however, no organized group coalesced to oppose him.

Furthermore, Hoover had outstanding specialists on the curatorial staff to assist Mr. Palm, under whom the Library & Archives quietly, but decisively, reclaimed its historic strength of pursuing special materials. The curator Maciej Siekierski, for example, went to Warsaw after the revolutions of 1989. Over two years, he gathered unique materials on Eastern Europe that could not be ordered through a catalog, bringing back an estimated 2.5 tons on resistance to Communism and its demise. One had to be there in person, cultivate a capacious network, and, not least, possess sufficient funding. In fact, Hoover's loyal donors appreciated the timely renewal of the original mission laid down by Herbert Hoover and the staff he had inspired, while at the same time the policy research side of the institution continued to flourish. Dr. Siekierski's massive enlargement of the already impressive Eastern European collection enabled the institution to continue to distinguish itself and to attract researchers from all reaches of the Earth. Mr. Palm relied on an expert staff to access and catalog copies of Soviet Communist Party materials at a staggering scale. What his back-to-basics reorientation did not do was upset the growing Hoover fellowship. Eventually, John Raisian, another economist who succeeded Dr. Campbell as director, would bring in a notable scholar, economic historian Paul Gregory from the University of Houston, to explore and showcase the new Soviet archival acquisitions. In the meantime, Mr. Raisian backed Mr. Palm unreservedly, allowing him to pitch his Soviet archives project to the Hoover Board of Overseers and other Hoover donors. Mr. Palm raised the first million dollars in five minutes.

Grace notes enrich the book's lucid prose. True, Mr. Palm's responses to critics can at times be weighted down with necessary monotony—largely because the original criticism was so tedious—but he is spot-on about the absolute necessity to set the record straight. Moreover, while treating the shenanigans and worse of rivals and opponents with his customary exactitude, as well as chagrin, rather than the vituperation some of them richly deserve, he gives credit where credit is due. A hallmark of the text is the named acknowledgment of all the people who together pulled off this remarkable feat of collaboration, from the American team Mr. Palm assembled, to the successful partnership with the British publisher, Chadwyck-Healey Ltd., and the numerous Russians working in the trying circumstances of the ongoing collapse that characterized the 1990s. In elucidating the many competing players and interests that got involved in the quest for the crown jewel papers of Communism, the author furnishes readers with an appreciation of the twists and turns on the Russian side and the misunderstandings that cropped up. The narration of the 1996 crisis arising out of intrigues in Moscow amid Yeltsin's weakness is one of countless valuable explications.

Mr. Palm's portrait of the work's central figure, Rudolf G. Pikhoia, is characteristically both savvy and scrupulously fair. A second vital contact on the Russian side also receives incisive and generous treatment: Sergei Mironenko, a historian of modern Russia and the head of the State Archive of the Russian Federation (GARF), who reported to Dr. Pikhoia of the archival administration. Eventually, after a quarter century of dedicated service, Mr. Mironenko would be ousted for using archival documents to debunk a Soviet deliberate falsification about World War II soldiers who supposedly died heroically in battle (some were found alive during the war). No one alive did more to declassify documents of Soviet-era history for public use. Working with him, Hoover Library & Archives acquired copies of the records of the Soviet labor camps known as the Gulag. This success followed Hoover's temporary wrangle with the publisher Chadwyck-Healey, an opening to an engaging second act of the drama.

The Gulag was rendered infamous by the transcendent work of Aleksandr Solzhenitsyn, *The Gulag Archipelago*, first published abroad. (Mr. Palm had the pleasure of meeting Mr. Solzhenitsyn when he visited

Hoover after his expulsion from the Soviet Union.) Mr. Solzhenitsyn managed to write his immortal three-volume literary investigation, as he christened it, of the labor camps, wielding them as metaphor for the entire Leninist-Stalinist system, without access to Soviet archives. He was compelled to rely, instead, on personal experience, official newspapers, and interviews with and letters from thousands of Gulag inmates. That said, much like the publications of Robert Conquest, Mr. Solzhenitsyn's work stood the test of time and the opening up of the once inaccessible secret materials.

Of course, anyone not afflicted with willful blindness knew Communism was a murderous tyranny. The formerly classified archives did not suddenly reveal it as a free society, a constitutional democracy with the rule of law, a dynamic market economy, and an open society. Still, on many fundamental issues of fact and matters open to interpretation, there is a decisive difference between experience or educated surmise and fully substantiated argument. Nothing provides evidence of a nasty regime's policies and their consequences better than the documents the regime itself produced in abundance (and hid). The avalanche of new information made available to scholars by Hoover affords additional insight into the operation of totalitarianism and the uncanny ways it enmeshed its victims in their own destruction, goading them to use their own agency to end the possibility of their continued agency. Exposed anew are the unfathomable depths of the system's moral squalor, the cruelty, barbarity, and treachery perpetrated in the name of the highest ideals. Indeed, the new documents also shed considerable light on the salience of ideas in defining an unfree society and the ideological commitment of the Communists, visible, finally, from behind closed doors in documents they never intended to be made public. The main secret to emerge from the Communist archives? They were Communists.

* * *

The account of the Hoover Institution's initiative offers an important contrast with the parallel Yale University Press project known as the Annals of Communism series, founded in 1992 under then Yale editorial and associate director Jonathan Brent. (The contrast with the style and content of Mr. Brent's own memoir, *Inside the Stalin Archives*, is instructive, too.)

The Yale project's lead recruited academics to choose and annotate the documents that the press published within its Annals series, and the choices invariably became contentious, given the positions scholars had adopted during the Cold War and the scores many of them now sought to settle. Questions arose about the selectivity as well as the interpretations. Because of the way he structured the Hoover project, Mr. Palm did not have to select some scholars, and not others, to make available the treasure trove of documentation from the Soviet era. In fact, he managed, wisely, to avoid not just the reality but the appearance of political bias by microfilming whole record series and files rather than individually selected documents and by providing open access right away.

That said, the Hoover initiative did arouse controversy of a kind: namely, charges in the Russian media against their side for allegedly selling, and against the American side for allegedly stealing, the nation's heritage. Accusations of bribes—false, in the case of Hoover—became commonplace as well. More substantively, prominent scholars in Russia sounded the alarm that the center of research on Russia would shift to Hoover and the United States. Such a "shift" could not take place, obviously, since it had already happened decades before, given the challenges of producing genuine scholarship within the Soviet Union on the country's history amid saturation propaganda and censorship. Nonetheless, to an extent, the lament was understandable in light of the difficulties, because of lack of resources, that citizens of Russia faced in capitalizing on the sudden opportunities that had opened up. In this context, Mr. Palm admits a serious mistake on his part: he neglected to engage Russian academics in the joint project.

Hoover could have, and should have, set aside funding to carry out academic work, including to support the publication of documents and monographs, offering stipends and recognition to key actors in Russia, many of whom were marginalized by the ongoing collapse in their homeland. The archival bonanza promised little or no glory for them. Mr. Palm's belated recognition of this oversight in 1996 came after a crisis had erupted in the joint efforts of Hoover and Russian institutions. When, belatedly, he did provide individuals on the Russian side with meaningful work, things went much more smoothly. In retrospect, this seems an obvious thing to have foreseen and done, but one must consider the whirl of tasks and pressures in the partnership across the ocean. The larger point is that Mr. Palm's admission typifies the book's open and self-critical tone, the heartfelt willingness to learn, in real time and retrospectively.

Nothing was smooth or easy. Petty jealousies, ill will, suspicion, and deception complicated implementation of the carefully structured legal agreements—and not just among Russian actors. Some readers might be disappointed that Mr. Palm does not relate these frictions in the form of zealous score-settling, but many will be inspired by his account's meticulously factual nature. Intrigues can fascinate, to be sure, but after the fact they can be as enervating to read about, piled one on top of each other, as they were to have experienced in real time. Mr. Palm describes the obstacles without some of the more grotesque details and frustrations, mercifully. Yet the key is that he and his staff, together with their Russian partners, overcame them. The cumulative effect of the book is an abiding sense that the extensive microfilming amounted to a historic achievement. (The failure to digitize emerges as tragic, with an explanation.) In the end, the book delivers an engaging story of a dramatic moment in time, a successful collaboration across cultures, a reliable record of who did what, when, how, and with what effects, and a gift to current and future generations.

* * *

Having copies of the archives of the Soviet Communist Party and the Soviet State end up at the Hoover Institution after the downfall of Soviet Communism would seem utterly logical. Where else but the world's premier repository of anti-Communism materials could the records of that ignominious experiment have ended up? But Mr. Palm demonstrates that it took vision, tact, and tenacity to make it happen, and to make it happen in an unreproachable fashion. Just listing the published scholarly contributions that resulted from this public good would require a book many times the length of Mr. Palm's terse volume. (As an example of the debts scholars already owe, I could point to my own trilogy on Stalin, much of which I researched at the Hoover Library & Archives.) Among the beneficiaries are the scholars yet to be born, who will be able to study the nature of "unfreedom" in remarkable depth and searing detail. Tyranny and its dangers are never far away, and the lessons obtainable at the Hoover Library & Archives never go out of date.

Charles Palm retired in 2002, after thirty-one years of service to the Hoover Institution. For his leadership in making these archives open forever, and his eloquence in setting out that captivating story, we can only be grateful. The arc of history bends toward research.

Stephen Kotkin
Kleinheinz Senior Fellow, Hoover Institution, Stanford University
Director, Hoover History Lab
Advisor to the Director of the Hoover Library & Archives
Birkelund Professor Emeritus, Princeton University

Chapter 1

A WINDOW ON HISTORY OPENS

A Twelve-Year Project

On December 25, 1991, the Soviet hammer and sickle flag came down from the Kremlin and the Russian tricolor flag went up in its place. The next day the Soviet Union was officially dissolved, and seventy-four years of Communist rule in Russia came to an end. Four months later, on April 17, 1992, the Hoover Institution concluded a historic agreement with the government of the Russian Federation to microfilm the records of the Soviet Communist Party and the Soviet State. During the next twelve years, the project copied ten million pages of documents onto 11,819 reels of microfilm, now deposited safely in the Hoover Institution Archives. In exchange, the Hoover Institution provided microfilm copies of its Russian archival collections to the Russian State Archives for use by scholars in Russia. It was one of the largest international archival exchange projects ever undertaken by an American academic institution.

Among the materials copied in Moscow were records of key policymaking bodies of the Soviet Communist Party, including the Party Congresses and Conferences, the Central Committee, and the Party Control Commission. The Hoover project also filmed records of the People's Commissariat of Internal Affairs (NKVD) of the Russian Soviet Federative Socialist Republic (RSFSR), a key state instrument that imposed Bolshevik rule on the Russian people; the massive records relating to the Gulag, the Soviet forced labor camps; and the 1992 trial records of the Constitutional Court documenting crimes of the Soviet Communist Party and its leaders. In addition, the project filmed the finding aids of all the filmed records as well as many of the finding aids of the other record holdings at the three participating Russian repositories. This collection of finding aids constitutes a reliable accounting of a large portion of the surviving records of Soviet Communism.

Hundreds of scholars from around the world have come to the Hoover Institution to use the materials copied in Moscow. Their research has covered a wide range of topics, including politics, economics, foreign relations, the Cold War, the operations of the Gulag, and purges and repressions, among many others. Dozens of books and countless articles based on the collection have been published. In addition, microfilm copies of all the materials produced by the Hoover project were marketed and distributed for sale by Chadwyck-Healey Ltd., a project partner that facilitated production of the microfilm in Moscow. As a consequence, libraries around the world have acquired the microfilms and made them accessible to hundreds of additional scholars.[1]

The Hoover Institution's decisive action during a brief window of opportunity permanently preserved on microfilm key records of Soviet Communism and made them widely available for research. In doing so, the Hoover Institution accomplished a principal mission envisioned by its founder, Herbert Hoover—documenting and bringing to account one of the most consequential ideologies of the twentieth century.

My memoir of this project is a story of opportunities seized, obstacles overcome, lessons learned, and a mission accomplished. It is also an account of a project that exposed a fundamental conflict in Russian society—on the one hand, a Russia, optimistic, ready to be reconciled to its tragic history, and open to collaboration with Western partners; and on the other hand, a second Russia, defiant, embittered by defeat, and distrustful of outsiders, even outsiders who came to help.

Project Beginnings

In May 1991, three months before the August coup that precipitated the collapse of the Soviet government, I invited Rudolf G. Pikhoia to the Hoover Institution. Pikhoia was the chairman of the Committee on Archival Affairs of the Council of Ministers of the RSFSR.[2] He was introduced to me by Alexander Shakai, who was vice president of the Russian-American University in Moscow. Shakai had informed me that Pikhoia would be in the United States and offered to convey my invitation to him. He did so, and Pikhoia accepted.

As deputy director of the Hoover Institution, I administered its Library & Archives, a major component of which was its East European and Russian Collections. Since the fall of the Berlin Wall in 1989, we had significantly expanded our collecting effort in Eastern Europe, and I was interested in the possibility of doing the same in Russia. I thought that Pikhoia's visit might lead to some promising collecting opportunities for our Russian Collection.

As the Soviet Union was still intact in May 1991, Pikhoia's domain was limited to the archives of the RSFSR, or the Russian Soviet Republic, as it was commonly called. The Russian Soviet Republic was one of fifteen Soviet socialist republics that made up the Soviet Union. Its leader was Boris Yeltsin, who was then chairman of the Supreme Soviet, its parliament, and who, on June 12, 1991, was elected the first president of the Russian Soviet Republic.[3]

The records of the Soviet Union itself, including those of the Soviet Communist Party, were then in the custody of the Soviet government, still led by President Mikhail Gorbachev. Despite glasnost, these records were mostly inaccessible—and under the Soviet archivists likely would remain so. Boris Yeltsin, on the other hand, represented the forces of democratic reform. I believed that if Hoover were to undertake any projects in Russia, it would be with Yeltsin's government, not with the government of the Soviet Union.

Pikhoia's visit was a success. We became friends instantly. He was from the Siberian city of Sverdlovsk (now Yekaterinburg), and I from the high plains of north central Montana, America's version of Siberia. I found him to be expansive in his thinking and confident in his position—very much unlike Soviet government bureaucrats with whom I had previously dealt. He was a historian of the eighteenth century—a period in Russian historiography less affected by Marxist orthodoxy—and had been the vice rector and chairman of the history department at Sverdlovsk University. Pikhoia was one of several Yeltsin associates who came from Sverdlovsk, including Pikhoia's wife, Lyudmila Pikhoia, Yeltsin's chief speechwriter. Yeltsin himself began his career in Sverdlovsk and from 1976 to 1985 had been the first secretary of the Communist Party of Sverdlovsk Oblast.

Pikhoia and his colleague, Vladimir P. Tarasov, spent two days with us, arriving on May 28 and departing on May 30. They were introduced to the Hoover Institution Archives and its staff and met the Hoover Institution's director, John Raisian. At the conclusion of the first day, I hosted a dinner at a local restaurant. In addition to Pikhoia, myself, and my wife, it included Hoover Senior Fellow John Dunlop; Olga Dunlop, a Russian specialist at Hoover, who served as translator; Anne Van Camp, Hoover's chief archivist; and Joseph Dwyer, the deputy curator of Hoover's Russian Collection. The dinner was a success. At it I proposed a three-part program of collaboration that Hoover and the Archives of the Russian Soviet Republic might undertake: a project to produce and exchange microfilms, a joint exhibit, and the creation of a digital database linking our two institutions. Pikhoia responded positively.

The next day I drew up a Letter of Cooperation, which spelled out these three elements: (1) "the exchange of archival documents on an equal basis"; (2) "a joint exhibit of archival materials on the topic of economic relations between our two countries"; and (3) "a project to catalog and enter data into the Research Libraries Information Network (RLIN) from the archives of the Russian Republic." It was the first cooperative agreement with an American institution that Pikhoia signed and the first step in what I expected to be a relatively slow-developing series of activities. After all, I had not secured funding for even one of these projects. Then, suddenly, everything changed.[4]

My wife and I were on vacation in the Maritime Provinces of Canada when the first news reports of the August 18 coup reached me. While President Gorbachev was in the Crimea, hard-line members of his government took control of the Soviet State. Resistance to the coup soon developed, led by Boris Yeltsin and his followers, among whom was our new friend, Rudolf G. Pikhoia. Initially, I was concerned about the well-being of Judith Fortson, Hoover's head librarian, who was in Moscow at a meeting of the International Federation of Library Associations and Institutions. I soon learned that Fortson was safe. In fact, like the dedicated librarian she was, she and her son had been out photographing the historic events taking place on the Moscow streets. I did not learn what had happened to Pikhoia until later, when he recounted his personal story of those days.

Yeltsin set up his command in the "White House of Russia"—the building that housed Russia's parliament, the Supreme Soviet of the Russian Soviet Republic. It was surrounded by tanks and soldiers ordered there by the leaders of the coup. Pikhoia was among those inside and was armed with a machine gun ready to defend the resistance. As I later reported to the Hoover Institution's Board of Overseers:

> Pikhoia stood by Yeltsin in the Russian White House, carrying a machine gun and overseeing telephone communications to the BBC and other news organizations. . . . When the coup was broken, Yeltsin immediately ordered the seizure of the Communist Party headquarters and all Party archives. Pikhoia led this effort . . . sealing the archives at Party headquarters and coordinating the efforts of city officials throughout Russia in seizing local Party archives. These quick actions saved countless numbers of documents from destruction.[5]

By September, conditions were sufficiently calmed down that I could send Dwyer to Moscow. His assignments were to meet with Pikhoia, to assess his situation, to ask whether he was still interested in the projects that we had discussed at Stanford, and, if so, to arrange for my visit to Moscow in order to move discussions forward. Not only was Pikhoia interested in advancing our relationship, Yeltsin had given him important new responsibilities.

Yeltsin's presidential decree of August 24, 1991, suspended the organs of the Russian Communist Party and placed the party archives under the control of Pikhoia's Committee on Archival Affairs—renamed the State Archival Service of Russia (Rosarkhiv) in 1992. Later in 1991, Rosarkhiv absorbed the former Soviet Main State Archival Administration (Glavarkhiv). As a consequence, Pikhoia and his committee were now in charge of a vast system of archival holdings, including eighteen federal archives and two thousand state and party repositories containing some two hundred million files amounting to billions of pages of records. Suddenly he was the person to see for Russian archives.[6]

I arrived in Moscow on November 18 with four team members: Van Camp, Fortson, Dwyer, and Alan Tucker, associate director of the Research

Libraries Group (RLG), the organization that operated RLIN. It was my first visit to that city, and I was surprised by what I saw. Russia was clearly a country in trouble. As my plane flew over the city making a nighttime approach for landing, I was expecting to see the lighted expanse of an urban area populated by several million inhabitants. Instead, I saw mostly darkness speckled here and there with isolated lights.

Inside the Sheremetyevo Terminal, emergency lighting lit our way. The interior spaces were cold and unheated. Police in military uniforms armed with machine guns lazily slung over their shoulders alerted visitors that Russia, while now on her knees, could still impose state authority. Beyond passport control and customs, we entered a public area filled with a surging crowd of people—some soliciting taxi fares and other business, some selling souvenirs, some begging for money. Fortunately, Tarasov and his driver, there to meet us, quickly came to our rescue. They escorted us through the crowd, loaded us into two government cars, and drove us into the city. After a bumpy ride over poorly lit and maintained roads, they deposited us at the Metropol, Moscow's historic and elegant hotel, where we resided for the next five days.

Back in May, I had only a vaguely formed plan for collaborating with the Russians. The Soviet Union was still intact, and the collecting possibilities, while improving, remained problematic. Now in November, as the newly appointed head of Rosarkhiv, Pikhoia was in charge of one of the most important bodies of secret, untapped historical records in the world. Moreover, he was part of a new government that seemed ready to embrace the ideals of an open and democratic society. A historic venture lay before us.

For this initial Moscow meeting my objective was twofold. First, I had to convince Pikhoia and his colleagues that we sought collaboration, not exploitation. Second, I had to demonstrate that collaboration with Hoover would successfully advance their agenda. Accordingly, I proposed two projects—two of the three projects outlined in the May Letter of Cooperation—that could achieve these two goals and that I was confident would elicit only positive responses. Implementing them, I thought, would begin the process of building trust.

The first project was a joint exhibit that we believed would create a spirit of friendship and goodwill, both among the cooperating archivists and with the Russian public generally. Van Camp, Hoover's archivist, came prepared with a coherent, attractive plan that developed the exhibit proposal we had discussed in May. She presented it effectively and persuasively. The theme was US-Russian economic relations in the first half of the twentieth century, including coverage of the 1921–23 humanitarian relief work headed by Herbert Hoover that saved millions of Russians from starvation. Both Hoover and the Russian side had rich holdings to support such an exhibit. In addition, since several Russian repositories had relevant materials, the exhibit would enable many Russian archivists from various archives to participate in the collaboration.

The subject of economic relations with the United States and the West generally was high on the agenda of the Russian government. It was forward looking and it was not offensive. Some dismissively called it "benign." I was fine with that description, because the exhibit itself was not the only object. In addition, its purpose was to build a confident working relationship with the Russian archivists and to create some goodwill among the Russian public. Ultimately, the exhibit did both. And, it had the additional feature of showing a positive connection between Herbert Hoover and Russia. Entitled "Making Things Work: Russian-American Economic Relations, 1900–1930," the exhibit opened in November 1992 at a high-profile Moscow venue—the Russian White House, home of the Russian parliament. It opened at the Hoover Institution the following year. A published catalog commemorated both openings.[7]

The second project I proposed would introduce automated technology into the Russian archival repositories. It involved entering cataloging data describing their holdings into RLIN, the principal database in the United States for the exchange of information among archival repositories. In the 1980s, I had participated in efforts of the American archival profession to develop a machine-readable format and standards for describing archives and manuscripts. The result of this work was the machine-readable cataloging-archives and manuscripts control (MARC-AMC) format. Subsequently, the Hoover Institution Archives became one of four repositories that first entered data into RLIN using this format. Since then, entering descriptions of archival and manuscript holdings into RLIN or other networks became—and continues to be—standard practice at most American archival repositories.

Bringing the Russian archivists into this electronic environment would make the finding aids and other descriptions of their archival holdings widely accessible. It would also enhance their technical capabilities and their connections to the professional archival community outside Russia. Tucker gave an expert demonstration of the RLIN system and presented a detailed plan of action for implementing it in Russia. The proposal had the desired effect. The Russian archivists could see the benefits of working with competent partners who were on the forward edge of archival practices.

Subsequently, in 1994, the National Endowment for the Humanities (NEH) awarded Hoover and RLG a grant of $377,177 to undertake a pilot project, which was successfully concluded in 1996. Unfortunately, the Russians did not follow up by continuing to enter catalog data into RLIN. Nonetheless, the project achieved my immediate goal—engaging Russian archivists with Hoover archivists in a confidence-building project.

As valuable as these two projects were in their own right, their main purpose was to lay the groundwork for a bigger objective. From the moment I sent Dwyer to Moscow in September, my goal was to bring out into the open for scholarly use the historical record of Soviet Communism and to do so under the auspices of the Hoover Institution. How could this goal not be paramount in my thinking?

For more than seventy years, the Hoover Institution, guided by Herbert Hoover's founding vision, had collected records on war, revolution, and peace. As a consequence, the Hoover Institution held the largest and most important collection of historical materials on Imperial Russia, the Russian Revolution, and the Soviet Union and Soviet Communism anywhere outside of Russia—including at that time some three hundred thousand volumes in its Library and more than one thousand individual manuscript and archival collections in its Archives. Herbert Hoover himself considered documentation and study of Marxism and other totalitarian ideologies to be central to the mission of his institution. If we succeeded in acquiring copies of the archives of the Soviet Communist Party and Soviet State, we would realize the founder's dream and honor all those before us who had labored at this task.[8]

The Letter of Cooperation that Pikhoia and I signed during his visit to Stanford in May 1991 listed "the exchange of archival documents" as a principal objective of our proposed collaboration. At the November meeting, however, I wanted to take a cautious approach to any discussion of copying large numbers of documents. I needed first to gain the Russians' confidence in us as reliable and equal partners who could be trusted to protect their interests as if they were our own. While I had a good understanding of Pikhoia's interests and objectives, I had not yet had a chance to assess the views of those around him, especially his key deputies and the directors of the repositories he oversaw. Making an aggressive proposal early on could unnecessarily create resistance from those who might otherwise support us.

I was keenly aware that every important publisher and all our key institutional competitors would be at his door seeking the same prize—the historical record of seven decades of Soviet Communism. Of the many attractive offers Pikhoia would receive, the one he was likely to accept would be the one from a partner he could trust. Everyone in Russia, including Pikhoia's government superiors, knew the value of the archives he oversaw. Managing this body of records—opening them to the Russian people and the world, utilizing them for the benefit of the Russian people, and preserving them as his nation's patrimony—was an immense responsibility. I wanted him to know first and foremost that I respected this responsibility and appreciated the uncertain, even precarious, position that he had assumed.

During the November meeting in Moscow, I shared with Pikhoia in a general way my interest in undertaking a large microfilming project but made no concrete proposal. He explained that he was being inundated with such offers. Most confusing to him were ambitious proposals to coordinate all the various Russian projects under the auspices of some international collegium. I was aware of the separate efforts at coordination by the Library of Congress, the Harriman Institute in New York, the International Institute of Social History in Amsterdam, and the Feltrinelli

Foundation in Italy. It seemed to Pikhoia that the would-be coordinators were all talk and no action. What he needed was a partner who would provide financial resources in support of his own priorities, not an international consortium that sought to organize the priorities of others.

In order to show him that Hoover could be such a partner, I asked if he would entertain an invitation to attend Hoover's upcoming Board of Overseers meeting in Washington, DC, scheduled for early February 1992. Pikhoia, of course, knew of Hoover's reputation as an academic institution with a long history in Russian studies. This reputation was an important element of his interest in us. In addition, I wanted him to meet some of our principal donors and to see the Hoover Institution in action. He responded favorably to my suggestion, and I promised that I would arrange for the invitation upon my return to California.

Meanwhile, I was given a firsthand look at the archives that might form the basis of a large-scale copying effort. As a result, I was able to make an initial assessment of their size and condition. The guided tour covered the two repositories holding the party archives. Entry into these sanctified spaces was a rare privilege. During the Soviet period, access to party archives was restricted to high party leaders, official historians of the Communist Party, and the Soviet archivists themselves. As a leading expert on Soviet archives has reported, "Only under very unusual and special circumstances has a noncommunist foreign scholar ever been admitted for research in Party archives."[9]

In 1991, the party records from October 1952 to August 1991 were held in the former headquarters of the Central Committee of the Communist Party of the Soviet Union on Kuibysheva Street (name changed to Il'inka Street in 1992), where Rosarkhiv established its offices. Rem A. Usikov, director of the Central Committee Archives, guided me through the entire facility. I was struck by the orderliness of the archives. The spaces were air-conditioned and protected from fire. The records were housed in file folders and stacked horizontally and neatly in closed steel cabinets. All folders were labeled, suggesting the presence of indexes and finding aids that facilitated their use.[10]

The second repository on the tour was the Central Party Archive and Marx-Engels-Lenin Institute, located in a different part of Moscow. It held the Soviet Communist Party archives from the party origins through October 1952, including a large collection of Lenin's papers as well as those of Marx, Engels, and other figures of the international socialist movement. The holdings of this repository also were well organized and preserved. I detected a strong sense of loyalty to its mission. One entered the building into an expansive lobby, at the center of which was a statue of Lenin. At its foot were freshly cut flowers, reminding visitors that the spirit of the revolution was still being honored in this last bastion of Soviet Communism.[11]

These two guided tours gave me the distinct impression—an impression later confirmed by others—that the records of the Soviet Communist Party had been conscientiously collected and preserved over the years and that very few of them had been lost or destroyed. As Mark Kramer, American historian and early visitor to the archives, noted, high party leaders never dreamed that their files would be shown to others, let alone be made public, and saw no need to sanitize or destroy them. When they realized their mistake, it was too late. The collapse of the Soviet Union was so sudden and Pikhoia's actions so decisive that no such action was possible.[12]

Pikhoia offered me a third tour, not of the archives but of central Moscow. He assigned an English-speaking staff person to escort me around town. My young guide walked me through the open markets on Old Arbat Street; passed by some government ministries; showed me the Memorial Museum, which housed a collection of memorabilia of Gulag prisoners; and took me shopping at the GUM department store, where I purchased a few souvenirs. At GUM I encountered the queues, the "inseparable feature of socialism," just as Bertram Wolfe had described them in his account of his visits to Moscow seventy years ago in the 1920s. In the first queue you found out the price of the item you wanted; in the second queue you got the paper receipt; and in the third queue you exchanged the receipt for your purchase.[13] I thought to myself: Would we encounter similar inefficiencies left over from the Soviet past once we began filming the archives? I filed the question away for later.

At the end of the walking tour, we returned to the Metropol. Since we finished the tour before my scheduled meeting with Pikhoia, I invited my guide to lunch in the hotel's upscale dining room. There we enjoyed a full-menu lunch and easy conversation until near the end as we were finishing our dessert. When I pointed out to my young friend that Pikhoia had arrived in the hotel lobby and was waiting for us, he answered, "He can wait." His remark startled me. Was this nothing more than a young man expressing his independence? Or did it reflect something more serious and general? Other visitors to Russia have noted the visceral contempt, usually suppressed until accidently and sometimes explosively revealed, with which ordinary Russians often hold those in authority. If the latter, how would such attitudes affect our project? It was yet another question I filed away for later. It was also a reminder that among all the other challenges we faced I was an outsider navigating a foreign culture.

On our final day in Moscow, I met with Sergei V. Mironenko, who would soon become the director of the State Archive of the Russian Federation (GARF), one of the main repositories under the administrative umbrella of Rosarkhiv. In the years that followed, Mironenko would become a reliable, effective, and energetic project partner. He told me that while Pikhoia was in a strong position, tensions and disagreements within Rosarkhiv and political factions generally could create friction for any cooperative project. While he mentioned no names, I concluded that Vladimir P. Kozlov, then the director of the Central Party Archive and Marx-Engels-Lenin Institute, might be our most serious internal critic. In these and later discussions, Kozlov had objected to large-scale microfilming and advocated a "gradual, stage-by-stage approach."[14] Given the uncertainties, it was a reasonable position. However, I did not think we had time for gradual approaches. Mironenko's advice coincided with my thinking. He advised us to move forward with all deliberate speed. It was my very definite intention to do so.[15]

Before we departed Moscow, Mironenko and his wife hosted a dinner party at their apartment. It was a lovely and warmly felt occasion. In addition to Mironenko, his wife, his young son, and his mother-in-law, those present included Fortson, Van Camp, Dwyer, Tucker, Kozlov, and me. Their apartment was small, but we all fit snugly in their living room, which also served as the dining room and, apparently, in one corner, as the mother-in-law's sleeping area. The baked chicken dinner was delicious and the conversation expansive. The contrast between the public spaces outside and the inside spaces of Mironenko's apartment was striking. The former were cold, dirty, broken down, and unloved. The latter were clean, comfortable, and homey, with evidence of a rich family life and history. It was the difference between despair and hope. The evening spent in the Mironenko family home, as much as any other experience in Russia, convinced me that, given its new burst of freedom, Russia would recover.[16]

When I returned to Stanford, I made my report to Raisian, Hoover's director, and outlined the program I had in mind. He agreed that we should move forward, and with his approval I invited Pikhoia to the Hoover Institution's Board of Overseers semiannual meeting in Washington, DC, on February 4–5, 1992.

Raisian had his own Russian initiative that he wished to discuss with the board and that he soon launched. Under his leadership, a team of Hoover economists, among them Annelise Anderson, Michael Bernstam, and Edward Lazear, made several trips to Russia during the early post-Soviet years, providing policy advice to the Yeltsin government on the transition to a market economy. The results of their work were published in 1995 in a book edited by Lazear, *Economic Transition in Eastern Europe and Russia: Realities of Reform*. The two programs—Raisian's team of public policy advisers and my archival project—operated independently but harmoniously and represented a comprehensive response to a world challenge, just what one would have expected from a research institution with a deep and abiding interest in Soviet affairs.[17]

At the February Board of Overseers meeting, Raisian presented both projects of the Soviet archives and of the economic transition. The board consists of distinguished men and women from business and government. It provides oversight and direction to the Hoover Institution and is the principal source of funding for the institution. Its meetings in Washington engage many of the leading policymakers in the nation's capital, including members of the president's cabinet, the president's White House staff, and Congress. I wanted Pikhoia to see that Hoover could harness the necessary financial resources to undertake a major international program and, if needed, the political influence to protect it. At the same time, I wanted the board to meet Pikhoia. In order to move the project forward, both our board and Pikhoia had to be convinced that the other side could deliver.

Pikhoia accepted our invitation and agreed to address the board. He was on the program with General Colin Powell, chairman of the Joint Chiefs of Staff; Richard B. Cheney, secretary of defense; Senator Robert Dole; and cabinet members Jack Kemp and Lamar Alexander. Also on the program were several of Pikhoia's Russian compatriots and high-ranking members of the Russian government: Vladimir Ispravnikov, chairman of the Supreme Economic Council; Viktor Sheinis, chairman of the Constitutional Committee of the Russian Parliament; and Andrei J. Kolosovsky, the Russian ambassador to the United States. In introducing Pikhoia, Raisian reported on my visit to Moscow and gave the full board its first exposure to our growing relationship with the Russian State Archives.

In his address, Pikhoia promptly announced the initial agreement that he and I had signed at Stanford in May 1991 as well as my visit to Moscow in November. He then described the scope of his authority over the archives of the Soviet State and Soviet Communist Party. He indicated his support for the two projects—the joint exhibit and the RLIN data-sharing project—that he and I had agreed to undertake. He went on to state that Rosarkhiv was ready to "make copies for publishing institutions both in Russia and for our foreign partners." This was precisely the message I wanted him to give to our board.[18]

During the two-day board meeting, I met with two board members who had the capacity and possible interest to provide immediate financial support for a large copying project in Russia. They were Herbert Hoover III, the grandson of President Hoover, and Richard M. Scaife, a longtime and faithful supporter of the Hoover Institution. I described the steps I had taken to lay the groundwork for a major copying project and my intention with their support to conclude an agreement with Pikhoia. Each immediately committed $500,000 to get the project started.

By then, I had worked out a plan with specific goals. It had the following elements: (a) a focus on the archives of the principal policymaking organs of the Soviet Communist Party and the Soviet State; (b) production of up to twenty-five thousand reels of microfilm amounting to twenty-five million pages of documents; (c) sale of microfilm copies to interested libraries through a microfilm publisher with whom Hoover and Rosarkhiv would partner; and (d) a commitment of $3 million—$6.5 million in 2023 dollars—over five years for project costs.[19]

On the same afternoon I met with Hoover and Scaife, I attended the meeting of the board's Executive Committee, a small subset of the full board, which held the principal responsibility for the institution's finances, budget, and programmatic direction. I repeated what I had told Hoover and Scaife, reported that I had a commitment of $1 million from these two overseers, and requested the board's approval of the project and continued financial support in case I was unable to raise the additional funds necessary to complete the project. Without debate, the Executive Committee gave its unanimous approval. I was grateful for its strong support but realized that I had just made a very large bet, both for the institution and for myself. Hoover's reputation and my own were now on the line in what was going to be a difficult, expensive, and high-profile enterprise.

Before taking the next step with Pikhoia, I had to address another relationship. The American Enterprise Institute (AEI), a public policy think tank in Washington with whom the Hoover Institution has had a long, friendly relationship, had invited us to join in an effort to gain access to the Russian archives. Working with Vladimir Bukovsky, a leading Russian dissident living in England, AEI had approached Pikhoia about producing a digital copy of the Soviet archives.

In an agreement signed with Pikhoia on September 11, 1991, Bukovsky claimed to represent a consortium of organizations, including AEI, the Hoover Institution, and others, that was prepared to "computerize the archives and publish them as collections of documents."[20] What he meant by "computerize the archives" was making a digital copy. His project differed from the digital project that I had proposed to Rosarkhiv in November. The Hoover-RLG project involved entering descriptions of archival documents—inventories and other finding aids—into the RLIN database, not making digital copies of the documents themselves.

Although I had not authorized Bukovsky to conclude such an agreement on behalf of the Hoover Institution, I was prepared to consider his proposal. On November 8, I met with Christopher DeMuth, the AEI president, and several of his colleagues, including Jeane Kirkpatrick, the former US ambassador to the United Nations, to discuss a possible collaboration.

I did not discourage them but soon formed doubts about their project and the wisdom of joining forces with them.

In a subsequent telephone conversation with DeMuth in December, I pointed out my concerns, noting serious technical issues in making a digital copy of Russian documents. AEI proposed to use optical character recognition (OCR) technology to capture the information in the documents. At that time, this technology was only 95 percent reliable, unacceptably low for archival purposes. In addition, AEI proposed to use computer programs to translate the information from Russian to English. Such programs were only 70 percent accurate. In addition, the AEI proposal was unclear about funding, access, and other questions.[21]

At the February Hoover Board of Overseers meeting, Pikhoia made it plain to me that he did not want to have anything to do with electronic scanning, and in any case he did not want to work with AEI. Pikhoia noted that AEI was not an academic institution or archival repository, and it had little history of interest in Russian archives. It focused principally on current public policy issues. I realized that if AEI were part of our proposal, all our efforts would fail.

In order to end the relationship with AEI, I enlisted the help of Robert Malott. Malott, the former CEO and chairman of FMC Corporation, was chairman of the Hoover Board of Overseers and also an influential trustee on AEI's board. He immediately saw the incongruity of the AEI role, noting that Russian history was not part of AEI's portfolio of interests. He contacted DeMuth and effectively ended its collaboration with Hoover and its venture into the world of Russian archives. Malott's timely intervention on our behalf was extremely helpful and much appreciated.

Bukovsky, however, was not done with us. He believed that the Russian government would not open its archives as promised and that it had already moved to hide the crimes of Russia's Communist past. He was especially concerned that Hoover's project would provide a public shield against legitimate criticism of these actions. Given the treatment he had received at the hands of Soviet authorities, it was understandable that he held these views, and he was not out of line in reminding us of our responsibility in this connection.

At Bukovsky's instigation, we received this reminder in the form of a thoughtful and friendly letter from Aleksandr Solzhenitsyn, who—along with his world standing—was an honorary fellow of the Hoover Institution. Raisian, to whom Solzhenitsyn's letter was addressed, replied respectfully. He thanked him for his interest, gave assurances of our commitment to open access, and noted the precautions we had taken. I feared that we might not be able to meet the high standards that Solzhenitsyn and Bukovsky had set for us, but I was committed to do our best. I also was convinced that Pikhoia had the same objective. I would not have undertaken the task ahead if I had thought otherwise.[22]

The 1992 Agreement

When the Hoover board meeting adjourned on February 6, 1992, Pikhoia and I agreed that we would meet in Moscow to flesh out and sign a formal agreement. We soon settled on dates—February 24 and 25. It was left to me to prepare the first draft of a legal agreement spelling out in detail the goals of the project and the obligations of each side. I had already lined up an outside law firm, Latham and Watkins, to help me write the agreement. Latham and Watkins had been recommended to me by John Stahr, a partner in its Orange County, California, office and a Hoover overseer. The firm assigned Robert Shanks to the task. During the next several months he worked effectively with me on all the legal issues relating to the project.

Assisting me on the Stanford side was Iris Brest of Stanford University's Office of the General Counsel. Brest had helped me on numerous legal matters relating to the Hoover Archives—deeds of gift, copyright, restrictions on access to documents, and the like. She had always been helpful, supportive, and very competent. She was so again during the drafting of the agreement and subsequently throughout the course of the project.[23]

A second task was selecting a publisher who would help produce, process, and market the microfilm. The publisher would in effect be a third partner. From the beginning I had someone in mind. In the mid-1980s, as Hoover's chief archivist, I had undertaken a project with a British microfilm publisher, Chadwyck-Healey Ltd., to copy the so-called Red Archive—a large collection of materials on the Soviet Union—at the Munich headquarters of Radio Free Europe/Radio

Liberty (RFE/RL). Charles Chadwyck-Healey, its chairman and owner, and I worked together effectively to negotiate an agreement with RFE/RL and carry out the project.

On a smaller scale and with fewer political overtones, the RFE/RL project resembled the Russian project before us. Moreover, Charles Chadwyck-Healey had a well-deserved reputation for taking on large, complicated projects. In fact, he had already put his oar in the Russian waters. Chadwyck-Healey met Pikhoia in February 1991, and in November, he began discussions to microfilm Russian archives. In December 1991, he and Pikhoia concluded an agreement to microfilm the papers of several leading figures of the Russian Revolution held in the Central Party Archive in Moscow, about a half million pages. Stories in the *London Times* and the *New York Times* reported the breakthrough agreement.[24]

After the Hoover board meeting in February and with Pikhoia's approval, I contacted Charles Chadwyck-Healey. I congratulated him on his Russian project and asked him if he wanted to be a partner in a much larger venture—one that would copy, not a half million pages, but twenty-five million pages. He was immediately attracted to the idea and saw advantages in the partnership. Hoover could provide strong financial backing, and Hoover's scholarly reputation, especially in the Russian field, would lend stature and credibility. With Chadwyck-Healey now on board and a draft agreement in hand, I was ready to return to Moscow. It would be another big test for this budding enterprise.

The February meeting took place at the former headquarters of the Soviet Communist Party, which Rosarkhiv now occupied. The participants on the Hoover side included Dwyer, Shanks, Richard Kahn, and me. Kahn headed the Moscow office of Latham and Watkins. The Russian side included Pikhoia, Vladimir P. Tarasov (head of the Department of International Relations of Rosarkhiv), Valery I. Abramov (deputy chairman of Rosarkhiv), Rem A. Usikov (director of the Central Committee Archives), Vladimir P. Kozlov (director of the Central Party Archive and soon to be appointed deputy chairman of Rosarkhiv), and Sergei V. Mironenko (director of GARF). From Chadwyck-Healey Ltd. were Charles Chadwyck-Healey, Natalia Volkova, Jana Howlett, and Edward Lee-Smith, a lawyer from Norton Rose, a law firm retained by Chadwyck-Healey. Volkova was a Russian citizen hired by Chadwyck-Healey to translate for him. Howlett was a Russian historian, Russian speaker, and a fellow of Jesus College, Cambridge University. She had previously done consulting work for Chadwyck-Healey and had known Pikhoia since 1989, when she met him at an academic conference he organized in Sverdlovsk.[25]

Our two days in Moscow were filled with intense discussions, guided by the thirty-page draft agreement that I had circulated beforehand. I was hopeful that the draft agreement would be readily accepted, but I was not surprised when we encountered questions, resistance, and counterproposals. We had to convince not only Pikhoia but his Rosarkhiv colleagues, including the directors of the three repositories that held the archives. Failing to get ready consensus, I sought at least to discover their bottom line. What exactly did they need? And could we give it to them? In discussions over the course of the two days, I came to understand more clearly the essential elements that had to be in any agreement that Pikhoia, on behalf of Rosarkhiv, might reasonably be expected to sign.[26]

First, the agreement had to reflect equality between the two principal partners. The Russian side, in its financially weakened condition, was sensitive to anything resembling exploitation. Second, the agreement had to affirm the scholarly nature of our collaboration and thus contribute to the restoration of Russia's national pride. The commercial aspect of the project could not be our primary consideration. Third, notwithstanding the above requirements, the agreement had at least to match the financial returns offered by competitors. The Russian state was financially bankrupt, and its State Archives badly needed funds.

The agreement that I had prepared generally met these requirements but not as fully or specifically as the Russian side wanted. It became clear after the first day that revisions, as well as a more extended exchange of views, would be necessary. As a consequence, we decided that a second meeting, which we scheduled for March (later changed to April), would be needed. However, as a result of our work during this first meeting, both sides realized that we had made considerable progress in laying the foundation for a successful collaboration. Accordingly, we concluded and signed a preliminary agreement, which we called a Statement of Intention.

In lofty language provided by Pikhoia, the Statement of Intention set forth the goals we sought to achieve. It emphasized our mutual desire to meet the "demands of society for historical information," to preserve archival documentation, to serve scholars, to improve access to information on Russian history, and to collaborate with historians, archivists, and other specialists. It identified the projects we wished to undertake: the joint exhibit, the RLIN database project, and the microfilming and exchange of Russian archives.[27]

The exchange of microfilm was not a new element. It was present in our very first discussions back in May 1991, but I had not yet spelled out the full scope of the exchange I had in mind. Late in the afternoon of the last day, I made my pitch. In return for the microfilms produced in Russia, we would give the Russian State Archives, on a reel-for-reel basis, microfilm of Hoover's entire collection of world-renowned Russian archives. It was an element that I intentionally held back until all other issues had been discussed. It was a dramatic offer that I thought would bring the Russian side wholly over to our side, and one that no other competitor could make.

My offer had the desired effect. It transformed a project producing a one-way flow of materials from Russia to America into a true collaboration of equals. It would provide ready access to Hoover's collections for scholars in Russia and would fill gaps in the archival record held in the Russian State Archives. I believed it would help Pikhoia persuade his colleagues at Rosarkhiv and others in Russia that the Hoover project was an exceptional opportunity. After I presented the offer, Pikhoia immediately reached across the table and shook my hand. We had a deal, at least in principle, if not in final language.[28]

Before we departed from Moscow, we witnessed an extraordinary event. In a large conference room in the former headquarters of the Soviet Communist Party, under portraits of Karl Marx and Friedrich Engels, Pikhoia held a news conference. Before numerous cameras and a hundred or so journalists from both Russia and abroad, Pikhoia announced that the secret archives of the former Soviet Communist Party and Soviet State would be opened for all to see. In his remarks, he said the Soviet government "had to systematically deprive our nation of its memory in order to justify its use of terror and force against the Russian people, even when its politics flew in the face of nature and common sense." Now, this memory would be recovered.[29]

For the first time, the Russian people would have access to their own history, and the world community of scholars would be allowed to conduct extensive research on the Soviet archives. It was a remarkable development. The Soviet flag had been lowered from the Kremlin on December 25, 1991, and only two months later, Russia took the first bold steps to reconcile itself with its totalitarian past and to embrace the practices and values of an open society. It was a privilege to be present at such a moment.

The project participants met again in Moscow during the week of April 13–18, when the final details of an agreement were negotiated and approved. It was signed by Pikhoia, Chadwyck-Healey, and me on April 17 and had the following component parts:[30]

- Production of up to twenty-five thousand reels of microfilm consisting of twenty-five million pages of documents from the holdings of three repositories under the jurisdiction of Rosarkhiv
- Unrestricted access to the microfilming workspaces in the Russian repositories for Hoover Institution and Chadwyck-Healey staff
- Selection of records to be filmed by an Editorial Board consisting of equal numbers of Russian and American historians and archivists, totaling six to eight persons
- Deposit of project microfilm at Rosarkhiv (one first-generation master negative and one positive copy), the Hoover Institution (one second-generation negative and one positive copy), and Chadwyck-Healey (a second-generation negative for printing and distribution purposes)
- Deposit of microfilm at Rosarkhiv of the Hoover Institution's collection of Russian archives equal in volume to the microfilm produced for Hoover
- Budget of up to $3 million provided by the Hoover Institution, covering the costs of production (project staff salaries, equipment, supplies, microfilm processing costs, negatives and positives for Rosarkhiv and the Hoover Institution), expenses of the Editorial Board, and microfilm copy of the Hoover Institution's collection of Russian archives for deposit at Rosarkhiv

- Publication on microfilm of documents expected to be of greatest interest to scholars (estimated to total five thousand reels) by Rosarkhiv and the Hoover Institution, marketed and distributed by Chadwyck-Healey Ltd. outside the territory of the former Soviet Union
- Retention by Rosarkhiv of the right to publish and permit others to publish printed editions of selected documents included in the microfilm, provided that Hoover would have the right of first refusal for any editions that Hoover might propose
- Hoover payments to the participating Russian repositories for labor at $60,000 per year totaling $300,000 over five years, based on an estimated labor cost of $12 per reel
- Royalties paid by Chadwyck-Healey equal to 40 percent of gross sales—27 percent paid to Rosarkhiv and 13 percent to the Hoover Institution
- Advance on royalties to Rosarkhiv paid equally by Chadwyck-Healey and Hoover of $100,000, half paid upon conclusion of the agreement and half upon approval of documents to be filmed
- Deposit of copies of the published microfilm (not to exceed five thousand reels) at the US Library of Congress and at the Novosibirsk Regional State Archives

In view of the complex nature of the project—one involving a newly formed archival agency of a government that had been born just months earlier, three repositories administered by that newly formed agency, a microfilm publisher in Britain, and an academic institution in California—the agreement held up remarkably well. Between April 1992 and July 1996, after which the 1992 agreement was replaced with a new agreement, only a few changes were made. Some simply clarified ambiguities in the agreement. Most of the others were changes requested by Rosarkhiv.

In a July 1992 annex, three revisions were agreed upon, as follows:[31]

- It was explicitly affirmed that the agreement did not grant Hoover the right to make an electronic copy of the project microfilm.
- The commitment to place copies of the published microfilm at the Library of Congress and the Novosibirsk Regional State

Archives was made contingent on sufficient royalties earned from microfilm sales.

- The publication rights granted to the Hoover Institution were clarified and recognized Rosarkhiv's exclusive right to publish, or permit others to publish, printed editions of selected documents from the project microfilm.

Early in my discussions with Pikhoia, I had raised the possibility of both a microfilm and a digital copy of the archives—a microfilm copy for permanent preservation and a digital copy for the convenience of users. In those years, however, our Russian partners had little familiarity with electronic data, and what they did know they did not like. Microfilm technology, on the other hand, was very familiar to them. It was not technically demanding, and expensive equipment and software were not needed to read it. Microfilm readers are simple devices, which were and still are present in all research libraries, including those in Russia.

The Russians also knew that data recorded on microfilm were much less easily manipulated than data recorded electronically. Moreover, in 1992, electronic scanning was in its infancy. Electronic media (optical discs) were very expensive, and optical character recognition, the technique for digitizing data, did not then make flawless copies. From the start, Pikhoia shut down any talk of electronic rights, and when he realized that we had not dealt with it in the April agreement, he asked that his concern be addressed in the July annex. As I had previously accepted his position on the matter, I readily agreed.

Another reason led us to microfilm. One of the principal objectives of the project was to provide the Russian repositories and Hoover with copies of the archives that met strict preservation standards and thus could form permanent collections in their holdings. In the 1990s, microfilm was the preferred medium for permanently preserving archives. Standards for microfilm preservation were well defined and accepted. We followed them all.

The most important standard was the use of silver halide microfilm. Under normal archival storage conditions, silver halide microfilm and the contents on it will last at least two hundred years, longer than the original paper records themselves would likely last. The only precaution necessary is maintaining two copies of the microfilm—one positive copy for use and one negative copy to be stored for permanent preservation and to be used only for making replacement use copies (microfilm gets scratched with frequent use). We furnished the Russian archives with both a positive use copy and a negative preservation copy. Thus, the microfilm produced by the Hoover project served two purposes: it made the Soviet archives widely available for research through publication of the microfilm, and it provided the Russian archivists and Hoover with permanent preservation copies of all the archives we microfilmed.

In a second revision, the July annex corrected an ambiguity that had mistakenly been included in the agreement. In one paragraph of the agreement, Hoover and Rosarkhiv were obligated to give copies of the published microfilm to the Library of Congress and the Novosibirsk Regional State Archives—Hoover to the Library of Congress and Rosarkhiv to Novosibirsk—provided royalties earned from sales were sufficient for the purpose. In a second paragraph, this responsibility was assigned solely to Hoover. The July annex removed the ambiguity by affirming the former arrangement. In the end, however, Hoover paid for both copies—not out of earned royalties but out of its project budget.

The third revision had to do with the publication rights that Rosarkhiv had granted to Hoover. In addition to our exclusive right to copublish the microfilm with Rosarkhiv, I had negotiated favorable treatment of any future request by Hoover for rights to publish printed, English-language, letterpress editions of documents selected from the microfilm. Hoover had a long history of publishing such works. While I had no publications immediately in mind, I wanted to secure rights for these projects in the future.

Language in the agreement, however, was broader than I had intended. It gave Hoover the right of first refusal for the publication of not only works proposed by Hoover but any work proposed by any other publisher. This was obviously unacceptable to Rosarkhiv. It would have given Hoover control over the intellectual property in the twenty-five million pages to be microfilmed, a sizable portion of the holdings in the participating repositories. As I never had any intention of exploiting our advantage in this way, I agreed to amend the agreement. Accordingly, the July annex limited our rights to projects proposed by Hoover.

A second annex, signed in August 1993, made further adjustments, all relatively minor. The number of microfilm cameras was reduced from fifteen to eleven; an additional $100,000 was allocated for equipment; the advance on royalties to Rosarkhiv was increased by $60,000 (subsequently renegotiated in June 1995); Rosarkhiv gave Hoover the right to copy microfilms that the Russian repositories had made in the years before our collaboration began; and a new schedule for Hoover's payments for Rosarkhiv's labor costs was established.[32]

As it happened, the inclusion of microfilms that the Russians had produced in previous years was not as useful as we had hoped. Some of the film that had been produced on German film met our standards. For the rest, the labor cost of checking for problems, refilming, and splicing the new film into the reels was higher than the cost of refilming the documents.

A third and final annex, signed in June 1995, had both minor and substantive changes.[33] The minor changes included the following:

- A paragraph describing seven subjects that would determine the selection of documents to be microfilmed was dropped. We decided that restricting the selection criteria in this way was unnecessary.
- We agreed to exclude documents containing current state secrets. We did not expect Rosarkhiv to violate the laws of the Russian government.
- Chadwyck-Healey agreed to return to Rosarkhiv within six months the negative microfilms that the Russian repositories had made in the years prior to our project and that we had agreed to include within the scope of the project.

The June 1995 annex made several substantive amendments to the agreement, as follows:

- Hoover's payment to Rosarkhiv was changed from a prepaid amount per year ($60,000, an amount based on the estimated production of five thousand reels at $12 per reel) to an amount determined by the quantity of microfilm actually produced and received. Additionally, the amount paid was increased from $12 per reel to $27 per reel for newly produced microfilm and $12 per reel for copies of existing microfilm. This change was agreed to in an exchange of letters in October 1994 and subsequently incorporated into the June 1995 annex. In return for the per-reel increase, Rosarkhiv gave up its claim to the $60,000 advance of royalties that had been provided for in the August 1993 annex. By basing payments on production, this amendment created a much-needed incentive to produce more microfilm and to do so more quickly.

- Hoover agreed to provide Rosarkhiv with a second copy of the microfilm of Hoover's Russian collections in order to place copies in both Moscow and Novosibirsk.
- Chadwyck-Healey increased its royalty payments to Hoover from 13 percent to 15 percent. Beginning in October 1995, Chadwyck-Healey began paying royalties to Rosarkhiv on a monthly rather than yearly basis.
- A production goal of 2,400 reels per year was set. Experience showed that our initial goal of five thousand per year was unrealistic.
- The term of the agreement was set at ten years or the production of twenty-five thousand reels, whichever was longer—a change from a five-year term, renewable by Hoover for a second five-year term. It was beneficial to our side because it reinforced our production goal.
- The paragraph on termination was amended to give Hoover the right to terminate the agreement before July 1, 1997, if Rosarkhiv could not fulfill its annual production goals. This change was intended to encourage an increase in production.
- The paragraph on intellectual property was amended to remove any restriction on Rosarkhiv's publication rights. This amendment did not affect Hoover's right to copublish the microfilm, but it did void our right of first refusal on publications of printed editions of microfilmed documents. This was a step back for Hoover. I conceded the point because at that time Pikhoia was coming under fire for allegedly having alienated Russia's rights over its own historic records. Of course, Hoover was still allowed to propose and negotiate the publication of printed editions of selected documents. What we lost was the right of first refusal on such publications. Rosarkhiv was now entirely and unmistakably free to conclude any agreements it wished involving publication of printed editions.

The numerous changes requested by Pikhoia during the life of the agreement refuted the charge, as one critic claimed, that Pikhoia "pampered" the Hoover project.[34] In negotiating the initial agreement, Chadwyck-Healey held firm at paying no more than 40 percent royalties total to Rosarkhiv and Hoover. In an early draft, these royalties were split evenly between us. By the time the agreement was signed, Pikhoia, who claimed to be a novice at bargaining ("It is the first time in my life that I have had to do any bargaining. It is not my profession," he said), had argued me down to 13 percent and Rosarkhiv up to 27 percent.[35] Not only did he win favorable terms in the initial agreement, but most of the subsequent changes to it went in his direction.

While Pikhoia vigorously defended his institutional interests, he wisely acknowledged the needs of his partners. He always met his obligations under the agreement, never criticized us in public, and never asked for any special favors. It was the identical posture that Chadwyck-Healey and I took. This mutual respect among the three partners was the project's essential foundation.

The Competition

The opening of the Soviet archives engaged the interest of historians and scholarly institutions around the globe. Most of this interest did not represent competition for us. Indeed, many projects involving the archives were entirely complementary. Among the most innovative and valuable of them was the set of activities undertaken by the Cold War International History Project (CWIHP) of the Woodrow Wilson International Center for Scholars in Washington, DC. In 1992, CWIHP concluded an agreement with Rosarkhiv and the Russian Academy of Sciences to give visiting scholars unrestricted access to declassified records at the Central Committee Archives. CWIHP followed this up with a three-part program—an archive of English translations of individual documents retrieved by scholars from the records on the Cold War; publication of the documents and scholarly works based on them in its CWIHP *Bulletin*; and international conferences. These initiatives advanced scholarship and enhanced interest in all projects relating to the Soviet archives, including ours. Indeed, the CWIHP *Bulletin* published several favorable accounts of the Hoover project.[36]

Our competition came from those who sought, as we did, to copy and publish entire record groups residing in the Moscow repositories, comprising millions of original documents—not English translations of a few hundred isolated documents, as the Woodrow Wilson International Center did. For such a prize I expected intense competition and was not surprised when we got it. Pikhoia received proposals from many sources—among them, the International Institute of Social History in Amsterdam, the Fondazione Giangiacomo Feltrinelli in Milan, the British Academic Committee for Liaison with Soviet Archives at Cambridge University, and the University of California–Riverside.

Our strongest competitor was Research Publications International (RPI), a microfilm publisher and subsidiary of Thomson Corporation, a Canadian media company.[37] RPI had put forward an offer in collaboration with the US Library of Congress. I did not become aware of the Library of Congress partnership with RPI until well into my negotiations with Pikhoia. Pikhoia, of course, had no obligation to inform me of his discussions with others, and did not do so until we had concluded our preliminary agreement in February 1992. The same could not be said for the Library of Congress.

James H. Billington, a distinguished historian of Russian history, was the Librarian of Congress. He had a deep interest in the Russian archives. In early December 1991, he called together a consortium of leading historians, librarians, and archivists, including me, to discuss ways in which American resources could be organized and coordinated to assist the Russians in what was going to be the monumental task of cataloging, preserving, and making accessible a massive body of newly opened historical records. It was called the International Committee of Scholarly Advisers, which Billington himself chaired. A subset of the committee met in London later in December, joined by Pikhoia and Howlett.

The International Committee of Scholarly Advisers, as Billington stated explicitly at the outset, was not created to undertake projects itself but rather to offer guidance and direction to those who did. As a member, I felt obligated to keep Billington informed of my negotiations with Pikhoia. I did so on five occasions: on December 2, 1991, at the meeting of the International Committee of Scholarly Advisers; on February 5, 1992, the last day of the meeting of the Hoover Board of Overseers, at which Pikhoia spoke; on February 21, before my departure for Moscow where I concluded the preliminary agreement with Rosarkhiv; and on February 28 and March 4, after returning from Moscow. At these meetings I shared with Billington, either directly or indirectly through his staff, the contents of the proposals I had made to Pikhoia.[38]

Billington did not reciprocate. At no time during this period did Billington inform me that he, on behalf of the Library of Congress and the International Committee of Scholarly Advisers, had joined with RPI in a proposal to Rosarkhiv—a proposal that was clearly in competition with Hoover. As I was a member of his committee, I was entitled to know that Billington was negotiating an agreement on its behalf. Thusly informed, I would have resigned from the committee and given up my obligation to keep its chairman informed of Hoover's proposals. Billington, of course, had every right to compete with us. But by receiving confidential reports from me on my negotiations with Pikhoia while keeping his own negotiations secret, Billington took advantage of my membership on his committee and by doing so gained an unfair competitive advantage.

I had heard rumors that RPI was in competition with us but learned of Billington's collaboration with RPI only on February 25. That is when Pikhoia showed me the RPI–Library of Congress proposal, dated February 21 and signed by Billington. (It was not signed by Pikhoia.) It referred to a meeting on February 4 of representatives of Rosarkhiv, RPI, and the Library of Congress. On February 5, the next day, I had met with Billington in his office at the Library of Congress and informed him of progress on Hoover's negotiations. Billington made no mention to me of the meeting he had held the previous day with Rosarkhiv and RPI.[39]

On February 21, the very day that Billington signed the RPI proposal, I met with two of his staff members, Declan Murphy and Irene Steckler, and shared with them in detail my plans for my upcoming meeting with Pikhoia in Moscow. I asked Murphy and Steckler if they knew whether RPI had made or planned to make a similar proposal to the Russians. Neither revealed Billington's partnership with RPI. Steckler acknowledged that she intended to travel to Moscow soon to meet with Pikhoia to discuss an RPI proposal. She did not describe the proposal or say whether the Library of Congress was either joining or supporting it. I assumed that she was going to Moscow simply to offer advice to Pikhoia as part of the advisory role assumed by the Library of Congress and Billington's committee of scholarly advisers.

Murphy then suggested that Hoover and RPI divide up the task and asked if Hoover would consider copublication with the Library of Congress, noting all the advantages to Hoover of such a collaboration. I made a countersuggestion—the possibility of naming Billington the chairman of the Editorial Board for the Hoover project—indicating that this would have to be approved by both the director of the Hoover Institution and Pikhoia.[40]

Shortly after the conversation on February 21, Billington informed Pikhoia that I had offered him the chairmanship of the Editorial Board. Of course, I had not done so. It was Billington's erratic actions that caused Pikhoia and me to exclude him from the Editorial Board altogether.

On February 28, upon my return from Moscow, having successfully concluded the preliminary agreement with Rosarkhiv, I received a phone call from Murphy wanting to know what happened in Moscow. By then, I knew from Pikhoia of Billington's deception. I informed Murphy and two other staff members also on the line (Bob Derker and Steckler) that my discussions in Moscow were successful. I also assured them that I wanted to carry out the project with Billington's support and to provide a role for the Library of Congress and Billington's committee.

Without telling them that I had seen Billington's name on the RPI proposal, I indicated that I needed some assurance that Billington had withdrawn from the RPI project and that I would not consider a future relationship if we were still in a state of competition. Murphy replied that Billington had never intended to exclude or compete with Hoover. Steckler then asked me to send her a copy of Hoover's latest agreement with Pikhoia. I declined and closed the meeting by asking Murphy to set up a telephone meeting for me with Billington.[41]

The conference call with Billington took place on March 4. Also on the line, at my request, was Don Wilson, the Archivist of the United States, who was well known to and friendly with both Billington and me. I wanted a witness to the conversation and, if necessary, a mediator. Murphy was on the line as well.

Billington began aggressively, gratuitously reminding me that I was a member of his International Committee of Scholarly Advisers and asking me to summarize my agreement with Pikhoia. I gave him a full description, including the promise to give the Library of Congress a complete copy of all published microfilm (not to exceed five thousand reels). Billington continued his offensive, stated that this was the first briefing he had received about the Hoover proposal, and accused me of not keeping him properly informed and of disregarding the role of his committee, of which I was a member. I replied that, on the contrary, I had kept him fully informed and cited the previous occasions at which this took place.

At that point I decided to reveal my cards. I said that I learned in Moscow that Billington, on behalf of the Library of Congress and the International Committee of Scholarly Advisers, had signed an agreement with RPI and Rosarkhiv to microfilm and publish Soviet archives. He immediately denied having signed any such agreement and said that he would never commit the committee to any commercial venture without consulting it. From this comment I concluded that he had not consulted any members of the committee. I then told him that I had seen his signature on the agreement. In fact, though I did not reveal it to him, I possessed a copy of his signed agreement.

His deception exposed, Billington changed his tone. Instead of accusations, he turned to questions, as follows:

- Who gets the twenty-five thousand reels expected to be produced by the Hoover project? I explained that there would be two sets of microfilm: the complete set containing everything microfilmed in Russia and a published set containing microfilms of most interest to scholars. Chadwyck-Healey, our commercial distributor, did not think that the complete set would be commercially viable. Our agreement with Rosarkhiv provided for the deposit of the published microfilms (not to exceed five thousand reels) at the Library of Congress and the Novosibirsk Regional State Archives. I added that I had no objection to giving the Library of Congress the complete set (all twenty-five thousand reels), provided Pikhoia agreed and provided I could raise funds to pay for it. In the end, Pikhoia did not agree to giving complete sets to either the Library of Congress or to the Novosibirsk Regional State Archives. Both institutions got the five thousand reels we promised.

- Will there be restrictions on the use of the microfilm produced by the project? I answered, "No."
- Will the project cover all "seven sisters"? The "seven sisters" referred to seven subjects identified by Billington's International Committee of Scholarly Advisers as being of most interest to scholars. The purpose behind the seven sisters was to direct research and other projects undertaken in Russia to seven prioritized subject areas. My answer to his question was "Yes." I went to Moscow with the idea of concentrating our efforts on what I considered to be the most important of these seven sisters—namely, the mechanisms of power. However, Pikhoia wanted us to take all seven. Reasonably, he opposed dividing up the seven subjects among various projects because initially he did not want to take on more than one large microfilming operation. Nonetheless, Billington accused me of "hijacking" the seven sisters. I pointed out that by adopting the seven sisters we were simply following the advice of his committee. Moreover, his RPI proposal also had named all seven sisters and thus, it would seem, effectively excluded Hoover and others from microfilming opportunities in these subject areas.[42]
- What will be the role of the Billington committee in our project? I said I was open to suggestion on coordinating the work of the committee and our Editorial Board. I saw no necessary conflict. I said that I would be open to overlapping membership of the committee and the Editorial Board.
- Does the Hoover agreement conflict with the effort now underway by the Library of Congress, the US National Archives, the International Research and Exchanges Board, and others to place six microfilm cameras in Moscow? I said I understood that the six cameras were an unconditional gift to the Russians. Billington emphatically said that they were not and suggested that the

Hoover project undermined this effort. I said that we were not going to microfilm every historically valuable document in Russia and that a useful purpose could be found for the six cameras. He did not explain how the Hoover project would undermine the work of his six cameras and the RPI project would not.

- Will he get a copy of the agreement? I promised to send him a copy.

I concluded the conference call by asking everyone to keep the details of the call confidential in order to allow Rosarkhiv and Hoover to present the project to the public in a complete and responsible way. I received no assurance from Billington. Instead, he said that a lot of people in Washington had an interest in the work of his committee and that he would have to reassess the entire situation. From Billington's concluding remark, I had to assume that everything disclosed in the phone call would be shared with his partner, RPI, and with others. I also had to assume that RPI might do what it could to undermine our project. I was not mistaken. Within days of the conference call, RPI was back in Moscow, uninvited by Pikhoia, pressuring him to abandon Hoover and sign the RPI proposal. He refused to do so.[43]

In order to counter Billington and RPI, Pikhoia and I agreed that we would have to go public with our agreement, even though we had not yet worked out all of the final details. Accordingly, on March 10, Rosarkhiv and the Hoover Institution jointly released an announcement of our agreement. It stated our plan to undertake "a comprehensive program for preserving on microfilm the archives of the former Communist Party of the Soviet Union and the State Archives."[44]

As an act of conciliation, with Pikhoia's approval, I sent a draft of the press release to Billington, asking him if he would like us to include a reference to the role of his committee. Through Murphy, he responded positively to this suggestion. Accordingly, we inserted a sentence stating that the project would be undertaken "in association with the International Committee of Scholarly Advisers chaired by U.S. Librarian of Congress, Dr. James H. Billington." On March 9, I faxed Billington a letter thanking him for his cooperation, confirming our intention to place a complimentary copy of the published microfilm at the Library of Congress, and pledging to explore the possibility of placing all project microfilm—published and unpublished—at the Library of Congress. I also informed him that the press release would be issued on March 10.[45]

By providing Billington advance notice of the date of our release, I intentionally gave him an opportunity to put out a release of his own on the Russian program of the Library of Congress. He took advantage of this opportunity. On March 11, the day our project made news in newspapers across the country, the *New York Times* published a well-placed story on the Russian projects at the Library of Congress and the Woodrow Wilson International Center for Scholars. It featured a photograph of Billington and numerous quotations by him on the Soviet archives and the work of his committee of scholarly advisers. Buried in the story was a one-sentence mention of Hoover's historic project to microfilm the Soviet Communist Party archives.[46]

I was not offended or surprised by the *New York Times* story. It was what I expected and, indeed, wanted. We did not need Billington as an enemy. Given his deserved scholarly reputation and his position as the Librarian of Congress, he could do us damage. Understandably, he may have felt upstaged, perhaps embarrassed, by the Hoover project, especially since he had invested his professional and public reputation in efforts to open the Russian archives—a development of international and historic importance. Indeed, his contributions deserved recognition. He had drawn attention to important issues related to the archives, organized scholars and others to set standards for dealing with these issues, and generously made available to the Russians and others the expertise of his staff. Anything I could do to acknowledge these contributions and promote his role would reduce future problems for Pikhoia and me. In fact, as far as I am aware, from that point he took no further actions that hurt our project, and on occasion he gave it his public support.

The five thousand reels of microfilm that Hoover had agreed to give to the Library of Congress were delivered in two installments—2,563 reels in May 1996 and 2,442 reels in October 1996. Hoover's gift saved the Library of Congress $470,000, the price it would have had to pay Chadwyck-Healey for a collection of five thousand reels of microfilm.[47]

I set forth five conditions of the gift, all accepted, as follows:

- Housing in reel boxes displaying the names of the three project partners (Rosarkhiv, Hoover, and Chadwyck-Healey)
- Issuing a joint press release announcing the gift of the microfilm
- No lending of microfilm on interlibrary loan
- No making microfilm or electronic copies
- No photocopying of contents of microfilm exceeding 5 percent of a reel

The latter three conditions were intended to protect the market value of the microfilm, which was especially important to Rosarkhiv and Chadwyck-Healey.[48]

The transfer of the microfilm concluded our obligations to the Library of Congress. After receiving the film, Billington wrote me a gracious letter of acknowledgment, stating that the Rosarkhiv-Hoover project microfilm was "an important contribution to the Library's collections" and was of "high interest to their researchers." Hoover's generosity and our sensitivity to Billington's interests ended the competition between us and brought us peace on an important front.[49]

A different approach was needed to resolve our differences with RPI. Following my phone call with Billington on March 4, as Pikhoia later related to me, RPI officials rushed to Moscow to revive their proposal. After Pikhoia rejected it again, he thought he was now done with them. Not so. He subsequently learned that RPI, without his knowledge or approval, had concluded agreements with two archival repositories under his jurisdiction. These agreements conveyed rights to materials that had already been conveyed to Hoover. Pikhoia reacted promptly to this challenge to his authority. He instructed his deputy to inform RPI that its agreements were null and void. Pikhoia's decisive action took no small amount of courage. RPI was owned by a powerful parent company, the Thomson Corporation, a media giant with buildings full of journalists and worldwide influence.[50]

I took my own action. On June 29, I met over lunch with Meg Bellinger, vice president of editorial development at RPI. She was attending the annual meeting of the American Library Association in San Francisco. She opened our conversation by asking my reaction to a new RPI proposal to Rosarkhiv that she had previously described to me in an earlier phone call. RPI intended to convert the card catalog of the Soviet Communist Party archives to a computer-based file, which RPI would distribute worldwide. She suggested that this effort would be compatible with the Hoover project. I expressed appreciation for her sharing this information with me. But I had to tell her that I would object to any proposal that would slice up the party archives into bits and pieces. The finding aids to these archives, including the card catalog, were an integral part of the records we were going to film. It was important that they be filmed together in an orderly way. She did not press the issue.

We then moved on to matters that I wished to discuss. I conveyed my displeasure with some of RPI's actions, especially to the extraordinary pressure it had put on Pikhoia, and made it clear that Hoover would protect its interests. Bellinger responded by suggesting that I would have done the same had I been in RPI's place. I, of course, objected to this suggestion. She then made no more arguments and promised to pass along my concerns to her RPI colleagues. After our meeting, as far as I was aware, RPI made no further attempts to challenge our agreement.[51]

With this battle won, I felt relief and not a small measure of triumph. A private educational institution allied with a handful of individual donors had just won a hard-fought, consequential contest with a competitor who had the backing of a large international media corporation and an influential institution of the federal government. With the competition behind us and an agreement in hand, the way was now clear for the next phase of the project and all the tasks it would involve: raising financial support, selecting the records to be filmed, assembling a project staff, and making the project operational in Moscow.

Chapter 2

BUILDING THE PROJECT

Our Donors

One of the advantages that the Hoover Institution has had in all its endeavors has been the generous support it has received from its loyal donors. From the beginning of the Russian project, this support enabled us to act quickly and decisively when such action was necessary. We received immediate and significant financial contributions from Herbert Hoover III through the Herbert Hoover, Jr., and Margaret Hoover Foundation and from Richard M. Scaife through the Sarah Scaife Foundation.

Shortly thereafter, additional major gifts came from six other donors: David and Lucile Packard Foundation, Jaquelin Hume Foundation, Lakeside Foundation, John M. Olin Foundation, Estate of Estelle Buel Simon (Alice Phillips Rose, trustee), and the Seaver Institute. Smaller gifts were received from numerous individuals and companies, including most notably from Henry Hoagland, the Archer Daniels Midland Company, George H. Hume, John Stahr, the Singer Company, and Margaret Soares. The project donors were both new and longtime supporters of the Hoover Institution, some going back to Herbert Hoover's time. The unity of support for the project was gratifying and encouraging. It was wind at my back.

In total, between 1992 and 2002, Hoover raised $3,185,161 for the project, all from private sources. These gifts paid for all project costs, totaling $3,159,666.[1]

In addition to gifts from donors, the Hoover Institution received royalties from the sale of the project microfilm, initially at 13 percent of total sales and 15 percent after 1995, totaling $750,000. Chadwyck-Healey, of course, had to incorporate the royalties paid to Hoover and Rosarkhiv into its calculation of the price of the microfilm. What it did not have to incorporate were the much larger project costs, paid by Hoover from gifts received from donors. Even when Hoover's costs increased during the course of the project, the increases never resulted in an increase in the price paid by customers for the microfilm. Had Hoover attempted to recoup project costs from the sale of the microfilm, the price would have been prohibitive. Thus, the generosity of the Hoover donors benefited not only Hoover but all the libraries and other customers who purchased the microfilm.[2]

In November 1992, Hoover director Raisian and I invited several project donors and members of the Hoover Institution's Board of Overseers to join us in a trip to Moscow. The occasion was the opening of our joint exhibit with Rosarkhiv. Entitled "Making Things Work: Russian-American Economic Relations, 1900–1930," the exhibit occupied prime space in the Russian parliament building. Before an approving crowd, Pikhoia and Raisian gave appropriate remarks, all of which were favorably covered in the Moscow press.

During their stay, our donors also met with several prominent Russian government leaders, toured the Kremlin buildings and other Moscow sites, and inspected the repositories holding the Soviet Communist Party archives. During the visit to the archives, one of our donors took down a document box and without permission opened it up. The Russian archivist guide nervously asked the donor to replace the box, but before doing so our Hoover translator read off one of the folder titles—"Caspar Weinberger, US Secretary of Defense."

Bringing wealthy Americans to Moscow in those days was not without risk. Crime was widespread, and official law enforcement was weak. We cautioned our donors not to bring large amounts of cash with them, and we hired private security protection to and from the airport for them. The Moscow security company even offered an escort tank, which I declined. The hotel where we stayed had extensive security—high fences around the entire hotel, armed guards at the perimeter gates, and plainclothes guards inside.

Fortunately, during the twelve-year project, only two untoward incidents occurred. The more serious of the two happened to Gordon Hahn, a Hoover research fellow who assisted me with assignments in Moscow. After exchanging some money in a Moscow bank, he was met outside by two armed thugs, forced into a car, and threatened. Acting quickly, Hahn offered them a small amount of American money and was released.

A somewhat comical but revealing incident happened to me. After a negotiating session with Pikhoia, he offered to take me back to my hotel in his government car. Within a block of our pulling away from the curb, a traffic cop waved the car to the side. I asked Pikhoia what the problem was. He said the cop spotted me getting into the car and, assuming I was a wealthy American, wanted a bribe. Pikhoia refused to give in. He said we would wait him out. After fifteen minutes or so, the cop waved us on, clearly annoyed that we had not paid his toll.

A second donor event occurred on March 23, 1993, the occasion of former British prime minister Margaret Thatcher's visit to the Hoover Institution. As part of the day's events, I organized a formal presentation to Rosarkhiv of 4,640 reels of microfilm of Hoover's Russian archival collections. The microfilm was the first installment fulfilling our promise to give the Russians copies of our holdings in exchange for the microfilms produced in Moscow. Pikhoia was present to accept the microfilm on behalf of the Russian nation. I instructed our staff to stack the microfilm boxes into a gigantic pile in Stauffer Auditorium for the ceremony. The pile conveyed to our donors the scope of the project they had paid for.

I introduced former secretary of state George P. Shultz, a distinguished fellow at Hoover, to make the presentation. He did so in his usual dignified and effective way before a gathering of members of the Hoover Board of Overseers, Thatcher, and other notables. Shortly thereafter, the microfilm was shipped to Russia. On May 21, a second ceremony was held in Moscow, attended by the US ambassador to Russia, Thomas R. Pickering.

Selecting the Records

By early June 1992, Pikhoia and I had agreed on the composition of the Editorial Board, which was assigned the responsibility of selecting the records to be filmed and setting the order of their filming. The records of the Soviet Communist Party and Soviet State numbered in the hundreds of millions of files. Even with an ambitious target of twenty-five million pages, we could hope to film only a fraction of the total. We needed the assistance of knowledgeable historians to help us make the selection.

The Editorial Board served a second purpose. Enlisting recognized experts to make the selections would blunt the charge of ideological bias that I thought might be made against us. For much of its history, the Hoover Institution has had a public reputation as a conservative think tank. Indeed, Herbert Hoover himself stated that a principal purpose of his institution was "to demonstrate the evils of the doctrines of Karl Marx."[3]

When the Soviet Union collapsed, he was vindicated in this view, and few scholars disputed it. Indeed, we certainly expected to find in the Soviet archives evidence of the evils and inherent failures of Soviet Communism. Most everyone else, including our Russian partners, expected the same. Nonetheless, it was important to put the project on a professional, scientific footing, isolated as much as possible from partisan bias. Placing the selection process in the hands of an expert Editorial Board helped to accomplish that objective.

To represent the Hoover Institution on the board I chose Robert Conquest, John B. Dunlop, and Terence Emmons. On the Russian side, Pikhoia chose Dmitri Volkogonov and Nikolai N. Pokrovskii. Pikhoia, the third Russian member, served as chairman. Jana Howlett, who became a consultant paid by Hoover to assist with the project, was appointed an ex officio member.

All members of the Editorial Board were distinguished scholars of Russian history. Conquest, senior research fellow at Hoover, was America's leading Sovietologist and author of *The Great Terror*, the definitive work on Stalin's purges, as well as *The Harvest of Sorrow* and *Stalin and the Kirov Murder*, among others. Dunlop, senior fellow at Hoover, authored *The Faces of Contemporary Russian Nationalism* and coedited *Solzhenitsyn in Exile: Critical Essays and Documentary Materials*. Emmons, professor of history at Stanford University, was author and editor of numerous books, including *The Formation of Political Parties and the First National Elections in Russia* and *Time of Troubles: The Diary of Iurii Vladimirovich Got'e*.

Members on the Russian side were equally distinguished. Volkogonov was special assistant to President Boris Yeltsin and chairman of the presidential commission assigned to examine the Soviet archives. He authored three biographies: *Stalin: Triumph and Tragedy*; *Lenin: A New Biography*; and *Trotsky: The Eternal Revolutionary*. During the Soviet period, Volkogonov led a dual life—inwardly a reformer secretly writing a critical biography of Stalin, outwardly a hard-line colonel general and head of the Institute of Military History. Pokrovskii was a member of the Russian Academy of Sciences and Russia's foremost expert on Siberia and peasant literature.

In addition to the Editorial Board, I drew on the expertise of Hoover research fellows Gordon Hahn and Semion Lyandres, both scholars of Russian history and politics. They spent time in Moscow examining the Russian archives, making recommendations for filming, and representing Hoover's interest at the three repositories.

The Editorial Board met four times: June 14, 1992, in Washington, DC; September 17–18, 1992, in Moscow; January 28–29, 1993, in Cambridge, England; and February 3, 1994, in Washington, DC. Pikhoia and I attended all these meetings. The recommendations of the Editorial Board were subject to the approval of Pikhoia and me as project directors. In the event, we approved their recommendations without reservation.[4]

The specific record groups selected and in fact filmed, together with the repositories that held them, included the following (dates are beginning and end dates of the records, not of the party or state entities):[5]

Record groups	**No. of reels**	**Repositories**
Party Congresses and Conferences, 1903–90	260 reels	RTsKhIDNI
Party Central Committee, 1903–71	2,460 reels	RTsKhIDNI
Party Control Commission of the Central Committee, 1934–66	973 reels	TsKhSD
People's Commissariat of Internal Affairs (NKVD), 1917–31	4,205 reels	GARF
Main Directorate for Places of Detention (GULAG) and related agencies, 1917–67	3,428 reels	GARF
Constitutional Court, 1918–92	24 reels	TsKhSD, APRF
Finding Aids	469 reels	RTsKhIDNI, TsKhSD, GARF

RTsKhIDNI (pronounced ertz-KHEED-nee) was the Russian acronym for the Center for the Preservation and Study of Records of Modern History, formerly the Central Party Archive and Marx-Engels-Lenin Institute. It held the party archives dated from the party origins through October 1952. It is now named the Russian State Archives of Socio-Political History (RGASPI).

TsKhSD (pronounced tse-KHAH-es-day) was the Russian acronym for the Center for the Preservation of Contemporary Documentation, formerly the Current Archive of the Soviet Communist Party Central Committee, usually referred to as the Central Committee Archives. It held the party archives dated from October 1952 to August 1991. It is now named the Russian State Archives of Recent History (RGANI).

GARF (rhymes with "scarf") was the State Archive of the Russian Federation, formerly the Central State Archives of the October Revolution, High Organs of State Power, and Organs of State Administration of the USSR and the Central State Archive of the RSFSR.

APRF, the Russian acronym of the Archive of the President of the Russian Federation (also called the Presidential Archive or the Kremlin Archive), was a repository that held Politburo files dating from 1919 to 1991, the papers of general secretaries and other top Soviet leaders, and the papers of President Gorbachev, as well as files (*osobye papki*) withdrawn from the main body of party and state records because they contained national security or political secrets.

Rosarkhiv did not oversee APRF. It was controlled directly by the office of President Yeltsin. A presidential decree dated September 22, 1994, directed the transfer of authority over APRF to Rosarkhiv, but it never happened and until recently few materials were ever transferred.[6] The other three repositories remained under the jurisdiction of Rosarkhiv throughout the duration of the project.

The records selected for filming reflected the Editorial Board's three principal objectives. First, we wanted to film all the finding aids at the three repositories and do so before any filming of the records themselves. Second, we focused on records documenting the mechanisms of power, by which we meant the decision-making and systemic operations of the central organs of the Soviet Communist Party and Soviet State. Third, entire record files were filmed. No attempt was made to select individual documents based on subject or other criteria.

The first objective was filming the finding aids and other guides that described and facilitated use of the records. It was our intention to microfilm the finding aids not just to those records we chose to film but the finding aids to all the holdings at the three participating repositories. We successfully did so at two of the three participating repositories: 326 finding aids at RTsKhIDNI and 2,150 at GARF. At TsKhSD, we filmed the finding aids of five key record groups (Fonds 6, 8, and 89, and selectively for Fonds 4 and 5).

Filming the finding aids first served several purposes. Having the finding aids in hand as we filmed the records enabled us to check for missing items. Additionally, in case our project was shut down prematurely, having the finding aids in hand ensured that at least we would have a reliable record of Russia's archival holdings on Soviet Communism. Once the project was completed, the finding aids became essential guides for scholars using the microfilmed records at the Hoover Institution as well as planning research trips to examine records at the Russian archives in Moscow.[7]

Documenting the decision-making and systemic operations of Soviet Communism was our second and most important objective. To do that we focused on the central organs of the Soviet Communist Party and Soviet State. While we did not film records of all central organs, we were able to film those of such key organs as the Party Congresses and Conferences, the Party Central Committee, the Party Control Commission, and the People's Commissariat of Internal Affairs (NKVD). In addition, we filmed the massive records relating to the Gulag, the system of forced labor camps that manifested the organizational attributes of Soviet Communism generally.

The Party Congresses and Conferences included representatives of all party organizations throughout the Soviet Union and met periodically to ratify the principal policies of the party and state. The Hoover project filmed the records of all but three of the Congresses, consisting of 220,000 pages dating from 1903 to 1990.[8]

When the Party Congresses were not in session, the Central Committee assumed their responsibilities. According to party doctrine, the Party

Congresses, and in their absence the Central Committee, constituted the apex of the Soviet Communist Party. Beginning in the late 1920s, when Stalin gained dominance, the actual apex of power was the Politburo. Nonetheless, as Mark Kramer's work shows, the records of the Congresses and the Central Committee are a valuable source for the study of Soviet policymaking. They document internal debate, reveal key information distributed to the party members, and record changes in policy.

Directed by the Politburo, the Central Committee oversaw party and government agencies and by extension the entire political and economic life of the nation. It elected the members of the Secretariat, which included the administrative departments of the party and was responsible for putting policies into effect. The departments prepared the background documents used by the Politburo and in so doing wielded influence on policymaking. More than two million pages of Central Committee records were filmed, including those of Central Committee party plenums (1918–41) and key departments of the Secretariat, including administration, finance and budget, statistics, census, defense, propaganda and ideology, and party organization. These records provide an in-depth picture of the operation of the Soviet Communist Party and of Russian society generally.[9]

The Party Control Commission supervised the lives of party members in minute detail, from their party transgressions to their private lives. It brought to account party members who violated party discipline, was instrumental in conducting the party purges of the 1930s, reviewed activities of local party organizations, and enforced party and governmental regulations. Its records thus document the operations of the most important actor in the Soviet State, the Soviet Communist Party. Approximately 825,000 pages, covering the period between 1934 and 1966, were filmed.

The People's Commissariat of Internal Affairs, often generally referred to by its acronym, NKVD, was one of the key instruments of Bolshevik rule. We filmed 3.6 million pages of NKVD records covering the first years of Soviet rule, 1917–30. During that period, the NKVD resided within the government of the RSFSR and did not oversee the secret police, the notorious body that terrorized party members and society in general. What it did oversee were virtually all aspects of the everyday lives of ordinary Russians and, in doing so, exhibited all the systemic deficiencies of Soviet

Communism. The records we filmed document provincial and local government, agriculture and industry, police and militia, labor unions, voluntary societies, labor camps, and prisons. NKVD forces guarded the borders, issued passports, kept track of foreigners; registered births, deaths, and marriages; and collected data on all manner of political, economic, and social activity.

The forced labor camps that began in 1918 and spread across the Soviet Union became the principal focus of the Hoover project during its second phase beginning in 1998. From 1918 to 1946, the camps were run by the secret police, which went through several reorganizations and name changes: Cheka (1918–22), GPU (1922–23), OGPU (1923–34), and NKVD (1934–46).[10] From 1946 to the end of the Soviet Union, they were run by the Ministry of Internal Affairs (MVD). The system of camps came to be called the Gulag, after the acronym for the Main Directorate for Places of Detention (GULAG), the NKVD department that ran the camps.

Hoover filmed three million pages of records on the Gulag from 1917 to 1967. They include records of all the government agencies that were part of the Gulag's administrative and judicial apparatus, as follows:

- Main Directorate for Places of Detention (GULAG) of the People's Commissariat of Internal Affairs (NKVD) and Main Administration of the Places of Confinement of the USSR Ministry of Internal Affairs (MVD), the agencies responsible for running the camps
- Council of People's Commissars, a ruling government body that oversaw the state police
- Ministry of Justice, Procurator's Office, Supreme Tribunal of the All-Russian Executive Committee and Supreme Court, which provided the veneer of judicial oversight
- Commission for Private Amnesty of the Presidium of the USSR Central Executive Committee
- Commission for Grievance and Requests for Pardons of the Presidium of the USSR Supreme Soviet
- Fourth Special Department of the USSR Ministry of Internal Affairs, which managed the mass expulsion of peasants from their homes during collectivization

- Department of Children's Labor and Educational Colonies, which operated children's colonies
- E. P. Peshkova Society (Committee for Aid to Prisoners) and the Political Red Cross, which offered some humanitarian aid to prisoners

The Gulag microfilms record every aspect of the system—the arrests, interrogations, judicial actions and oversight, transportation, camp life, uses of forced labor, economic impacts, disease, repression, and deaths. They include the full range of documentation: secret police records, policy memoranda and minutes of meetings; laws, decrees, and judicial rulings; regulations and instruction on camp administration and operations; lists of prisoners; budgets and personnel data, reports on the vast industrial and agricultural enterprises operated by the GULAG administration; data on hunger strikes, escapes, executions, and mass rebellions; lists of grievances and grants of amnesty; documents on camp culture and educational activities; and records on health, disease, and death rates.

The focus on the central organs of the Party and State accomplished our principal objective—to document the systemic operations of Soviet Communism. During the early scramble for Russian archives, many of those seeking access were looking for sensational revelations on controversial topics—the 1939 Molotov-Ribbentrop Pact, the Kennedy assassination, the 1968 invasion of Czechoslovakia, Soviet spies, and the like. Others wanted to establish a Nuremberg-type prosecution that would expose evidence of wrongdoing by Soviet leaders. While we did not turn down a chance to get such materials, we had a different objective.

From the beginning I did not think that Rosarkhiv, even under the administration of its open-minded director, Rudolf Pikhoia, would ever give us or others access to the Soviet Union's most sensitive state secrets—secrets that might have contained sensational revelations. The Russians opened a great many records, all of which had been closed for decades. But the records of the Politburo, the KGB, and other security agencies, with the exception of those materials in the Gulag records and Fond 89 (noted below), remained closed to us and everyone else. I did not spend much time and effort trying to get them. What I did think the Russians would open and in fact did open to us, freely and expeditiously, were the everyday records of party and state agencies—the housekeeping records of Soviet Communism.

While not always sensational, such records document the inner workings of the system, their effect on the life of the country, and thus the essential nature of Soviet Communism, including its systemic failures and tragic costs. Beyond the crimes of individual Communist leaders, our project sought to expose a system—its goals, organization, and operation. What in its nature made Soviet Communism and its system of government inherently ruinous, corrupt, and inhumane? The ordinary administrative records of the organs of state power, I thought, would answer that question.

In addition to these two objectives—copying the finding aids and documenting the central organs of the Party and State—we had a third objective, namely, filming the entire contents of each record file. We rejected the idea of selecting individual documents within record series based on subject. The International Committee of Scholarly Advisers, chaired by Billington, which had named seven distinct subject areas as priorities, emphasized a subject approach, which I felt had four shortcomings:

- It would have involved an extraordinary amount of time and effort. The delay and expense would have been fatal to our efforts.
- It would have meant treating individual documents as discrete units detached from considerations of their origin and of their relationship with other records created by the same agency. The evidential value and meaning of records are derived in important ways from these factors. Documents are best understood within the context of surrounding records, not singly as isolated pieces.
- It would have focused mainly on individuals, events, and episodes, not on the inner workings of the system. Understanding the system required an examination of the organizations that comprised it, and understanding these organizations required an examination of their records, preserved in their original order and completeness. It is the full, unabridged, and undisturbed body of its records that gives evidence of an organization's goals, policies, decisions, procedures, functions, performance, and operations.

- It would have exposed us to a charge of bias. Picking and choosing individual documents would have left readers wondering what was omitted and why.

Instead of the individual document level, our selection was made at the *fond*, *opis*, or *delo* (pluralized as *fondy*, *opisi*, and *dela*, respectively) level. In American parlance, *fondy* correspond to record groups (the largest groupings of records in the hierarchy of archival organization), *opisi* to record series comprising record groups, and *dela* to folders within series. Most of our selections were made at the *fondy* or *opisi* levels; the selection of some records at GARF relating to the Gulag were made at the *dela* level. By filming entire record files, we let the records speak for themselves.[11]

Our decision to film complete record files paid off by enabling valuable, detailed case studies and organizational histories of party organs and government agencies. Many of these studies were conducted under the direction of economic historian Paul Gregory, a research fellow of the Hoover Institution. Gregory led a team of young scholars who produced dozens of works that analyzed the internal operations of various Soviet Communist Party and Soviet State institutions. They cataloged and assessed the systemic elements of Soviet Communism and by doing so documented the inherent flaws of a collectivist system.[12]

The recent works of Gregory and others, of course, were not the first to examine the systemic nature of Soviet Communism. The preeminent such study was Merle Fainsod's *How Russia Is Ruled*, published in 1953 and again in 1963. Fainsod's influential book inspired a generation of scholars who sought to dissect and understand the institutions that comprised the Soviet system. All of these earlier works, however, had a fundamental flaw, one their authors all acknowledged. They were undertaken without access to the actual records of the system. Without such access, these scholars could not reach agreement even on the most fundamental question: Were the Soviet institutions qualitatively different from Western institutions, or did both work in relatively similar ways? The opening of the Soviet archives and the access to complete record files provided by the microfilm collection have given scholars the means to address again this question and others that Fainsod and his generation raised but could not fully answer.[13]

In one case, we departed from our twin objectives of documenting the mechanisms of power and filming complete record files. Well into the project, Pikhoia offered us Fond 89, "The Communist Party of the Soviet Union on Trial, 1918–92." These records consisted of evidence gathered for the 1992 trial involving a lawsuit brought by the Communist Party against Yeltsin's decrees of August and November 1991, which dissolved the party and transferred its records over to the government. The trial was held before the Constitutional Court of the Russian Federation from July to November 1992. The records numbered about twenty thousand pages, including more than two thousand declassified secret and top-secret Politburo, Central Committee, secret police, defense, and foreign relations documents.[14]

Fond 89 was a departure from our selection criteria in two ways. First, it focused on individuals and events, not the systemic features of the organs of the Party and State. The purpose of the trial records was to reveal the most sensational crimes of individual party leaders, and they did so—among them the World War II Katyn Forest massacre, the 1956 invasion of Hungary, the 1968 invasion of Czechoslovakia, the 1980–81 crisis in Poland, the downing of Korean Air Lines Flight 007, and the handling of the Chernobyl disaster.[15]

Fond 89 departed from our selection criteria in a second way. As a group of records selected by government lawyers trying the case, it constituted a collection of individual documents drawn from various record groups of which they were a part. In contrast, our focus was on whole record groups or series, not single isolated documents.

Despite these considerations, I agreed to include Fond 89 in our project. I did so for three reasons: the trial was an important event in Russian politics during the Yeltsin presidency; the documents came largely from record groups that otherwise were denied to us; and its size was relatively small (twenty-four reels). I am glad we filmed them. Fond 89 became one of the most used parts of the collection.

Facsimiles of six documents from Fond 89 are reproduced in the photo section of this book and show why these records were so compelling. One shows financial support of Comintern (Communist International) agents in foreign countries amounting to millions of rubles as early as 1919–20.

A Politburo resolution, dated July 10, 1937, confirmed twenty-three thousand citizens shot and fifty-one thousand sent to the Gulag in just two days. A Central Committee resolution, dated March 5, 1940, and signed by Stalin and Soviet leader Kliment Voroshilov, reported the execution of 14,700 captured Polish officers and others at Katyn and other camps. The minutes of a Politburo meeting, dated March 4, 1968, show large sums of money transferred to communist parties in Spain, Denmark, and Guatemala, among others.

Other Fond 89 records show the progressive decay of the Soviet system. For example, a KGB report dated July 25, 1962, recorded the extent of internal resistance to the government both internally and abroad: 7,705 discrete pieces of opposition literature circulated clandestinely during the first six months of 1962. In the final months of the regime, Politburo meeting minutes reveal a government splintering into factions, ending in an epic struggle between the hard-line reactionaries led by Yegor Ligachev and Vladimir Kryuchkov and the reformers led by Mikhail Gorbachev.[16]

All records selected by the Editorial Board and approved by Rosarkhiv were materials we wanted. But we did not get everything we asked for. Three record groups we wanted but did not get were the records of the Politburo, the Comintern, and the US Communist Party. When I requested these records, Pikhoia refused to include them in the project. The only Politburo documents we filmed were those in Fond 89.

The Comintern was an international organization of communist parties founded in 1919 by Lenin to seize leadership of the world socialist movement. Because the records included documents originating with other national communist parties in Europe and elsewhere, Pikhoia did not think he had the authority to include them in the project without their consent. Pikhoia gave us a similar answer to my request to copy the records of the US Communist Party, which had been shipped from the United States to Moscow in 1939 for safekeeping.[17]

Other records that were beyond our reach were materials restricted by law, primarily documents closed for reasons of national security or privacy. All governments observe such restrictions. While we pushed hard for openness, I recognized that Pikhoia himself faced limitations on his authority in this area. On January 14, 1992, for example, Yeltsin issued a decree barring the release of Communist Party materials dated after 1981. It also closed records of decisions of the Secretariat of the Central Committee dated after 1961, as well as other records dated after 1961 relating to international affairs, defense, and national security matters.[18]

Subsequent decrees and laws followed. On July 7, 1993, the Law on the Archival Fond of the Russian Federation and Archives, the first archival law in Russian history to be enacted by the legislature, set forth the basic regulations on archives. While guaranteeing public access, it established a thirty-year restriction for most records and a seventy-five-year restriction on personal privacy documents. This law was accompanied a month later by the "On State Secrets" law, which gave control over records access not to Rosarkhiv but to the government agencies that created the records. In September 1994, a presidential decree established a declassification commission with authority to set access policies relating to the Communist Party archives and records transferred from the Presidential Archive. As our project focused on the party archives, this commission was of concern to us. It was chaired by Sergei N. Krasavchenko, first deputy director of the presidential administration.[19]

Pikhoia had good relations with the officials in the presidential administration and the new declassification commission, which included Dmitri Volkogonov, who was a member of our Editorial Board. Even so, aside from documents in Fond 89, we had no success getting records of the Politburo and limited success getting records housed at TsKhSD—those dated after October 1952. It did not help that TsKhSD staff had been accused of releasing classified documents to a foreign researcher, an unfortunate incident that led in 1993 to the dismissal of its director, Rem Usikov, and to the closure of TsKhSD's reading room. Usikov's replacements, first A. S. Prokopenko and then Natalia G. Tomilina, were understandably very cautious about opening up materials.[20]

Going into our negotiations with Rosarkhiv, we knew that some Soviet archives were beyond our reach because they were not under Rosarkhiv's control. In addition to the holdings at the Presidential Archive, these included the records of the KGB, the military and Ministry of Defense, and the Foreign Ministry. Pikhoia told me that initially he expected to have jurisdiction over the KGB archives, but before he could act, the Federal Security Service (successor to the KGB) regained control.

While many secrets doubtless remain hidden in the Soviet archives still closed, what was opened and made available to us was remarkable and consequential. While Soviet history was generally known before the archives were opened and filmed, historians now have the evidence to confirm their accounts, fill in the details, and expand their understanding. Moreover, the evidence contained in the microfilmed records ensure that the history of Soviet Communism can no longer be denied, whitewashed, or falsified. It is possible to dismiss interpretations. It is not possible to dismiss documentary evidence.

A word must be said about the goal set for the number of pages to be microfilmed and reels produced—i.e., twenty-five million pages on twenty-five thousand reels of microfilm. At the beginning of the project, when I wrote the agreement, I did not know the record groups that the Editorial Board would select or how many pages they would occupy. Thus, the goal I set in the agreement—twenty-five million pages—was not based on an informed or careful count. Nor did it represent a criterion against which the success of the project should be judged. Rather, it was calculated simply to give the Editorial Board enough range to accomplish its main objective—to capture the historical record of the policymaking organs of government, whose records, I knew, numbered in the millions.

In addition, I wanted to present a number that would signal our commitment to preserving Russian archives, that would attract the attention of Hoover's donors and supporters, and that would cause our competition to pause, if not retreat. Most of all, I wanted to engage fully the working capacity of our Russian colleagues and the financial resources that I could bring to the enterprise. I did not want to leave anything on the table. My number did not scare away the competition but did accomplish the other objectives.

All members of the Editorial Board deserve much credit for the success of the project and the scholarship it produced. Especially noteworthy, however, was the work of Emmons and Howlett, both of whom spent considerable time in Moscow examining the holdings of the three participating repositories and working with the Russian archivists. The knowledge they gained by these efforts and their recommendations were essential factors guiding the deliberations of the Editorial Board.

Making It Work

Negotiating and concluding an agreement, pacifying opponents, raising financial support, and selecting records for filming were only the initial tasks of the project. Staffing the project, setting and managing a budget, buying and shipping equipment and supplies, setting up equipment in three Moscow locations, training microfilming crews, microfilming records, processing microfilm, authorizing and executing payments, preparing catalogs, distributing and marketing the microfilm, and furnishing the Russians with matching microfilms of Hoover's Russian Collection—these were the necessary tasks that lay ahead of us.

At Hoover I retained overall direction of the project. Assisting me were several Hoover staff: Judith Fortson, head librarian; Cathy Aster, preservation officer; Anne Van Camp, archivist; Elena Danielson, who succeeded Van Camp as archivist; Joseph Dwyer, deputy curator of the Russian Collection; Dena Schoen, librarian and Russian specialist; Lora Soroka, archival specialist; and my administrative assistants, Kathleen Power and Lois Christopherson. All performed ably and professionally.

The most important of these was Fortson, who for many years had managed Hoover's preservation program as preservation officer, who was a leading expert on archival microfilming and who now was head librarian. She was responsible for setting up and overseeing technical operations in Russia as well as assisting me in numerous administrative chores. She was my indispensable chief deputy throughout the project, and her wise counsel and innumerable and invaluable contributions were essential to its success. When Fortson retired in 2000, near the end of the project, Cathy Aster, Hoover's preservation officer, ably assumed her project duties.

Van Camp was responsible for making the microfilm accessible to scholars in the Hoover Archives reading room, overseeing the preparation of guides to the microfilm, and independently managing the Hoover-Rosarkhiv joint exhibit and RLIN database project. Danielson succeeded Van Camp in 1996 and did so effectively. Dwyer provided curatorial advice as needed and on occasion served as my translator. Soroka was newly hired at Hoover to prepare guides for the microfilm as it arrived at Hoover. Her detailed descriptions were published in the Online Archive of California. In addition, the Hoover Institution Press published her guide to Fond 89, the records of the Constitutional Court of the Russian Federation relating to the 1992 trial of the Communist Party of the Soviet Union.[21]

Schoen was my principal translator and, along with Fortson, was present at many of my meetings with Pikhoia. In addition to her exceptional language skills, Schoen contributed astute observations, especially about the Russians we encountered and their ways of thinking and behaving. Most importantly, she understood that as a translator she had to be an extension of me. She had to know my intentions, my negotiating strategy, and my concerns. Her diligence in preparation and her ability to read my mind under pressure as negotiations ebbed and flowed were crucial. She did all of this while effectively translating my words from English to Russian and Pikhoia's words from Russian to English.

I had two administrative assistants during the course of the project: Kathleen Power until 1994 and Lois Christopherson thereafter. They helped in countless ways—coordinating communications between me and the numerous partners, agents, and others involved in the project; wiring money transfers; and organizing and managing the extensive project records, among other tasks. Communicating with our partners in Russia was especially challenging. The Russians did not use email during those years, and the surface mail was useless. We relied mostly on faxes. Since the Russians often turned off their fax machines at night, we had to fax them materials at odd hours. Their machines seemed to fail frequently. We used the telephone as well, but that also had limited value because of the nine-hour time difference.

In addition to Hoover's own staff, I leaned heavily on Jana Howlett, a fellow of Jesus College, Cambridge, with whom Hoover concluded a consulting contract. In addition to her language skills and scholarship, she brought to the project her familiarity with Russian archives and a good relationship with Pikhoia, which enabled her to mediate differences. Howlett assisted both Chadwyck-Healey and me in negotiating the agreement with Rosarkhiv, attended all summit meetings of the three partners, often served as translator for the three of us, and served on the Editorial

Board as an ex officio member. Her other assignments included coordinating operations in Moscow, communicating information and issues among the three partners, troubleshooting and solving on-site problems, and providing other logistical support in Moscow for both Chadwyck-Healey and Hoover. She did so by making numerous trips to Moscow, writing detailed reports, and employing local helpers. Her contribution to the success of the project was as important as any made by others.

Especially valuable to Howlett's efforts in Moscow was the work of Natalia Volkova, whom Howlett hired in September 1993. Volkova worked half-time for the Hoover project and half-time for a separate project run by Chadwyck-Healey. The cost of her salary was split evenly between Hoover and Chadwyck-Healey. Volkova periodically gathered up the exposed microfilm and shipped it to the Chadwyck-Healey microfilm production company (CHMPS) in England. She was an invaluable source of information about the problems and issues that developed at the microfilming sites.

The project was a three-legged stool. It remained upright when each of the three partners performed its function and became shaky when any one of them faltered. Rosarkhiv gave direction for the project in Moscow and oversight of the three participating Russian repositories. The repositories provided on-site labor and supervision and, of course, the records themselves. Hoover provided the conception, organization, direction, financial backing, and management, and shared responsibility for supervision and troubleshooting problems. Hoover paid for all project costs—equipment and supplies, labor (both Russian and our own), film processing and development costs, meeting costs, and Editorial Board expenses. All key decisions were made by Pikhoia and me as the lead partners after consultation with Charles Chadwyck-Healey.

The project could not have succeeded without the third leg of the stool, the Chadwyck-Healey publishing company and its enterprising chairman, Charles Chadwyck-Healey, who served as a project director along with Pikhoia and me. In 1992, the Chadwyck-Healey staff included Alastair Everitt, managing director; Steven Hall, sales and marketing director; Don McCrae, group finance director; Alison Maynard, financial controller; Dave Chapman, production manager, and his assistant, Reuben Starling;

and Inga Huld Markan, administrative assistant.[22] (See appendix A for Charles Chadwyck-Healey's account of the project.)

Charles Chadwyck-Healey always acknowledged Hoover as the lead partner. As he wrote to me in January 1995, "This is Hoover's project . . . set up at your initiative, and Chadwyck-Healey was brought in as an enabler and marketing specialist." While Pikhoia and I accepted responsibility for all major decisions and their consequences, we always regarded Chadwyck-Healey as an equal partner.[23]

Chadwyck-Healey Ltd. provided the know-how and flexible management that was necessary to create and operate a microfilming project from scratch in a difficult environment. The Chadwyck-Healey team set up the equipment and operations at the three Russian repositories in Moscow (assisted by Hoover's Fortson); coordinated the shipment of exposed microfilm from Moscow to its production company in Bassingbourn, near Cambridge, England; spliced in all the leaders, trailers, and targets (e.g., title page and copyright notice); maintained quality controls over the production and processing of microfilm; prepared the published catalog; and marketed and distributed the microfilm for sale.[24]

As Charles Chadwyck-Healey described it to me in a letter, "Microfilming is not rocket science, it is not very creative and it is not very complicated but to do it well does need enormous attention to detail by pragmatic, down-to-earth people who do not mind spending time on small, mundane items of management." As a small company with an informal management style, Chadwyck-Healey Ltd. provided the flexible, on-the-spot decision-making skills needed to deal with the many and varied problems that we faced in an unstable Russian environment.[25]

Chadwyck-Healey Ltd. was not entirely suited to the project. Like other microfilm publishers, it normally published collections limited in size and densely packed with high-value documents. Such publications yield sufficient sales to realize profits. Its main customers were research libraries, few of which could afford the high price of an 11,000-reel collection—one that would yield its value not immediately but over many decades of use.

The huge number of records copied by our project presented significant challenges to Chadwyck-Healey's marketing staff. As Steven Hall, its sales and marketing director and from 1994 its managing director, wrote to me, "The lack of selectivity makes it very difficult to sell such an enormous body of material." Hoover's main goal was to copy as much material as possible; Chadwyck-Healey's main goal was to realize a profit. It was a credit to Charles Chadwyck-Healey and his staff that they persevered despite being exposed to significant financial risk on uncertain ground.[26]

Making the project work took all the resources that the three partners had in their arsenals. Hoover and Chadwyck-Healey had their essential roles. But of course we had to make it work at the three participating Russian repositories. Without them we would have had no project. They housed the archives and employed the staff who prepared the records for filming and operated the cameras and other equipment. The tasks they performed constituted the heart of the project, but it came with challenges.

Equipment issues were the first challenge. The equipment list was impressive: eleven Recordak MRD II cameras, three Dukane microfilm readers, two Alos duplicators, one Extek duplicator, three Prostar processors, one Allen processor, three inspection stations, a computer and laser printer, and miscellaneous items. Even the miscellaneous category was quite extensive: spare parts, line stabilizers, eye loupes, sump pumps, and book cradles. When we learned that many of the records we wanted to copy had already been microfilmed by the Russians in previous years, we had to reallocate some of our funding for additional equipment needed to duplicate the Russian film.[27]

Next, we had to ship the equipment to Russia, which turned out to be more difficult than we expected. The airline that transported the first shipment off-loaded it in London and sent it on to Moscow by surface, causing further and unnecessary delay. Once in Moscow the equipment had to clear customs. Again, more delay. Russian customs officials held up the first shipment for weeks. Eventually, the Rosarkhiv staff was able to obtain a waiver by declaring the equipment foreign aid for economic development, a device we used effectively for subsequent shipments.[28]

Then, once received, the equipment had to be installed. Chapman and Starling from Chadwyck-Healey and Fortson from Hoover spent several weeks in Moscow assembling the equipment and installing it in the three Russian repositories. In doing so, they encountered and resolved numerous issues—water supply, plumbing, lighting, and voltage variation, among others. It was like going into an undeveloped country. They could depend on nothing, and they took with them every possible item they would need to install and operate the equipment—tape, tool kits, pipe fittings, glass plates, black fabric, paper for the computer and laser printer, and processing chemicals. One pleasant surprise was the ability of the Russian staff. They were impressively adept at dealing with unusual or nonexistent plumbing connections and weak or erratic electrical systems. Finally, by the end of June 1993—more than a year after the agreement was signed—all equipment was ready for use.[29]

According to our plan, our Russian partner took responsibility for furnishing the staff and supervision needed to microfilm the records—all, of course, at Hoover's expense. It was a logical approach. The Russian archivists had custody of the records themselves and legally could not have delegated responsibility for preparing them for filming. Because these two tasks—preparation of the records for filming and the filming itself—required coordination, we thought it advisable that the Russian managers and staff perform both.

With cameras we provided, the Russian staff filmed the records. The exposed film was then developed, also in Moscow. We considered sending the exposed, undeveloped reels to Cambridge for processing, but decided that this had too much potential for damage to the images, especially since it was almost impossible to maintain tight control over shipping into and out of Russia. Once the developed film was received at the Chadwyck-Healey lab, every frame was checked, and written requests for corrections were faxed back to Moscow. The Russian staff then refilmed the pages that had been filmed incorrectly and shipped the corrections back to Cambridge, where they were spliced into the appropriate reels. Most of the problems requiring correction related to density, focus, poor alignment, chemical stains, faulty splices, omission of targets, improper filming sequences, or gaps in filming.[30]

Because the collections being filmed were located in three separate repositories, it was not possible to centralize all microfilming operations in one location under one supervisor. The day-to-day supervision was the responsibility of each repository. We did not send a supervisor from Hoover, though both Hoover and Chadwyck-Healey staff made frequent trips to Moscow to check on work and to troubleshoot. Howlett, who made the most visits to Moscow, had free access to the filming sites, as did Volkova, her local assistant who gathered the microfilm for shipment and reported problems that needed attention.

Hoover made periodic payments for the labor costs incurred by the three Russian repositories. In order to get the project going, an initial payment of $60,000 was made up front before any production occurred. Subsequent payments were tied to production and paid upon delivery of the film to Chadwyck-Healey. The payments varied over the course of the project from $12 per reel in 1993 to $27 per reel in 1994 to $40 per reel in 1998.

At the height of the project, twenty-five full-time project staff were employed at the three repositories—eleven camera operators, eleven technicians who prepared documents for filming, and three supervisors. Total payments for labor (microfilming, binding and rebinding volumes, and management) from 1992 to the end of the project amounted to $630,000. All our payments to the Russian repositories were paid in dollars. The repositories paid their employees in rubles. Thus, any advantage gained from the chronically weak ruble went to the repositories, not to Hoover.[31]

Since we did not receive internal budgets or expenditure statements from the Russian repositories, I did not know the extent to which our labor payments covered actual expenses. However, my estimates suggested that they did so with much to spare. The number of staff employed fluctuated from twenty-five when all three repositories were filming (1993–95) to no more than twelve when only GARF was filming (1996–2003). By our estimate, the average salary of a full-time staff member was the equivalent of $100 per month. In addition we paid project staff the equivalent of $20 per month as a bonus. Assuming twenty-five staff for three years and twelve staff for eight years, salary costs plus benefits at 50 percent and bonuses would have totaled no more than $350,000, considerably less than the $630,000 we gave the repositories to cover labor costs. This extra amount enabled the repositories to realize an estimated $280,000 for indirect (overhead) expenses, a rate of 80 percent. I did not begrudge the high overhead charges. Like the staff bonuses, they incentivized production.

Transferring funds to Rosarkhiv and the three repositories was sometimes problematic. The Central Bank of Russia, which approved the exchange of foreign currency to rubles, often delayed payments for inordinately long periods of time—once for as long as four months in 1992—before finally issuing payment.[32]

Initially, our funds were sent to Rosarkhiv, which distributed them to the three participating repositories. In 1994 and thereafter, we sent funds for labor directly to the accounts of the three repositories doing the work. Once the money was received by Rosarkhiv or the repositories, it was up to Pikhoia or the directors of the three repositories to spend it. At that point, we at Hoover had little knowledge of or influence over how they distributed these funds. Any oversight of their budgets and expenditures by us would have been seen by them as unwarranted intrusion into their internal affairs. All we could do was judge the results, try to identify and overcome problems, and, if necessary, withhold future funds.[33]

Over the course of the project, the Russian staff produced a massive amount of microfilm. Indeed, without the contributions of the Russian staff who prepared the documents for filming and operated the cameras, nothing that we did on our side would have mattered. We owed much to their work. Initially, however, as filming began, we had to overcome a few obstacles—camera heads placed in the incorrect position, records filmed in the wrong order, out-of-focus images, and reduction ratios failing to match the size of documents, among others.[34]

The absence of normal business practices and the residual attitudes from the Soviet system accounted for other obstacles. Customs clearance of our shipments of supplies and processed microfilm was a continual problem—partly because of bureaucracy at the Moscow airport, partly because of inexperience of the Russian staff, and partly because of communication breakdowns among the three partners. One shipment of supplies from California to Moscow was delayed a full year—from November 1995 to November 1996—before Rosarkhiv managed to obtain clearance.

On another occasion, a shipment of microfilm headed for Cambridge for processing waited six months at the Moscow airport—December 1996 until May 1997—before GARF could clear it through customs. Chadwyck-Healey at one point threatened to withhold its monthly advances on royalty payments unless the Russians resolved the problems at customs. If Hoover's payments to the Russian repositories for labor costs had not been tied to the receipt of microfilm, the delays might have been even longer. Fortunately, we lost only one shipment of microfilm—169 reels containing images of one hundred thousand pages of documents in September 1995.[35]

Russian management deficiencies created other problems. Dilatory recruitment of camera operators; inadequate instruction in operating the equipment; bad morale caused by pay differentials among the repositories; delays in acting on instructions from the Editorial Board; filming of records not approved by the Editorial Board; and reassignment of staff to tasks not related to the project—these were some of the shortcomings of a management bureaucracy struggling to adjust to a new project with foreign partners.[36]

Many of these issues were internal matters that the Russians had to sort out for themselves, and eventually did. Aggressive intrusion by us would have been ineffective and resented. They knew their work culture better than we did. However, we did take two intrusive but necessary remedial steps.

The most important of these was giving bonus payments to project staff. The bonuses supplemented the salaries they received from their Russian employer. Initially, I hesitated to approve the bonus arrangement because it involved us in the internal personnel affairs of the Russian repositories. Problems did in fact occur. The most troubling and persistent effect was resentment from Russian staff who were not assigned to the Hoover project and who thus received no bonuses. I agreed to implement the bonus payment arrangement only after Howlett and Chadwyck-Healey told me that production would not come close to our expectations without it.[37]

The bonus payments were made at first through Howlett, who was reimbursed by Hoover. After the repository directors objected to direct payments from Howlett to staff, the bonuses were paid by the repositories as part of their regular salaries. The payments were twenty dollars per person per month, equivalent to 20 percent of their monthly salary of $100 per month. The bonus payments had their desired effect. They improved morale, kept staff from departing, and significantly improved production.[38]

The Russian staff working on the Hoover project benefited in another way. Because Hoover paid their salaries, project staff could work and be paid even when regular staff were put on leave without pay during long vacation periods. Government agencies, for example, closed down the entire month of August, during which regular staff received no pay.[39]

A second remedial step was to convince Pikhoia to assign to specific staff the responsibility for coordinating project operations in the three repositories, including maintaining equipment, instructing new staff, and troubleshooting problems. He accepted our suggestion and appointed Nina Yakovlevna Ivanovskaia to this task with the title of project technical director. She performed well under difficult conditions.[40]

Misunderstandings, inevitable in any joint project and especially one involving relations between persons of different nationalities, languages, and cultures, also had to be overcome. For example, our Russian partners objected to the name that I assigned to the project—namely, the Russian Archives Preservation Project. They insisted on the removal of the word "preservation." In American professional archival parlance, the word refers to long-term preservation, a normal and ongoing function of any archival repository. For the Russians, it meant rescue of records in imminent danger. They did not want the project name to imply that the records in their custody needed rescuing by foreigners. I, of course, accepted the change and henceforth used the new name, Russian Archives Project.[41]

Another miscue was a comment I made to GARF director Sergei Mironenko early in our relationship. I suggested that the Soviet government had lacked legitimacy because its founding 1917 revolution and its subsequent authority were never validated by free elections. I thought it was an innocent remark and accepted truth, even in Russia. Mironenko responded sharply that I was mistaken. In his view, the Soviet Union held legitimate authority. I did not pursue the topic and never attempted again to engage the Russians in anything resembling political conversation.

We also had to accommodate government record policies that differed markedly from our own. For American archivists, freedom of information is a uniformly accepted goal, and the declassification of restricted government records is a routine and regular activity. In the new Russia, these things had to be newly established in law and practice. As the chairman of Rosarkhiv, Pikhoia had the responsibility of managing Russia's transition from the recordkeeping practices of a secretive totalitarian state to those of an aspiring liberal democracy. While his efforts at reform were not as successful as we would have liked, his record in this regard was admirable. Pikhoia encouraged the adoption of new laws and regulations, applied them with few missteps, and maneuvered skillfully within the bureaucracy.

From time to time, Pikhoia faced serious challenges from within the government, brought on by media attacks. In July 1993, the Federal Security Service—the successor to the Soviet KGB—inspected his repositories and questioned his staff about the release to and subsequent publication by a foreign scholar of a classified document. The document in question came from TsKhSD and purported to show larger numbers of American POWs in Vietnam than previously thought. The Russian media exploded, and the archives had to close during the investigation. It was an extraordinary reaction to what was essentially an accidental release of a document that was embarrassing only to a previous administration. The incident was a reminder to us that the nationalist media could easily whip up passions involving the nation's archives. It happened again in 1994, when President Yeltsin's political enemies in the parliament demanded and got an investigation of Rosarkhiv. Pikhoia and Rosarkhiv were subsequently cleared of all charges.[42]

We were sensitive to the problem of national security classified records. Before any materials were filmed, they were screened by Russian archivists for documents that fell into restricted categories. Such documents were either declassified before filming or removed and not filmed.[43]

In this connection, a curious incident occurred. During one of our Moscow visits, Howlett asked Chadwyck-Healey and me to take a walk with her outside the hotel where our conversation could not be heard by others. She reported that she had found on our microfilm some documents that referred to the location of strategically important mineral deposits. The documents were clearly sensitive and probably highly classified. She thought it unlikely that the screeners had inadvertently missed them and speculated that their inclusion might have been a trap set to discredit the project and Pikhoia. We immediately notified our Russian colleagues and removed the materials from the microfilm. We followed this policy on other occasions when such documents were found.

The problems with shipping, customs, banks, staffing, communications, management, and national security matters were challenging, but they did not fundamentally threaten the project and were all overcome. It was an outside event beyond our control that put us in peril. In the parliamentary election of December 1995, the government opposition parties won 53 percent of the vote, while the government's supporters won only 38 percent. The biggest winner was the Communist Party of the Russian Federation (KPRF), which nearly doubled its 1993 vote—12.4 percent—to 22.1 percent in 1995. A *New York Times* headline announced a "Communist Comeback." The Yeltsin government was now in serious political trouble, as was Pikhoia, Yeltsin's appointed chairman of Rosarkhiv.[44]

Chapter 3

THE WINDOW CLOSES AND OPENS AGAIN

Crisis, January 1996

As early as September 1995, Howlett reported to me that Pikhoia was nervous about the upcoming December parliamentary elections. He had good reason. The Yeltsin government was under extreme pressure. The war in Chechnya that began at the end of 1994 turned sour in 1995. In June, 126 hostages taken by Chechen terrorists were killed in a failed rescue attempt. In July, Yeltsin had a major heart attack (two more followed in October and late December). Public opinion polls in late 1995 showed support for him at a mere 5 percent. It did not help Pikhoia's position in government circles that Lyudmila Pikhoia, his wife and Yeltsin's speechwriter, had lost much of her influence at court. In September 1994, she had joined other staff members in signing a letter admonishing President Yeltsin. As a consequence, she had been denied access to him for six months.[1]

In early December, Howlett asked me if our agreement could be legally terminated and what the consequences might be. Pikhoia had expressed to her his apprehension, especially about possible claims Hoover might make if the Russian side terminated the agreement. I sensed that he was no longer able or willing to protect the project. When the election results came in, I braced for the worst. It came in Pikhoia's letter to me of December 28, 1995, announcing that Rosarkhiv was ending the agreement. The tone of the letter was completely unlike Pikhoia—distant, reproachful, and short. In the opening sentence, he signaled that he was speaking not for himself but on behalf of his governing board. It was clear that he was now no longer calling the shots.[2]

Pikhoia's letter cited four reasons for terminating the agreement:

- The agreement placed restrictions on the selection of documents to be filmed.
- It lacked sufficient financial incentives.
- It lacked any programs for joint teamwork by Russian and foreign scholars and archivists drawing on the archives.
- It contradicted current Russian laws and a new Russian law on international information exchange, passed by the parliament on December 8.

The letter concluded by stating that the agreement was being terminated on the basis of "force majeure" as provided for in paragraph 23. It argued that because of the Russian laws, Rosarkhiv was "forced" to end the agreement.[3]

From my perspective, most of the complaints had little validity. None was cause for abruptly terminating the agreement. From the beginning, we had always been open to amending the agreement to accommodate concerns and had done so several times. In spite of this aggressive move, I resolved again to remain positive and open to an accommodation. At the same time, the reasons given for ending the agreement demanded refutation.

The letter mistakenly charged that the agreement placed restrictions on Rosarkhiv and its subordinate institutions in the selection of documents for microfilming. It was true that the Editorial Board selected the documents to be filmed. Its work was a collaborative effort by American historians picked by me and Russian historians picked by Pikhoia. But the board was advisory. The agreement stated explicitly that its selections required the approval of both Rosarkhiv and Hoover. As head of Rosarkhiv, Pikhoia retained complete authority, alone or in consultation with repository directors, to propose records for filming or to disallow the inclusion of any records selected by the board. In fact, he did both when he included Fond 89 and when he refused to include the records of the Comintern and the US Communist Party.

The Russians complained that the Editorial Board included none of the repository directors. This was also true, but again nothing in the agreement precluded Pikhoia from appointing anyone he wished to the Editorial Board, including any of the repository directors. He simply chose others instead. Even after he made his initial selections, he could have changed the composition of the Russian side at any time.

The letter charged that the agreement lacked sufficient financial incentives. By any measure, the agreement was exceedingly generous. Hoover paid for all project expenses, including the salaries of Russians working on the project, ample administrative overhead, and the cost of equipment and supplies; gave the Russians royalties of 27 percent, nearly twice as high as the going 15 percent rate for such projects; gave generous advances on royalties; gave the Russians use and preservation copies of all microfilms produced; gave a free copy of all published microfilms to the Novosibirsk Regional State Archives; and gave Rosarkhiv two free copies of the Hoover Institution's own Russian archives. No other microfilming project in Russia came close to matching the financial terms we provided.

An inherent problem in any publishing enterprise is the delay in realizing royalties. The problem was especially acute for us. Selling thousands of reels of microfilm was not an easy job. It took time. Of the $1.35 million in royalties that the Russian side earned in sales by the end of the project in 2004, only $324,000 was earned by June 1996. Had more royalties come earlier in the project, they may have tempered the opposition. From the perspective of the Russians, given the financial stress they faced, their impatience on this score was understandable, if regrettable.

Some of our Russian colleagues were especially aggrieved that the project had not provided opportunities for their professional scholarly endeavors. In addition to the $3 million microfilming project, they wanted Hoover to fund a program of research activities for Russian and foreign scholars. At the time, it seemed to me an irrelevant complaint. The usual parameters of microfilming projects, both ours and every other such project I was aware of, did not include research grants to scholars. What they really wanted was a second and separate program. For that they had no cause to end the microfilm project but only to send me a proposal for an additional project. It would have been readily received and easily managed.

Inexperience with commercial matters and international collaboration on the Russian side was a disadvantage for them. But it was also a disadvantage for us. It affected the attitude of some of our Russian colleagues toward the project and us. For them, no matter what we provided, it never seemed to be enough. If the other side was winning, they had to be losing. When your partner does not know if he has a good or a bad deal, seeks to change the scope of a project already agreed upon, fails to take into account the interests and limitations of the other side, or threatens termination without prior discussion, the partnership breaks down.

The most serious charge was that the Hoover project had violated Russian law. A new, startling, and entirely baseless accusation, it made even less sense than the other complaints. At no time during the previous four years had our Russian collaborators said that the agreement was in violation of any Russian law. Moreover, the termination letter cited no specific laws other than one that had recently been passed by the parliament, on December 8, but had not yet been signed by the president. It gave no explanation of precisely how the agreement violated either any current laws or the pending law. In fact, Hoover was never in violation of any Russian law.

The Russian law on government records directly relevant to the Hoover project, which was enacted in 1993, set forth provisions on restricted and national security classified information. Since the Russian archivists screened all records and removed any restricted documents before they were filmed, we were always in compliance with this law. On the one or two occasions when we discovered restricted documents in the microfilm, they were brought to the attention of the Russian side and removed. Moreover, the 1993 Russian law permitted the export of copies of unrestricted archival documents. Neither this law nor any subsequent Russian law or presidential decree ever specifically named the Hoover Institution or our project with Rosarkhiv.[4]

Accusing us of violating the law appeared to have two purposes. First, it added another reason for ending the agreement. Secondly, as they argued, it gave them the means to end it legally within the terms of the agreement. Paragraph 23 of the agreement contained a standard force majeure provision for excusing harm caused by actions taken in circumstances beyond one's control (acts of God, war, etc.). The Russians argued that they could end the agreement on the basis of force majeure because Russian law, which was beyond their control, forced them to do so. They were mistaken in their interpretation of the force majeure provision. That clause related to performance of duties and liability for failing such performance. It did not relate to termination. A separate paragraph (6[c]) dealt with termination. This latter paragraph enabled either side to terminate the agreement without cause by giving six months' notice.[5]

The charge that we were in violation of Russian law and their choice of the force majeure paragraph instead of the no-fault-termination paragraph was a curious development and raised the question of why they chose this gambit. Why contrive a false, hurtful charge by invoking the force majeure paragraph when the no-fault paragraph was a simple and obvious way to end the agreement? Two possible answers, I concluded, were to incriminate Hoover or to create a bargaining chip for something they wanted. If the first, we faced a very hostile crowd indeed and stood little chance of revising the project. I even wondered whether it was safe for me to be in Russia at all. If the second, we still had a chance to save some form of the project.

Pikhoia's letter concluded with his opinion that representatives of Rosarkhiv, the Hoover Institution, and Chadwyck-Healey should meet soon in Moscow. At that meeting, the letter asserted, Rosarkhiv would "present for discussion new principles for the organization of collaborative scholarly work on the archival collections as well as the microfilming of documents and the exchange of archival information." Chadwyck-Healey and I agreed to meet with Rosarkhiv on January 11 and 12, 1996.

My objectives for the upcoming meeting were threefold. First, I would state Hoover's refusal to accept termination of the agreement on the basis of paragraph 23 and insist that it be terminated, if that indeed was Rosarkhiv's intention, on the basis of paragraph 6(c). The force majeure clause in paragraph 23 implied that the Hoover Institution had been in violation of Russian law for the past four years. This was entirely unacceptable to us and, I presumed, would be unacceptable to Pikhoia, since he too was being accused of breaking the law. Second, I would seek continuation of the project for the six-month period provided for in paragraph 6(c), during which time microfilming would be allowed to proceed to logical stopping points. Third, I would try to conclude a new agreement acceptable to all. To accomplish these objectives, I was prepared to offer generous terms.

During this time I was in constant touch with Howlett. During the past four years, she had gained the confidence of Pikhoia, and since the crisis broke, she had been speaking with him frequently about his reaction to it. It was Howlett who suggested that the three of us—Pikhoia, Howlett, and me—meet at a neutral site to discuss the upcoming Moscow meeting. She suggested either Prague or Budapest on January 6, 7, or 8. We settled on Prague on Sunday, January 7. We stayed at separate hotels and met at a quiet restaurant about a mile from my hotel. While the meeting was certainly legal—Pikhoia still had the authority to represent Rosarkhiv and I to represent Hoover—it was necessary to keep it secret. Pikhoia was being attacked in the Russian press for having approved and protected the Hoover project. Had it become known that Pikhoia met with me prior to the meeting with his full board, his enemies would have accused him of all sorts of crimes.[6]

At Prague I laid out my plans for the January 11–12 meeting. I wanted Pikhoia to know that I was not going to blow up the relationship with him or his colleagues and that my intention was to terminate the agreement on mutually acceptable terms and negotiate a new agreement. Knowing my intentions, he could deploy whatever influence he had left to bring about a resolution that would harm neither of our institutions.

From him I wanted to know definitively that the current agreement could not be saved. I assured him that I was willing to fight for it, if we had any reasonable chance to save it. But I did not want to waste my time or his defending a lost cause. He confirmed that the agreement was dead, that he was no longer in a position to protect it, and that the only question was whether it would be allowed to die in peace or in anger. We departed with our usual firm handshake, but we knew that this was the last time we would speak with each other with the confidence and empathy that had always in the past characterized our relations and that had been an essential element in launching a noble project and making it work.

The meeting in Moscow took place as planned on January 11 and 12. When I arrived at Rosarkhiv headquarters, I was led, not to Pikhoia's office to meet with him individually as was our usual practice, but to a large conference room. There waiting for me on one side of a long table was the entire membership of the Rosarkhiv Collegium—Pikhoia, his first deputy-director, second deputy-director, manager of the international department, deputy manager of the international department, manager of the administration department, deputy manager of the administration department, a Rosarkhiv consultant, and directors of the three repositories whose records we had been filming. If I had not already known it, this picture would have told me that Pikhoia was no longer in charge. Decisions were now being made by the whole collegium.[7]

On my side of the table were Chadwyck-Healey, Howlett, Schoen, Volkova, and Herbert Hoover III. Hoover was the grandson of President Herbert Hoover and a leading member of the Hoover Institution's Board of Overseers. Through his family foundation, he was one of the principal financial backers of the project. He had a deep interest in the project as well as in the Hoover Library & Archives generally. I relied on him in many ways. He asked if he could accompany me to Moscow for the meeting, and I gladly agreed. Throughout the trip he contributed welcome moral support and never questioned my strategy or performance.

After a short introduction by Pikhoia, in which he summarized the accomplishments of the project and the recent legislative actions, I presented Hoover's position and outlined three possible outcomes:

1. Ending the project on the basis of force majeure, as proposed by the Russian side. I argued that force majeure based on Hoover's supposed violation of Russian law was unjustified. The accusation was harmful to our reputation, came without forewarning or prior consultation, and was not supported by any legal opinion. Moreover, paragraph 23 of the agreement, in which force majeure is mentioned, applied only to performance and liability for failure of performance. It did not apply to termination, which was provided for in paragraph 6(c). If Rosarkhiv wanted to end the agreement, I said, it could do so without accusing Hoover of violating laws. If Rosarkhiv insisted on force majeure as a basis for ending the agreement, Hoover would consider this action a breach of contract and a basis for Hoover's terminating the agreement. In that

case, Hoover would reclaim all the equipment, withhold labor and royalty payments, and refuse to fulfill the equal exchange of microfilms. I then submitted a letter from our legal counsel, Morrison & Foerster, stating the opinion upon which my statement was based.[8]

2. Ending the agreement on the basis of paragraph 6(c). Paragraph 6(c) provided for the termination of the project by either Rosarkhiv or Hoover, simply by one party giving six months' notice to the other. No cause or reason needed to be cited. From the beginning of the project, it was understood that either partner could end the agreement if in its discretion it concluded that the project was no longer in its interest. I indicated that Hoover would respect Rosarkhiv's decision to end the project on this basis and would seek to do so on friendly terms, as follows:

   a) Rosarkhiv would keep two-thirds of the equipment and one-half of the remaining supplies.
   b) Hoover would match on a one-to-one basis microfilm produced by the project with microfilm of either Hoover collections or available microfilms from the US National Archives, as specified by Rosarkhiv.
   c) Hoover and Chadwyck-Healey would honor their obligations with respect to payment of labor and royalty payments.

In return I asked for the following:

a) Any press release announcing the end of the project would be approved by all three parties.
b) During the six-month period between the notification and the end of the project, Rosarkhiv would establish reasonable end points at which filming would stop and would continue to film until those end points were reached, as required by the agreement.
c) Rosarkhiv would send copies of project microfilms to the Novosibirsk Regional State Archives as provided for in the agreement.

3. Continuing the project by revising the agreement to address the concerns expressed in the December 28 letter. Hoover would work with Rosarkhiv and its legal counsel to make the agreement compatible with the new Russian law, if in fact that became necessary. Hoover would agree to enlarge the Editorial Board to include directors of participating repositories. Hoover would agree to an immediate meeting of the reconstituted board to review and revise the current list of materials to be filmed. Hoover would reduce the goal of the project from twenty-five thousand reels to 12,500 reels and increase the labor payments from $27 to $40 per reel.

After my presentation, members of the collegium retired to a separate room to discuss the three options among themselves. When we reassembled, several participants from the Russian side expressed views on the positives and negatives of the current project and the way forward. To my surprise and relief, they did not bring back the force majeure argument or the charge that we were in violation of Russian law. The hostility evident in that argument was also absent. After all their opinions were aired, Pikhoia asked me to submit in writing a list of the three options. I wrote a one-page list that Howlett and Schoen translated into Russian and presented it to Pikhoia.

After some additional deliberation, the collegium decided on option two. Rosarkhiv would rescind the December 28 letter and instead give notice of termination of the agreement on the basis of the no-fault paragraph 6(c). In addition, Rosarkhiv offered to negotiate a new agreement during the six-month period between the date of notification and the date of final termination. I accepted the notification to terminate as well as the offer to negotiate a new agreement. A memorandum of mutual understanding summarizing these actions was prepared by Chadwyck-Healey and me (a version prepared by Kozlov was rejected) and signed on January 12 by Pikhoia, Chadwyck-Healey, and me. While the memorandum ended our agreement, it also opened the door for a second chance. We were still in the game.[9]

I drew several conclusions from the January meeting. First and foremost, the project agreement failed to survive because Pikhoia failed to survive, figuratively speaking. His authority depended on the strength of the Yeltsin government, which came under serious threat as a result of the December parliamentary election and negative public opinion fomented by a hostile media. Not only Pikhoia but several other key reformers in Yeltsin's government lost their jobs—Foreign Minister Andrei Kozyrev, Finance Minister Anatolii Chubais, and most importantly, Sergei Filatov, Yeltsin's chief of staff and Pikhoia's main source of support in the Yeltsin administration.[10]

Some of our American critics claimed that the election had no causal relationship to the rebellion within the Rosarkhiv Collegium. The sole causes, they said, were a bad agreement, Hoover's mistakes, and a failed leader. The December election, they said, was an unrelated "coincidence"—that the rebellion sprang forward on its own, independent of politics. This claim was puzzling. While the specific grievances against Pikhoia and Hoover within Rosarkhiv were indeed unrelated to election politics, the rebellion was not.[11]

The election was not a trivial event. It was won by parties opposed to Yeltsin, including a rejuvenated Communist Party. They threatened the very existence of the Yeltsin government and did so by flying the flag of nationalistic opposition to Western interference in Russian affairs. The election results created a hostile public environment and inspired an avalanche of hateful, xenophobic attacks from the media.

In this atmosphere, a high-profile American project to copy sensitive Russian archives was an easy target. The political upheaval that followed encouraged the opposition within Rosarkhiv to act and destroyed Pikhoia's ability to protect either the project or himself. It gave opportunity and force to the Rosarkhiv rebellion. If the Yeltsin forces had won the December election, can anyone doubt that Pikhoia's position would have been strengthened and that the opposition would have remained silent or disappeared altogether?

Initially, when I received Pikhoia's letter terminating the agreement, I thought our Russian partners feared the actions of a new Communist government, one that would reimpose restrictions on government record policies, end collaborative projects with foreigners, and punish those who had engaged in them. It is possible that some members of Rosarkhiv were so motivated. However, once in Russia, I heard no such concerns. I then looked for other motivations.

I soon came to the conclusion that the Hoover agreement—while certainly a target—was not the prime target of the rebellion. All the complaints so forcefully stated in Pikhoia's letter ending the agreement—restrictions on the selection of documents, insufficient financial incentives, lack of opportunities for Russian archivists and scholars, and even the violation of Russian law—were easily refuted or addressed. Indeed, during the January meeting, the Rosarkhiv Collegium hardly defended any of them.

By the end of the meeting, the atmosphere was positively friendly. The Russian side even opened the door to continue the partnership. After Pikhoia departed, new agreements in fact were signed, and all their concerns were addressed and resolved. Had the Hoover agreement been so intensely hated, as our critics in the media and elsewhere claimed, no reconciliation would have been possible. Rosarkhiv would have simply ended the agreement and ceased contact with us entirely.

So if not primarily about Hoover, what was this rebellion all about? Why the dramatic letter with all the grievances when a brief notice invoking the agreement's no-fault clause would have easily and quickly ended the agreement? Why the media attacks, in which at least one member of Rosarkhiv participated? Why the exaggerated complaints to our other critics, both in Russia and in the United States? What purpose did all the drama serve? It certainly was not needed to deal with us.

It became clear to me that the frenzy served one overriding purpose: to get rid of Pikhoia, their boss. The Hoover agreement was the means for attacking and disposing of Pikhoia. By the January meeting, at which point Pikhoia was mortally wounded, the agreement had served its purpose. With Pikhoia dealt with, the Russians became friendly, even open to a new agreement. Only Kozlov remained aloof, still decisively opposed to large-scale microfilming and generally critical of the Hoover project.

Perhaps the most revealing tell in the rebels' strategy was the charge that the project violated Russian law. This was a spurious charge, as was the use they made of it. Given the no-fault clause in the agreement, the charge was clearly not needed to end the project. When we suggested that they consult with legal counsel in the Russian legislature to see if our agreement in fact was in violation of an existing or proposed law, they showed no interest in doing so. That response told me that the accusation of illegality was insincere and served a hidden purpose. That purpose, I concluded, was to put Pikhoia under threat. As it was his signature on the purported illegal agreement, the charge amounted to an accusation of unlawful action by him. I imagine it got his attention. He would not have been the first Russian state archivist to face Russian justice.

Russia has always been hard on its weakened leaders, as Pikhoia learned firsthand. In Russia, contempt for authority is barely beneath the surface. I recalled the comment by the young man who guided me around Moscow in 1991. "He can wait," he said of Pikhoia, his boss, who was waiting for us to finish our meal at the Metropol.

The media was especially brutal. A January 1996 article in *Izvestiia* was typical of the contemptuous attacks. The article accused Pikhoia of "selling raw meat from the archives" and compared it to "selling crude oil." It made the overwrought claim that the Hoover project enabled American scholars to earn huge profits from publishing scholarly works based on the archives.

Pikhoia's subordinates did not create the media attacks, but at least one took part in them. Kyrill Anderson, director of RTsKhIDNI, complained to a reporter of the *Moscow Times* that the Hoover project was "robbing Russia blind."[12] In another interview, Anderson said, "We [directors] barely figured in the negotiating of the [Hoover] contract." Decisions on what to film, he said, were dictated by a Russian-American Editorial Board, of which he was not a member. But it was not Hoover that kept them out of the negotiations or off of the Editorial Board. It was Pikhoia. And it was not Hoover that prevented the realization of their other objectives.[13]

Could they have gotten rid of Pikhoia without the dramatic termination of the Hoover agreement? Perhaps, but an aggressive attack against us gave them their best chance. Ending a high-profile international agreement attracted the attention of the frenzied media and put maximum pressure on Pikhoia. He was closely associated with the project, and ending it "amounted to a vote of no confidence," as one observer noted.[14]

Ending the agreement quietly would not have had the same effect. He likely could have survived that. Ending the agreement aggressively and publicly was far more effective. It excited the media. As a foreign enterprise, we were easy prey for the xenophobic attacks. They weakened us, and as Pikhoia was associated with us, they weakened him too. The election destroyed Pikhoia's defenses. The attack on Hoover finished him off.

Why did his opponents within Rosarkhiv want to get rid of Pikhoia? From my vantage point, I saw a capable, flexible leader who consistently advanced the interests of his organization. Of course, I was not sufficiently familiar with the internal politics at Rosarkhiv to know the whole story. Clearly, they did not think they could get what they wanted with him in charge. With all the Western interest in the Soviet archives swirling about, perhaps they saw opportunity passing them by. Some of the repository directors resented the centralization of authority in Rosarkhiv, which kept them from concluding deals on their own. That Pikhoia was an outsider from Sverdlovsk and not a member of their Moscow inner circle may have added to the distance between them.

Whatever the reasons, in the end I do not think they gained much, if anything, by the change in leadership. The new agreements they negotiated with us were not that different from the one Pikhoia got and could just as easily have been concluded with Pikhoia in charge. The deals they got from others were not any better than ours, and likely not as good. Moreover, the centralization they disliked largely continued under Pikhoia's successors.

I drew another conclusion from the trauma. It became clear to me that some members of Rosarkhiv did not fully share Pikhoia's vision for the archives. They seemed to be not as motivated as he was by the ideal of making the archives freely available to as many scholars as possible. During the January meeting, the one point they continued to make was their objection to massive filming of entire record groups, which they said benefited mainly American scholars. They stated that such projects did not adequately leverage the value of their collections for themselves.

For what purpose did they want to leverage their collections? Most of all, they wanted projects—letterpress documentary publications, elaborate guides, conferences, etc.—that would employ their individual talents and enhance their individual scholarly reputations. They wanted projects that would pay them individually and that would produce scholarly works with their names on them. I have not been alone in making this observation. Patricia Kennedy Grimsted, a frequent and knowledgeable visitor to Russia during these years and herself a scholarly collaborator with Russian archivists, noted that "Russian archivists . . . want to be included in the bylines and receive part of any potential royalties."[15]

Self-interest motivates most human endeavors. Indeed, I should have foreseen this need. Early on, through the exhibit and RLIN projects, we had effectively engaged the interest of the middle and lower levels of the Russian staff. I had miscalculated in believing that preservation of, and open access to, large bodies of records would be motivation enough for the professional archivists who were in charge. I had assumed mistakenly that Russian archivists were much like American archivists, who achieve professional status from contributions to their institutions, service to users, and work in their professional associations. The American archival profession is primarily a service profession. Russian archivists, on the other hand, especially those at the top of their profession, see themselves as independent scholars as well as administrators. Contributions to their institutions and their profession are certainly important, but what is equally meaningful to them is recognition for the scholarship they achieve as individuals.

While I do not think my failure to recognize this need for scholarly opportunities was responsible for the rebellion, the issue needed to be addressed. It was a lesson learned. I filed it away for future use—too late to help with the current crisis but, as it turned out, useful in the future when we got another chance.

On January 18, one week after my meetings in Moscow, I received a letter from Pikhoia notifying me of his resignation as the head of Rosarkhiv. Yeltsin did not dismiss him. In his five years of public service, he had achieved a great deal for his country. Some argued that his reform of the archives and his efforts to gain financial support for them were insufficient.[16] From my vantage point, however, I saw an energetic, committed leader who faced an unprecedented challenge—namely, administering and reforming a government agency burdened by the embedded attitudes and practices of the failed state that preceded him and doing so in an economy that was barely alive. I saw a leader who was not afraid to keep or appoint strong leaders to serve under him, a leader who treated his staff with respect, and most importantly, a leader who held a commanding vision of returning Russian history to its people and who set goals and priorities to realize it.

One can look at what Pikhoia failed to achieve and measure it against an ideal. I prefer to look at what he did achieve and measure it against what he started with. During the tumultuous aftermath of the coup d'état, he seized and then opened the records of the Soviet Communist Party. He expanded professional practices and standards in Russia and drafted legislation for post-Soviet archives. He opened two major international exhibits of Russian archives, one at the Library of Congress and one at the Hoover Institution. The latter was also shown in Moscow at the parliament building. And he undertook ambitious collaborative projects with the Hoover Institution and others—projects that produced preservation microfilm of large quantities of archival records in his custody, secured for Russian scholars microfilm of valuable archival collections located outside of Russia, and obtained necessary financial resources for his institution during a time of need. He could look back with just pride on this notable record of achievement.[17]

In January 1996, when notice was given to terminate the 1992 agreement, the Russian side agreed to continue some limited filming at the three repositories until July. We wanted something we could call a finished product. Accordingly, the agreed plan was to replace microfilm that had been lost in shipment or that contained faulty images and to end filming at logical points. GARF, under Mironenko's direction, was the only repository that fulfilled the whole of this promise. It replaced film with faulty images and continued to film new materials. RTsKhIDNI replaced faulty film but made little effort to end filming at logical points or to film new materials. TsKhSD stopped filming altogether.[18]

The agreement signed in April 1992 came to an end on July 16, 1996. During that time the project produced 6,707 reels of microfilm totaling 5.7 million pages of records and spent $1.5 million. Copies of the microfilm were deposited for preservation and scholarly use at the three Russian repositories and at the Hoover Institution. Of this total, Chadwyck-Healey identified 2,450 reels for sale and inclusion in its published catalog. By the end of 1995, Chadwyck-Healey had realized $1.2 million in total sales, of which 27 percent ($324,000) went to the Russian side and 13 percent ($156,000) went to Hoover. The Library of Congress and the Novosibirsk Regional State Archives each received gifts of the published microfilm.[19]

At that point we could have ended our relationship with the Russian archives and been reasonably satisfied with what we had achieved. I was certainly tempted to do just that. Instead, we pressed on, encouraged by the positive attitude of our Russian partners who expressed interest in negotiating a new agreement, taking into account the lessons learned from our previous collaboration. It did not take long to get started.

In April 1996, at the Hoover Institution, I began discussions with Vladimir A. Tiuneev, Pikhoia's replacement as head of Rosarkhiv, and Mironenko, the director of GARF. On October 10, 1996, at Cambridge, a framework agreement was concluded among Hoover, Chadwyck-Healey, and Rosarkhiv. It stated our intention to undertake collaborative projects, defined the scope of those projects, established an oversight Editorial Board, and—under Rosarkhiv's umbrella—permitted Hoover and Chadwyck-Healey the right to negotiate separate agreements for new projects directly with individual repositories administered by Rosarkhiv. I was informed that all three repositories—GARF, RTsKhIDNI, and TsKhSD—wanted to sign up with us again. In the end, only GARF eventually did so.[20]

The October 1996 principals' meeting in Cambridge also resolved all the loose ends from the 1992 agreement. Hoover allowed Rosarkhiv to keep two-thirds of the equipment, including nine microfilm cameras, and all remaining supplies, not half as earlier stipulated. Chadwyck-Healey agreed to continue paying royalties on the sale of microfilm produced under the old agreement. The final accounting of Hoover's labor payments to the three repositories was accepted by both Hoover and Rosarkhiv. Rosarkhiv promised to replace faulty microfilm produced by its side. Hoover agreed to meet its remaining obligation to match the microfilm received from Rosarkhiv, either by providing more reels of microfilm of its own collections or by acquiring microfilm of records at the US National Archives.[21]

The improving political atmosphere was an important factor in realizing better relations with our Russian partners. On July 3, 1996, President Yeltsin unexpectedly won reelection with 54 percent of the vote, defeating Gennadii Zyuganov, the KPRF (Communist) candidate, who got 41 percent.[22] This turnaround in our fortune is what I had hoped for when I sought to end the 1992 agreement on generous terms.

The termination of the 1992 agreement and apparent collapse of the project had been a disappointment to our donors and other supporters. Stanford president Gerhard Casper and university provost Condoleezza Rice were especially supportive. Rice in particular had taken a strong interest in this and our other projects in Russia. Moreover, I very much valued her opinion. She was an expert on Russia, an astute and influential colleague, and a steady source of advice. So, when Yeltsin was reelected and the Russians restarted our work together, I was much relieved.

Even though relations with the Russians improved after Yeltsin's reelection, things were not the same. The termination of the first phase of the Hoover project closed a period of reform for the Russian archives. The xenophobic hysteria took its toll. The Hoover project was not its only casualty. Among them was the Crown Publishing contract to produce a series of books based on the Soviet KGB archives, which was canceled in the summer of 1996.

After the resurgence of the Communists in December, as one scholar noted, "the process of declassification of secret documents slowed considerably. . . . Individual scholars often ran up against unscheduled closures of archives, power outages, sudden decisions to deny access to documents that had been declassified, and exorbitant copying charges."[23] While the window of opportunity in Russia was closing, it had not yet closed entirely. So we decided to press ahead, but with more realistic expectations and a better understanding of our Russian partners.

Interregnum, 1996 to 1998

The Russian repository most willing to continue collaboration was GARF. Once we concluded the framework agreement with Rosarkhiv, negotiations with its director, Mironenko, got underway. Meanwhile, GARF continued to film records of interest and did so at the same pace it had achieved before the breakup. During the interim between the end of the first agreement in 1996 and the second agreement in 1998, GARF produced 1,794 reels of microfilm.[24] I was, therefore, not in any great hurry to conclude a new agreement.

Mironenko moved deliberately as well. Among other considerations, he did not want to get ahead of the other members of Rosarkhiv. After the recent political upheaval, Rosarkhiv, while generally supportive, was understandably cautious and became more so after Vladimir P. Kozlov, Pikhoia's former deputy and nemesis, replaced Tiuneev as head of Rosarkhiv in November 1996.

Chadwyck-Healey, on the other hand, was eager to have a new agreement. He could not sell GARF's newly produced microfilm without the copyright approval that a new agreement would provide. He also became increasingly frustrated by GARF's inability to overcome the Russian customs restrictions that held up shipments of microfilm to CHMPS. During this period, he appealed to both Mironenko and me to move more quickly, and at one point in late 1996 described the relations among us as "descending into chaos."[25]

The tension between Chadwyck-Healey and Hoover during the interim period—i.e., between the end of the first agreement in January 1996 and the signing of the agreement with GARF in June 1998—reflected our differing interests. As a commercial enterprise, Chadwyck-Healey wanted microfilm to process in its processing plant—services paid for by Hoover—and microfilm to market and sell to customers. Hoover's interest, on the other hand, was the preservation of the historical record. For Hoover, the microfilm produced by GARF during the interim was just as important as that produced during the earlier phase, while for Chadwyck-Healey it was microfilm that he could not sell.

Chadwyck-Healey's proposed solution to overcome the long delay was to send more emissaries to Moscow. "Not having Jana [Howlett] regularly going to Moscow and reporting back the gossip and the hard information," he wrote in one of his email messages, "was one of the reasons" for our problems. Chadwyck-Healey was justified in his complaint about communications. On one occasion, a Chadwyck-Healey manager asked GARF to approve a change in labels used on the microfilm boxes; it took GARF five months to reply. On another occasion, Chadwyck-Healey asked for clarification on GARF's bank account numbers into which earned royalties could be safely deposited. It took one letter, two phone calls, and two faxes before GARF responded. And it was not uncommon to wait months before GARF could clear customs for shipments of microfilm to Cambridge.[26]

The communication shortcomings notwithstanding, I did not think that Chadwyck-Healey's proposed solution was the answer. As effective as Howlett had been during the first four years of the project, I did not think that the problems we were now encountering could be solved by more information. Only Mironenko could resolve the problems with Russian customs and the shipments of microfilm to Cambridge. We also depended on Mironenko to resolve the problems we had with the Russian banks, which often held up deposits of Hoover and Chadwyck-Healey money transfers into GARF's account. Howlett did not have the same rapport with Mironenko that she had with Pikhoia, and she had none with Kozlov, Mironenko's new boss at Rosarkhiv.

During the interregnum we had a different relationship with Rosarkhiv than we did in the first four years. Pikhoia could always be counted on to work with us constructively. Kozlov was less predictable. He led a divided Rosarkhiv, which had a veto over any agreement negotiated by Mironenko. During a visit to Moscow in early 1998, one of my helpers learned that some members of Rosarkhiv harbored an "anti-western and anti-Hoover sentiment" and had proposed changes in the proposed GARF-Hoover agreement in order to scuttle it. As in Pikhoia's administration, the centralization of authority in Rosarkhiv was a restraint on the repository directors, including Mironenko. When Pikhoia was in charge, centralization worked in our favor. Now it sometimes created problems that were beyond our capacity to fix. We depended on Mironenko to fix them, and, through his patience and bureaucratic skill, he eventually managed to do so.[27]

As problematic as the long delay was, things were not as bad as Chadwyck-Healey feared. In the end, we lost only one shipment of microfilm (which GARF redid), and we never lost any money from wire transfers. While communications during this period were not ideal, they were maintained. I had a regular correspondence by email and fax with Mironenko, and I did in fact send emissaries to Moscow, including Gordon Hahn, whom I hired to help me coordinate this and various other projects in Russia. Hahn's reports routinely went to both me and Chadwyck-Healey.

More importantly, I continued to convene meetings of the principals (Chadwyck-Healey, Mironenko, and myself) during this period—April 1996 at Stanford, October 1996 in Cambridge, March 1997 in Moscow, and June 1998 in Cambridge. Eventually Mironenko brought Rosarkhiv along; resolved the customs, shipping, and banking issues; and fulfilled all the interim production goals we had set. Two years after the end of our first agreement, conditions were finally set for phase two of the project.

Phase Two: The 1998 Agreement

In June 1998, an agreement with GARF was signed. A worsening Russian economy no doubt contributed to the sudden interest from the Russian side. In May 1998, the RTS (Russian Trading System) stock index dropped to 200 from its high of 572 on October 6, 1997, and fell to a new low of 38 points on October 2, 1998. During the second week of May, the price of oil—Russia's main source of foreign currency—fell to $12 per barrel, less than half its price in January 1997. The GDP for 1998 dropped below $1.3 trillion, the lowest point in the Yeltsin presidency. Inflation for 1998 was 84 percent. On August 17, the government defaulted on its debt. In good news for our Russian partners, the dollars we furnished them were worth a great deal more to them after the default. The exchange rate went from 6.3 rubles to the dollar on August 17 to 21 rubles to the dollar on September 21.[28]

The new agreement with GARF focused on its records relating to the Gulag, the vast system of forced labor camps established by Stalin that imprisoned millions of his own people. The Gulag archives give a full picture of the forced labor system in the Soviet Union and establish once and for all the historical record of one of the greatest criminal episodes in human history. In so many ways, the history of the Gulag is a history of

Soviet Communism. It was an extension of Soviet society—the last stop in a continuum of terror. As Anne Applebaum has noted in her history of the Gulag, it was "the quintessential expression of the Soviet system." At least eighteen million people out of a population of one hundred million adults passed through the Gulag between 1929 and 1953, and its 476 camp complexes comprising hundreds of individual camps were an integrated and significant sector of the Soviet economy.[29]

The archives of the Gulag are thus a rich resource for the study not just of the Gulag, but of Soviet Communism generally. The systemic problems and outcomes were similar for both. It was this opportunity to capture the essence of Soviet Communism, as we did in filming the party and other archives during the first phase of the project, that attracted me to the Gulag archives and, from my point of view, justified the continued investment of Hoover's resources in Russia.

The agreement included the following elements:[30]

- GARF would microfilm the records relating to the Gulag from its beginning in 1918 to the end of the Stalinist period in 1953, up to 1.5 million pages. Hoover would pay for supplies and for labor (filming, unbinding and rebinding volumes, and management) at $40 per reel. Hoover supplied all the equipment, most of which was already in place.
- GARF and Hoover would publish the microfilm, and Chadwyck-Healey would market the film, paying royalties to GARF at 27 percent and to Hoover at 15 percent of gross sales.
- Rosarkhiv, GARF, and Hoover would produce and publish in Russian a six-volume letterpress documentary history of the Gulag, consisting of Gulag documents organized by subject and selected primarily from GARF's holdings but also including relevant materials from the Hoover Institution Archives. Hoover would engage editors for each volume at its expense and pay the printing and other publication costs totaling $120,000.
- GARF and Hoover would establish an Editorial Board, each organization naming and paying the expenses of its representatives.

- GARF and Hoover would not provide copies of the produced microfilm to the Novosibirsk Regional State Archives or to the Library of Congress, as was done under the 1992 agreement.
- At GARF's expense and direction, Hoover would provide microfilms of collections either at Hoover or at the US National Archives, matching the number of microfilms produced by GARF. This provision preserved the exchange aspect of the relationship, but GARF in fact never requested any microfilms.

A letter of understanding was attached to the agreement and signed on the same day. It clarified three elements of the agreement: (1) the Editorial Board would be advisory only and have no administrative role; (2) Hoover's total payments to the documentary editors would be capped at $60,000; and (3) GARF agreed to finish microfilming one of the record groups it had agreed to film in the earlier 1992 agreement. In October 2000, an annex to the GARF agreement was concluded. It provided for the filming of up to 2.5 million additional pages and a seventh volume of the documentary publication.[31]

In order to help Mironenko obtain approval of the agreement from Rosarkhiv, I acquiesced in naming Rosarkhiv as one of the publishers of the seven-volume documentary, along with GARF and Hoover, and in including Kozlov on the Editorial Board. During the final negotiations with Mironenko, I also agreed to put certain of Hoover's conditions into a letter of understanding between Hoover and GARF, rather than into the agreement itself. Mironenko told me that Kozlov was still against large-scale microfilming. If we changed any terms of the draft agreement that Rosarkhiv had already approved, he would have to go back to Rosarkhiv, which would likely hold things up for several more months. Lastly, I accepted his request that we not issue a press release announcing the new GARF-Hoover agreement. He feared that his opponents at Rosarkhiv would use the publicity against him.[32]

During the new agreement we filmed some three million pages. Moreover, we achieved this objective without having to change the main terms of our relationship. Except for the documentary publication that employed Russian senior archivists as editors, the terms of the GARF agreement were essentially the same as those that existed in January 1996, when the Russian side ended the 1992 agreement. It included large-scale microfilming, the shipment of microfilm copies abroad, an Editorial Board, the commercial publication of microfilm, provision for an exchange of microfilms, and similar financial incentives.

Once we concluded the new agreement, all the objections about violations of Russian law, which seemed to be such a big problem in January 1996, vanished and never reappeared. It is true that the Russian government enacted a new law on information and international collaboration, as anticipated by the Russian archivists. It took effect in July 1996. However, it was so vague that no one was sure what it restricted and what it allowed. We all assumed it did not apply to our project and went on our way without any adverse consequences. The biggest difference between January 1996 and June 1998, aside from our inclusion of the documentary publication project, was the absence of political turmoil. Yeltsin had won reelection and the overheated political atmosphere had cooled.[33]

During negotiations with GARF, Mironenko was in parallel negotiations with Jonathan Brent of Yale University Press to undertake an English-language single-volume documentary publication on the Gulag. The three of us—Mironenko, Brent, and I—discussed the possibility of combining the two projects. However, Yale declined to name Hoover as one of the publishers of its edition. In the end, we all concluded that the two projects would function better independently. In 2004, GARF and Hoover published their Russian-language documentary on the Gulag in six volumes, and in the same year Yale published a one-volume English-language edition. The Yale volume, which included about a hundred documents, was primarily a monograph by its author, Oleg V. Khlevniuk. Hoover fellow Robert Conquest wrote its foreword.[34]

Under the new agreement, microfilming operations proceeded much as they had under the old agreement, with two important exceptions. First, Hoover no longer needed to employ its own staff in Moscow, which under the first agreement gathered up the film produced at the three participating repositories, arranged the shipment of the film to Cambridge, and repaired and maintained the equipment. GARF assigned its staff to take care of these tasks. As filming was underway at only one repository, the coordination that was needed when three repositories were involved was no longer required. Consequently, I ended our contracts with Volkova and the other Russians we had employed to perform these services under the old agreement. I did so reluctantly, as they had done their jobs effectively and had made an important contribution to the project.

The Gulag project differed in a second way. The work of the Editorial Board was greatly reduced, as it was not needed to select materials to be microfilmed. We already knew what we would film at GARF—namely, the records on the Gulag. During the first two years of the agreement, the Russian side of the Editorial Board met only once, in January 1999; the Hoover side of the board met only twice—in January 1999 and in August 2000.

During the Gulag project, the primary role of the Editorial Board was overseeing the seven-volume documentary, which was published in 2004 and 2005. While the actual selection and organization of the documents were done by the individual volume editors—under the direction of Mironenko, who was executive director, and Khlevniuk, who was the coordinator—the Editorial Board provided valuable guidance and advice. For example, Terence Emmons, a Hoover member of the board, noted the absence of stated common principles of selection and organization of documents across the volumes, without which their utility would be limited. Emmons, who expressed these concerns in written form to the Russian editors, presented them in person at a meeting of editors and board members in Moscow where his concerns were specifically and effectively addressed.[35]

The collaboration with GARF proceeded smoothly. Mironenko was genuinely interested in working with us. He believed in the value of preserving his collections on microfilm and making them widely available for scholarship by microfilm publication. I never detected any ambivalence in his attitude or commitment to our collaboration. Our work together met or exceeded all our goals and did so on schedule.

While the GARF project on the whole was successful, some of the problems we had previously experienced arose again and sometimes exasperated us. Banking issues continued. In August 1998, the Russian bank that held GARF's account crashed, as did many other Russian banks during the economic crisis of 1998. In February 2000, the wire transfer instructions furnished by GARF failed to work, jeopardizing a $20,000 payment to GARF. Finally, as a last resort and with GARF's approval, Chadwyck-Healey set up an account for GARF at a bank in the United Kingdom where it deposited all royalty payments due to GARF as well as Hoover's payments to GARF for labor and supplies. Chadwyck-Healey would periodically send money to GARF as it was needed. These wire transfers were always problematic, but at least GARF did not have to depend on shaky Russian banks to hold the bulk of its funds.[36]

Communications with the Russian side also remained a problem. Between August 1999 and July 2000, I sent Mironenko several faxed letters requesting information about what was being filmed at GARF and received no answer until July 23, 2000. Under the agreement, GARF was asked to send monthly reports on its work and to submit requests for monthly payments but sent none for the first five months. I concluded that this was just the way Russians managed their affairs. While frustrating, it did not substantially affect the end result.[37]

In addition to the microfilms of the Gulag archives, GARF and Hoover successfully produced and published in 2004 a six-volume letterpress documentary entitled *The History of Stalin's Gulag*, with forewords by Aleksandr Solzhenitsyn and Robert Conquest. A seventh volume was published in 2005.[38] Its editors compiled key documents from the archives held at GARF as well as records from the former KGB, from the St. Petersburg Memorial Society—a private organization in Russia that gathered up personal papers from former Gulag prisoners—and from the Hoover Institution Archives.[39]

Working with Mironenko and GARF during the interregnum (1996–98) and the Gulag phase (1998–2004) of the project realized valuable results. We added 5,112 reels of microfilm to the 6,707 reels produced in the first phase, and we produced a seven-volume documentary publication. Together, the microfilm and publication told the tragic story of Russian life in the twentieth century—the unspeakable suffering of the victims, the iniquities of the perpetrators and of the ideology that motivated them, and the lessons from history for the rest of humanity.

For Russia, the Gulag microfilm and documentary publication were tangible steps toward reconciliation with its history. The choices of Aleksandr Solzhenitsyn and Robert Conquest to author forewords to the seven-volume publication—two writers who dramatically exposed the history of Stalin's terror and its Gulag—represented both an acknowledgment of the evil that was done and an awakening of conscience that could help heal the wound.

Chapter 4

THE CRITICS

Critics in Russia

Throughout the life of the project, our Russian partners were subjected to criticism from the Russian media, often poorly informed, one sided, and harsh. For us in the West, such criticism was business as usual. For them, however, apprehension of public criticism was understandable. They were breaking new ground in so many ways—collaborating with foreigners, opening heretofore closed government records to foreign scholars, signing commercial contracts, and sending microfilm of valuable historical archives outside the country. They were accused of selling their country's patrimony, taking bribes, providing favored treatment to foreign scholars, and much more. Most of these specific accusations were contrived, but the underlying grievance was real and deeply felt.

The Russians had lost the Cold War, and their country was prostrate. A former world power with a great history had been humbled and its national pride deeply wounded. As much as we tried to frame our project as one of collaboration between equals, the Russian media presented it as one of commercial exploitation by unscrupulous foreigners. The headlines in the Russian press stoked this theme: "Archival Piracy," "Goats in the Garden," and "How Much Is Our History Worth?" These stories repeatedly failed to distinguish between the acquisition of original documents, which we never sought, and the production of copies. The benefits to Rosarkhiv, Russian scholars, and the Russian people were rarely mentioned. Instead, the stories gave full voice to the opposition.[1]

An especially virulent article early in the project expressed the depth of the anger:

> The Hoover project . . . is an act of betrayal of Russia's fundamental national interest by the Yeltsinites, [as part of the] unconditional capitulation of this regime in the face of victorious America which, as a victor country, is taking materials and spiritual values of the vanquished country in amounts and of a quality sufficient . . . to preclude any possibility of national resurgence.
>
> As soon as these archives arrive in America, hordes of historians, military, intelligence agents, and social engineering specialists will converge on them to extract the precious ferments and to use them for the good of America and as poison against Russia.[2]

We put up arguments. The Hoover project never in any way undermined the government's sovereignty over its archives. The Russian archivists retained total physical control of their records. Rosarkhiv retained the right to approve or reject the microfilming of any records. We took out only copies, not the originals. We observed all Russian laws, including those relating to national security and restricted documents.

Moreover, even after agreements were duly signed, we repeatedly met every reasonable request from our Russian partners to amend them. We raised labor payments from $12 to $27, then to $40, per reel over the course of the project; we gave up the right of first refusal on the publication of documentary works; we incorporated and paid for documentary publications desired by the Russian side; we adjusted microfilming goals downward; we held back publicity to protect our Russian partners; we changed the royalty payments schedule from annually to monthly; and we offered to buy microfilms from the US National Archives in lieu of microfilms of Hoover's collections to meet the matching requirement. Such actions, however, were ineffective against essentially emotional responses. We just had to endure them.

Not all the opposition can be dismissed as angry xenophobia. We also received reasoned criticism. We addressed that as well. The most serious such criticism came from an unexpected source—Yuri N. Afanasiev, a noted historian, founder of the Democratic Russia movement, and rector of the Russian State University for the Humanities (RGGU). As a scholar and democratic reformer and someone who had supported Yeltsin over Gorbachev, he might have been expected to support us. Instead, he forcefully attacked the project in *Izvestiia, Komsomolskaya Pravda,* and *Frankfurter Allgemeine Zeitung.* Afanasiev feared that the "transfer of copied materials would move the center for the study of Russian history to the United States—the Hoover Institution." He argued that Russian scholars should have the "first access to the archives of the fatherland." Repeating our now familiar arguments, Pikhoia responded in an article in *Izvestiia,* in an interview in *Rossiiske vesti,* and in person at an open meeting of the Scientific Council of RGGU, at which Afanasiev was present.[3]

Robert Conquest and Terence Emmons, my Stanford colleagues and members of our Editorial Board, also responded. Conquest described the Hoover project as an "archival bonanza" and "a service to the scholarly community." In an article in *Moscow News,* entitled "I Don't Understand You, Gentlemen," Emmons pointed out that privileged access was a policy of the old Soviet regime and that equal access benefited all scholarship. Historian Robert W. Davies agreed, stating, "The availability of basic documents in the West . . . is far more likely to encourage postgraduate students and teachers to take up research on Russian history, and visit Russia for more material."[4] Eventually, Afanasiev was won over. In 1998, he was invited onto the Editorial Board of the Gulag project, to which he made valuable contributions.

In the battle between those who embraced the values of open access and universal scholarship and those who held on to the values of privileged access and exclusion, both sides appealed to national pride. Initially, the open access side showed some strength. When Pikhoia announced the opening of the Communist Party archives in February 1992, he was cheered. The history of Russia, he said, would be accessible to the Russian people and the world.

Unfortunately for our side, the opponents of the Hoover project soon gained the upper hand and were more effective in invoking national pride than we were. What mattered most to the Russians who opposed us was the exposure of their history to the harsh judgment of outsiders and the complicity of its own government in facilitating that exposure. In effect, the Hoover project made the Russian government a partner in exposing the Soviet Union to an outside audit—something many Russian citizens not surprisingly found offensive. Reconciling a nation to its history, especially a history that is as dark and tragic as Russia's and that outsiders helped to expose, is hard medicine to swallow. Those able to do it were our allies, but they were in a definite minority.

What surprised me was not so much the critical reaction but its harshness. In my first interview with the Russian media, when our agreement was announced, the first question to me was, "How much did I have to bribe Pikhoia to get this deal?" Instead of some acknowledgment of Hoover's generous terms and expression of friendship, I got hostility. Equally surprising to me was the contempt for Pikhoia evident in the question. It was my first introduction to the conflict in Russian society between its openness to the West and Western values represented by Pikhoia on the one hand, and enmity toward foreigners and deep disdain for those in authority on the other.

We tried to soften the project's effects on Russia's national pride—through joint exhibits, exchange of microfilm, favorable royalty and labor payments, a joint Editorial Board, frequent revisions of agreements, and the RLIN project—but our efforts were never enough to assuage the resentment of our Russian critics. It was probably beyond our capacity to do so.

Should we have not attempted such an ambitious project? Should we have offered more modest goals, as others did? Should we have stayed out entirely? In answering these questions, I can only challenge our critics to measure the costs against the benefits. The costs were damage to Russia's national pride, antagonism against the West, and loss of exclusive control by the Russian government over copies of its records and their interpretation. The benefits were enhanced scholarship on Russian history made possible by worldwide access to a massive archival resource; the permanent preservation on microfilm of millions of pages of Russian archives; the repatriation to Russia of many important archival materials, including copies of Hoover's Russian collections; and the knowledge gained by Russian archivists of Western archival institutions, practices, and standards. In my opinion, the pain was bearable and temporary, and the gain was substantial and permanent. As long as our partners at Rosarkhiv were willing to bear the pain, then we at Hoover, I concluded, should do the same.

Critics in the United States

The opposition eventually made its way to the United States. In the May/June 1996 issue of *Perspectives*, published by the American Historical Association (AHA), J. Arch Getty, an American scholar of Russian history at the University of California–Riverside (later at UCLA), authored an article on the Soviet archives and a follow-up letter to the editor in a later issue. In them he cataloged all the complaints against Pikhoia and the Hoover project that were circulating in Russia. These included a full array of voices: scurrilous gossip from an unnamed source, published opinions from serious critics, and criticism coming from within Rosarkhiv. His purpose, he stated, was to be a "messenger," conveying to the American audience the context for understanding the rebellion against the Hoover project. My reply, published in the December 1996 issue of *Perspectives*, addressed his message.[5]

At the time I was not happy to see Getty's article, because it brought all the criticisms we were receiving in Russia to America. Now we had to do battle on two fronts. Looking back, however, I can see that it served useful purposes. The Russians were entitled to their say, and interested Americans wanted to hear from them. Additionally, it identified all the criticisms in one place and gave me a forum to reply. I address them again here, not so much because they are unusually deserving of refutation but because they were representative of the attacks on the project.

First, Getty stated that "the National Endowment for the Humanities and other Western funders . . . generously supported Hoover, often to the exclusion of the other on-going Russian-American collaborations." Hoover did, indeed, receive generous support, but this support had no exclusionary effect. The microfilming project was financed entirely by foundations and other donors with long histories of support, not for Russian projects as such but for the Hoover Institution. Few, if any, of these gifts would have been available to other institutions. Thus, the Hoover project actually increased financial support for Russian studies, not decreased it.

Funding from the NEH, which might conceivably have gone to other institutions for Russian projects, was a very small portion of the funds Hoover received for its work in Russia. Moreover, the NEH grant was made jointly to Hoover and to the Research Libraries Group and had nothing directly to do with the Hoover microfilming project. It was made solely to support a project undertaken cooperatively by Hoover and RLG to link Russian repositories electronically to a bibliographic database in the United States.

Second, Getty said that Hoover intended to microfilm "virtually the entire collections of the three most important Moscow political archives." Our Russian critics also made this claim, maintaining that Hoover had been given favored "exclusive, monopoly status," closing off opportunities for others.[6] These claims were false. We never received favored, monopoly status. The Hoover agreement was not a no-bid contract. We won an open competition fair and square, and we won because we made the best offer. After we concluded our agreement, we opposed other institutions only when they sought to copy the same materials our project intended to copy. At no time did Hoover propose to microfilm the entire holdings of any repository. Such a project would have been completely impractical, for those repositories held billions of pages of documentation. Hoover's actual project goal sought to produce twenty-five million pages. We managed to copy about half that number. We left plenty of room for other projects.

In fact, opportunities for others abounded. While the Hoover project was by far the biggest such project, we were certainly not the only ones copying Russian archives. Several institutions successfully undertook archival copying and publishing projects with Rosarkhiv or its subordinate repositories. In May 1994, RTsKhIDNI concluded an agreement with Inter Documentation Company, a Dutch publisher, to publish microfilm of the records of seven Comintern congresses and thirteen plenums held between 1919 and 1935, as well as the finding aids of the Comintern archives. Primary Source Media (formerly RPI) produced several microfilm publications, including, at TsKhSD, records of the Plenums of the Central Committee, 1941–90 (181 reels and 690 microfiches) and records of the International Department of the Central Committee, 1953–57

(126 reels); and at GARF, the intercepted correspondence from the Special Department of the Police, 1906–17. The Library of Congress microfilmed the records of the US Communist Party held at RTsKhIDNI.

Third, as Getty reported, our Russian critics claimed that Hoover offered the Russians, in exchange for the microfilm it received, a substantially smaller number of microfilms of Hoover's holdings. This was untrue. At the conclusion of the first agreement with Rosarkhiv in July 1996 (in subsequent years the Russian side made no requests for matching microfilm), Hoover had received 6,707 reels containing 5.7 million pages from Russia. In 1993, we delivered to the Russians 4,640 reels containing 4.5 million pages from our collections.

In order to meet our remaining matching obligation, I offered to either give Rosarkhiv additional microfilm of Hoover's collections or purchase for them microfilm of collections of interest elsewhere. Pikhoia and some of his colleagues had mentioned an interest in microfilm of US Department of State records on Russia that were available from the US National Archives. On September 19, 1996, Tiuneev (representing Rosarkhiv) accepted this offer and promised to make a selection of microfilms from a list I had furnished him. Three years later, at a meeting with Chadwyck-Healey in Moscow on April 12, 1999, Kozlov (Tiuneev's successor) admitted that his side had not yet made a selection from the list I had provided. By the end of 2001, the Russians had still not given us their selections.[7]

Then, in 2002, in fulfillment of Hoover's matching obligation, the Russian side agreed to accept microfilm of additional collections from Hoover's Russian Collection (1,499 reels) as well as from the Museum of Russian Culture in San Francisco (516 reels). The Russians received these materials in October 2002—bringing the total number of microfilm reels provided by Hoover to 6,655, containing approximately 5.7 million pages, and thus meeting our contractual obligation.[8]

Some of our critics claimed that the Hoover collections microfilmed for the Russians were not comparable in value to the Russian collections microfilmed for Hoover. They said the Hoover collection consisted mainly of papers generated by Russian émigrés. While a sizable part of Hoover's archival holdings included such papers, a significant part consisted of records generated by Russians in Russia or by Russian governmental agencies. Among them were the records of the Paris office of the Tsarist Secret Police (206 boxes), the records of the Russian Imperial and Provisional Government embassies in Paris (37 boxes) and Washington, DC (474 boxes), the Boris I. Nicolaevsky Collection on Menshevik and other revolutionary leaders (811 boxes), and the General Peter Wrangel Papers on the Russian Civil War (174 boxes).[9]

The Russian archivists must have wanted these collections. Instead of taking these and others, they could have accepted our offer to provide microfilm of records at the US National Archives. They declined to do so.

Fourth, Getty repeated a statement made to him from an unnamed official at one of the participating repositories to the effect that his repository had received "not one kopek" from Rosarkhiv, Hoover, or Chadwyck-Healey. Getty also cited "the universal perception in Moscow academic circles . . . that millions of Hoover dollars have disappeared while those doing the project's work have received nothing." These statements were demonstrably false. Rosarkhiv received two initial payments, one for start-up costs ($60,000) and one as an advance on royalties ($100,000). All subsequent payments went directly to the individual bank accounts of the repositories. By June 1996, when Getty's article was published, Hoover had paid over $200,000 to cover all staff and overhead costs, and Chadwyck-Healey had paid over $324,000 in royalty payments—a total of $524,000.[10]

What could the Russian archives have done with $524,000 in 1996? In that year, the monthly salary of a government worker on average was equivalent to $185. The twenty-five persons employed by the Russian repositories for the Hoover project were mainly entry-level employees who received less than that amount—the equivalent of $100 per month plus a $20 bonus. Even at the higher $185 rate, the $524,000 would have paid for forty-seven employees for five years.

At the conclusion of the project, in 2004, total payments equaled $630,000 for labor and overhead, and $1.35 million in royalties, totaling $1.98 million. Assuming the same average 1996 monthly salary (that is, $185 per month per employee), $1.98 million would have paid the salaries of eighty-nine employees for ten years. In other words, this single microfilming project enabled three Russian repositories to cover a substantial part of their entire budgets and thus to weather a decade of economic turmoil.[11]

Fifth, our opponents raised the question: "Why should Russia permit foreigners to buy Russia's cultural treasures?" The charge, of course, was nonsense. The originals of all records microfilmed in Russia always remained in Russia, where they still reside. Moreover, at Hoover's expense, two copies of the microfilms (a preservation negative and a positive use copy) were sent to the Russian repositories—not "eventually, maybe," as some suggested, but as soon as they were produced. A microfilm copy was also deposited at the Novosibirsk Regional State Archives for use by Russian scholars in that distant region of the country.

Sixth, Getty elaborated Afanasiev's complaint that access to Russian archives for American scholars was inherently unfair to Russian scholars because Americans have the financial resources to take greater advantage of such access. When Pikhoia announced the opening of the Soviet Communist Party archives in 1992, he proclaimed that the materials would be accessible on an equal basis to all the world's scholars without regard to citizenship. This was a noble goal—one that had long been endorsed by scholars in the United States and elsewhere. Knowledge has no boundaries. Scholarship—wherever and by whomever it is done—benefits everyone. Restricting access in order to offset a disparity in economic resources would ultimately be harmful to scholarship everywhere.

Seventh, writing shortly after the termination of the 1992 agreement, Getty characterized the Hoover-Rosarkhiv project as being in a state of complete collapse, stating that the governing board of Rosarkhiv "rose up in rebellion against Pikhoia and Hoover . . . denouncing him and the Hoover project." That was an exaggerated half-truth. While it was true that the Rosarkhiv governing board voted to end the project in December 1995, that same board rescinded its December termination letter and, in its place, approved a "memorandum of mutual understanding" on January 12, 1996. In that memorandum, Rosarkhiv continued the project for another six months and affirmed a desire to negotiate a new agreement. All parties noted "the importance and value of the Agreement concluded between them on 17 April 1992 in expanding and raising the effectiveness of archival documentation."[12]

Eighth, Getty noted that Hoover had concluded an agreement with Rosarkhiv rather than directly and individually with the three participating repositories, as their directors would have preferred. In this criticism, Getty and others who made it were right; it was a lesson learned. During the second phase of the project, we had two agreements: one with Rosarkhiv authorizing us to make separate agreements with repositories and a second one with GARF. Although Rosarkhiv had the right to intervene and did so, this arrangement worked better.

Finally, Getty asked if there were not valid questions about the propriety of relationships between public archival organizations on the one hand and private and commercial organizations on the other. He did not make or cite any accusations of wrongdoing by either Hoover or Chadwyck-Healey but felt the matter deserved attention.[13]

Getty had not been alone in expressing this concern. In April 1995, a year before Getty's letter, a Joint Task Force on Archives of the American Association for the Advancement of Slavic Studies (AAASS) and the AHA issued a report on the Russian archives. It dealt with many issues related to the Russian archives, but cast its eye most critically on the relationships between private and commercial organizations, on the one hand, and state archival organizations in Russia, on the other. In this part of the report, the Hoover project came in for some unfriendly treatment.

The joint task force report identified "worrisome tendencies" of Russian archival repositories engaged in commercial microfilming and other publication projects and named Rosarkhiv's project with Hoover and Chadwyck-Healey among those to be concerned about. The "worrisome tendencies" were selling publication rights to commercial publishers and succumbing to commercial incentives. These tendencies, it claimed, "open the door to practices that are either explicitly illegal or that violate implicit codes of scholarly and archival ethics." It offered no examples of illegal or unethical wrongdoing by the Russian repositories or any commercial projects.[14]

Accusations against Hoover of committing illegalities had been made before, and seeing accusations insinuated in this report now was thus a concern to me. At the time, after consulting with Raisian, Hoover's director, and other colleagues, I decided not to respond publicly. Since Hoover had not been accused of any overt criminal or unethical activity, the report was merely offensive, not ruinous. Moreover, any response from me would have created only more distracting friction, to no good effect. Now, however, looking back, I think the issues raised in the report deserved more attention.

First, with respect to selling rights to commercial publishers, the report did not accurately describe the relationships among the three Hoover project partners. Rosarkhiv did not sell publication rights to Chadwyck-Healey, our commercial partner, though doing so would not have been an unusual or improper thing to do. Archival repositories everywhere routinely grant publication rights to commercial publishers in exchange for royalties. They do so without incurring accusations of illegal or unethical practices. Evidently, according to the AAASS-AHA Joint Task Force, such publishing arrangements when undertaken by Russians are suspect.

In any case, with respect to the Hoover project, Rosarkhiv and Hoover, not Chadwyck-Healey, were the publishers of the project microfilm. Chadwyck-Healey was the distributor. As distributor, it assisted with production and marketed and sold the microfilm. As publishers, Rosarkhiv and Hoover retained final authority over the microfilm publication. Together we approved the selection of materials filmed, making adjustments throughout the course of the project. The Russian staff prepared all materials for filming and used cameras and other equipment provided by Hoover. Every other detail of the publishing process, including the content and design of all marketing literature, the design of the microfilm boxes, and the price charged to customers, had to be approved by Rosarkhiv and Hoover. In other words, along with Hoover, Rosarkhiv performed all the duties and responsibilities of a publisher. The arrangement, in my opinion, was and remains a model to be followed, not a model to be avoided.

The task force report identified a second "worrisome tendency"—succumbing to commercial incentives. Its discussion was brief and undeveloped, but two possible reasons for its concern were apparent. First, the task force was worried, as it had stated earlier in its report, that the difficult economic conditions in Russia during the 1990s enhanced the temptation to engage in illegal or unethical practices. Second, by linking "commercial incentives" to illegal and unethical practices, the task force appeared to assume that commercial endeavors are more prone to bad behavior than other endeavors and, therefore, warrant special scrutiny. Neither reason—neither enhanced temptations nor suspicions of commercial endeavors—justified invoking a supposition of wrongdoing.

It was certainly true that the Russian economy at that time was rife with illegality. As many observers have noted, bribes, extortion, and protection schemes were common.[15] However, a crime requires more than conditions favorable to temptation. It requires actors. Making the assumption, without offering any evidence whatsoever, that the leaders at Rosarkhiv, Hoover, or Chadwyck-Healey, with or without favorable conditions, might be unable to resist temptation and commit crimes or unethical acts was unjustified. Many of our angry critics in Russia had low opinions of us, as previously described in this chapter, and the conditions in Russia made it easy for them falsely to accuse us of crimes. Giving voice to these unfounded and undeserved accusations, even if we were not incriminated overtly, amounted to incrimination by innuendo.

The task force seemed to think that commercial activities by their very nature open the door to illegal or unethical behavior. But commercial enterprises are no more likely to engage in illegal acts than noncommercial enterprises. In fact, they are subject to restraints that greatly reduce the incentive to do so. Good reputations are essential to success in business, and firms go to great lengths to protect them. Additionally, commercial enterprises are accountable to laws that apply specifically to business activities abroad—both laws in the countries in which they do business and laws in their home countries that apply to their foreign commercial activities. During the 1990s, when Hoover was operating in Russia, US organizations that were engaged in any form of commercial activity abroad—as well as their foreign partners—were subject to the US Foreign Corrupt Practices Act. This law was applicable worldwide and rigorously enforced. British firms were subject to a similar law.

Commercial interest in the Soviet archives was only one incentive at work in Russia in the 1990s. Opening these archives was an event of historic importance. It attracted players of all sorts and with varying motivations. Glory, adventure, professional advancement, selfless idealism—these and others were at play on both sides. Any of them could have led, and in a few cases perhaps did lead, some to engage in bad behavior. The individual researchers, for example, who bribed archivists in Russian reading rooms to obtain access to documents and gain an advantage over others—a practice the task force reported—were not motivated by commercial incentives. Neither, I believe, was James Billington, the Librarian of Congress, when he misled me. The Soviet archives were an enticing prize. We all sought it, but we did not all succumb to bad behavior to get it.

The Hoover project was a legal enterprise in all its facets and endeavors. More than that, the project met the highest professional standards. The AAASS-AHA Joint Task Force report contained a list of these standards, which it recommended for microfilming projects in Russia. We followed them all:

- We filmed the entire contents of record files (except documents restricted by law), in order to provide a true, unbiased, and comprehensive copy.
- Records were inaccessible only during the actual filming process and were immediately returned for general use thereafter.
- The Hoover project did not gain preferred access to records or restrict access to users in any way.
- In our public statements we endorsed and defended the AHA standard "that open access to archives be maintained to scholars of all countries."
- We issued periodic press releases informing the scholarly community of our plans and progress.
- We established an Editorial Board of distinguished historians—both American and Russian—to insure adherence to scholarly standards.
- Finally, by providing the Russian side with microfilm copies of Hoover's Russian collections, we sought to make the project one of archival collaboration rather than one solely of commercial interest.

The AAASS-AHA Joint Task Force report failed to give us credit for meeting any of these standards, and it included only a single statement acknowledging the good works of those who invested financial resources in opening the Russian archives. Without commending specific institutions, it stated that "microfilming and publication ventures . . . vastly expand the opportunities for scholarship."[16] Beyond that, nothing. One might have thought that these two professional organizations would have made a point of encouraging investments in Russian studies and would have expressed more generous and specific appreciation for those who made them.

During the 1990s, the Hoover Institution's contributions to Russian studies were not limited to our projects with Rosarkhiv. In 1991–93, with a grant from Hoover, Michael McFaul, then a visiting research fellow at Hoover, conducted 134 oral history interviews with Russian political leaders on the transition to democracy and deposited them in the Hoover Institution Archives.[17] In 1997, in a joint project with the International Democracy Foundation (Moscow), headed by Alexander Yakovlev—the intellectual father of perestroika and glasnost—the Hoover Institution funded the compilation and publication of seven volumes of documents from the Soviet archives on various aspects of Russian and Soviet history. In 1998, the Hoover Institution and the Gorbachev Foundation (Moscow) undertook a joint project that produced oral history interviews of leading participants in both Soviet and US governments concerning the policies and events that brought the Cold War to an end. Moreover, throughout this period, Hoover continued to acquire vast quantities of archival and other special materials for its Russian Collection, including the vast archives of Radio Free Europe/Radio Liberty, all open to scholars of every persuasion.

Looking back, I prefer to recall the generous support the project received from individuals. When Pikhoia was under attack in December 1995, Emmons, Hoover Senior Fellow John Dunlop, and I asked scholars of Russian history to join us in a public letter of support for Pikhoia. The letter mentioned the Hoover project as well as several others that Pikhoia had undertaken with American partners. Seventy-eight scholars from leading universities and other academic institutions signed it. It stated the following:

> In this time of uncertainty, we, the undersigned American scholars and archivists of Russian affairs, wish to express our appreciation for your efforts over the last four and a half years—specifically your efforts toward opening the archives of the Soviet period for scholarly research, and generally for facilitating international scholarly cooperation. . . . We congratulate you, Rudolf Germanovich, for your contribution toward consolidation of international norms of archival access and cooperation in Russia and wish you further success in that work.[18]

Chapter 5

MISSION ACCOMPLISHED

Last Chapter

The last chapter of the story was written by Elena Danielson, who replaced me as head of the Hoover Institution Library & Archives when I retired at the end of December 2001. I was the last of the three principals to exit. Pikhoia resigned in January 1996. In 1997, Charles Chadwyck-Healey sold his production operations to Micromedia, a company owned by Bell & Howell. On October 7, 1999, he sold his three publishing companies to Bell & Howell Information and Learning, which changed its name to ProQuest Information and Learning in 2001.[1]

Toward the end of 2001, I could see that the prospects for continued engagement with the Russians had dimmed considerably. Russian politics and attitudes toward foreigners were heading again into very negative territory. Interest from our British partner also weakened. In October, Steven Hall, who was senior vice president at ProQuest, informed me that based on current sales he "could make no commitment on the level of royalties to Hoover and the [Russian] Archives on any further stage of the project."[2]

In my exit interview with Danielson, I advised her against taking on any further collaborative projects with Rosarkhiv or its subordinate repositories. I suggested that the materials they might offer for filming would probably not be worth the expense, that fundraising for such work would be difficult, and that other prospects in Russia were more promising.

Before I departed, I tried to complete as many of the remaining project tasks as I could. One was dealing with a complaint by Kozlov that Chadwyck-Healey had failed to make all its required royalty payments and to deliver all the promised sets of the project microfilm to the Russian repositories. On July 10, 2001, and again on September 5, 2001, Hall gave

Kozlov a detailed accounting of the royalty payments, including the date, amount, and wire transaction of each payment, and of the shipments of microfilm sets. When Kozlov claimed he never received Hall's letter, Hall sent him a second copy on October 3. Since we received no further complaints, Hall's actions evidently settled the matter.[3]

A second task was to obtain a firm commitment from the Russians on a date certain for the completion of all project work. On August 22, 2001, Kozlov stated that preparation of the collection of documents for the seven-volume documentary publication would be completed before the end of the year. He also reported that microfilming was scheduled to be completed in six to seven months. Thus, by the end of 2001, it seemed clear that most of the production work for both the documentary publication and microfilming would be completed.[4]

A third task was to prepare a final status report for my successor. It listed the remaining unpaid expenses of the project that would come due after I left. They amounted to $669,600, including payments for the printed documentary edition ($140,500), payments to GARF for production costs ($247,800), payments to Micromedia for its production costs ($177,600), and payments for producing microfilm of Hoover's collections for GARF ($103,700). All of the funding to pay these bills was in place.[5]

One final task I hoped to complete was to meet with Kozlov, Mironenko, and Hall to inform them in person of my retirement and to deal with any remaining issues. Kozlov also wanted a year-end meeting. Hall and I proposed a meeting in Cambridge, England, or Moscow in October, but Kozlov's schedule did not permit it. I would have liked to close my time with the project with a farewell meeting, but it was not to be.

Of course, some unfinished tasks remained. They included writing introductions to the documentary volumes, paying unpaid bills, resolving remaining production issues, issuing a press release on the completion of the project, and writing a final report to donors, all of which I necessarily left to my successor. Danielson navigated through these waters with her usual grace and skill. In 2004, six volumes of the documentary, entitled *The History of Stalin's Gulag*, were published. Danielson, representing Hoover, joined with others for a celebratory seminar at Harvard University to mark the occasion. The seventh volume was published in

2005. The publication was awarded the 2005 Silver Medal for Human Rights by the Russian Federation.

Final Accounting

When we began the project with Rosarkhiv in 1992, Jana Howlett prophesied: "This project will launch a new era of Russian history. The period of emotive ideology in the writing of Russian history is now past. Now, at long last, long-argued conclusions can be grounded in documentation."[6] No longer confined to secondary sources and interviews of émigrés, historians can now base their research on the archival record. Soviet Communism cannot escape the documentary evidence now safely and permanently preserved on microfilm and available for all to see.

Since the records were first made available for research in the Hoover Institution Archives reading room, more than five hundred registered scholars have requested and examined more than eleven thousand reels of microfilm from the collection. Many more scholars at all the libraries that purchased the collection have also gained access to the collection. Countless books and articles on Soviet history have now been written based on these materials, and countless more will be done by future generations of scholars.[7]

The numbers show the magnitude of the accomplishment. The project produced microfilm images of approximately ten million pages held on 11,819 reels of microfilm. Stacked in one pile, ten million pages would reach 3,650 feet in height, equivalent to about six and a half Washington Monuments. Thirty-five libraries purchased varying numbers of the microfilm, and four libraries—British Library (London), Bavarian State Library (Munich), National Diet Library (Tokyo), and Harvard University (Cambridge, Massachusetts)—purchased complete sets, thus making the collection widely available to scholars. In addition, Hoover donated five thousand reels each to the Library of Congress and the Novosibirsk Regional State Archives. And, of course, complete sets reside at the Hoover Institution and at Rosarkhiv in Moscow.

The total cost to Hoover was $3.16 million. At 32 cents per page, it was a good investment for a priceless collection. We also had the satisfaction of knowing that had we not done the project, it may not have been done at all, certainly not with the voluminous result we achieved. For the customers who bought the microfilm collection, it was an even better deal. They paid 12 cents per page and endured none of the frustration.

For the Russians, the numbers were as impressive as they were on Hoover's side, if not more so. The Russians received royalties, labor and overhead payments, equipment, two complete sets of the microfilm (one positive and one negative copy), a set of five thousand reels sent to the Novosibirsk Regional State Archives, and microfilm copies of Hoover's Russian archival collections, altogether valued at $2.96 million, as follows:[8]

Royalties (27 percent of $5 million in total sales)	$1,350,000
Labor payments for microfilming, disbanding, and rebinding volumes, and management	630,000
Preservation negative and positive use copy of all 11,819 reels	450,437
Positive copy of 5,000 reels for the Novosibirsk Regional State Archives	91,900
Positive copy of Hoover's Russian Collection and Museum of Russian Culture Collection, 6,655 reels	122,319
Equipment	250,000
Payment to authors/editors of seven-volume documentary on the Gulag	70,000
Total	**$2,964,656**

Even our most persistent Russian critic, Vladimir P. Kozlov, Rosarkhiv's chairman from November 1996, acknowledged the value of the project to the Russian archives when he stated: "[Income from the project] gave the archives the opportunity to somehow survive during the economic turmoil of those years. Thanks to the money received, Rosarkhiv managed to redirect budget money to support the functioning of other federal archives during those difficult years."[9]

Numbers, of course, are not the only measure of success. For Russia, opening the Soviet archives and joining in the Hoover project were first steps toward a free society. By their actions, the Russian archivists established a documentary basis for a more truthful, objective understanding of their nation's history, without which no country is truly free. For twelve years they navigated past all the criticisms, frustrations, and problems, aided by two partners—one American and one British—who persevered alongside them.

After a promising beginning, when the hammer and sickle came down from the Kremlin tower, the journey toward a free Russia soon stalled. Indeed, by the end of the 1990s it had turned decidedly backward. Yet, if past is prologue, Russia may one day turn again to the optimistic, outward-looking side of its national character. If it does, the Hoover project's most important contribution may turn out to be the example of international collaboration it set—in what was done both well and less well—for Russia's next burst of freedom.

For the Hoover Institution, the microfilming of the records of the Soviet Communist Party and Soviet State represented the culmination of efforts over many decades by Hoover librarians and archivists to collect the history of Soviet Communism. In Moscow in November 1991, when I first laid my eyes on the rows of metal shelving holding the massive archives of the Soviet Communist Party, I saw a chance to realize one of Herbert Hoover's most intensely felt aspirations and one of the founding missions of the Hoover Institution—documenting an ideology that produced nearly a century of tyranny over the Russian people and that menaced liberal and democratic values everywhere. I think it would not be too much to claim for the Hoover Institution, especially for all those who supported and worked on the project: mission accomplished.

Appendix A

RED ARCHIVES

Charles Chadwyck-Healey

Note to the reader: This account was first published in *Publishing for Libraries: At the Dawn of the Digital Age* by Charles Chadwyck-Healey (London: Bloomsbury, 2020). It has been revised, expanded, and edited for republication in this volume. Chadwyck-Healey founded the Chadwyck-Healey publishing group in the United Kingdom in 1973 as a publisher of research material in the humanities and social sciences on microfilm, CD-ROM, and the internet for purchase by university, public, and national libraries throughout the world. The group also included publishing companies in the United States, France, and Spain.

* * *

Jana Howlett was a lecturer in Russian history at Cambridge University and had been our neighbor when we first moved to Cambridge in 1976. Her mother was English; her father was Czech. In the 1960s she moved with her mother and stepfather to Beijing, where she attended Chinese and Russian secondary schools. As a postgraduate student and later lecturer she had spent many months working in Russian archives. In May 1990 she was invited to a medieval history conference in Sverdlovsk in the Urals organized by the then head of the history faculty, Rudolf G. Pikhoia. She took some reels of our microfilm to Sverdlovsk and brought back some Russian microfilm and a list of illuminated manuscripts that might be published in facsimile.

Shortly after, I was approached by a library automation company that wished to sell a library management system to the Russian Academy of Sciences Library (BAN) in Leningrad. BAN did not have the foreign exchange to pay for it, and the company asked me if I would visit the library at its expense and advise on how it could earn foreign currency by publishing facsimiles of its most important books, manuscripts, and microfilms or CD-ROMs of collections in the library. I asked Hans Fellner, who had been a director of my company and now worked in the Book Department of Christie's, the auction house, to come with me, as I needed his expertise in identifying the most important rare books and illuminated manuscripts. With his demanding workload, a week in the USSR was a substantial commitment. We flew to Leningrad in February 1991 and spent several days in BAN, one of the largest libraries in the USSR, looking at their finest books and manuscripts, but we could not find anything suitable for republishing in facsimile for a Western market. Nor was there anything obvious for publishing on microfilm or on CD-ROM. We did agree to market and sell copies of their *Catalogue of Foreign Language Books and Periodicals to 1930*, which was already on microfiche.

We went on to Moscow, and through an introduction by Howlett I was able to meet Pikhoia, the historian with whom she had discussed potential microfilming in Sverdlovsk. He was now the head of the Committee on Archival Affairs in the government of the Russian Soviet Federative Socialist Republic (RSFSR).

Howlett had also arranged for a friend, Natalia Volkova, to act as interpreter and guide while we were in Moscow and for a driver to chauffeur us in his small, battered Lada. Pikhoia was friendly and quite different from how I expected a senior Russian official to be. He proposed that we should microfilm archives and books on several themes, including the industrialization of Russia from Peter the Great to the 1930s and the development of Siberia and the Far East from the sixteenth century.

We did not sign a letter of intent with Pikhoia until May 1991. In August 1991 came the coup that attempted to depose Mikhail Gorbachev. The coup failed, thanks to opposition organized by Boris Yeltsin. Gorbachev resigned as president of the USSR on December 25, 1991, but by then the USSR had already ceased to exist, with its constituent republics having already claimed their independence. The former RSFSR was the largest of these, and Yeltsin became the head of the new Russian government.

Pikhoia was now a junior minister with responsibility for all the state and party archives on Russian territory, with the exception of the KGB archive. In the autumn of 1991 he came to Cambridge and we met again with Howlett. He suggested that we publish on microfilm the personal papers of the leaders of the Russian Revolution (*Leaders of the Russian Revolution*, or the *Leaders* project), most of whom were members of the first Soviet. These included Trotsky, Molotov, and seven others. The archives would carry out the microfilming for us but, unusually for manuscript material, they would be published on microfiche.[1] This may have been because there were microfiche cameras in the archives that could be put to use for this project. I sent Pikhoia a draft agreement. A Russian version and English translation came back quickly, with few changes, and we signed on December 17, 1991.

When our press release went out to the wire services, I found myself experiencing "fifteen minutes of fame." If I had read our press release more carefully, I should have realized that it implied that we had signed an agreement with the Russian government in which everything, including secret material, was going to be microfilmed on an exclusive basis. "All," "secret," and "exclusive" are trigger words for journalists. The phone rang all day as news agencies and broadcasting services like CNN wanted interviews and quotes. The next day there were articles in all the broadsheets and foreign newspapers. The London *Times* published articles two days running, while the *New York Times* stated:

> The company said it had reached an agreement with the Russian government to microfilm the entire archives, which some have estimated include more than 70 million documents. . . .
>
> In winning the contract Chadwyck-Healey has gained the publishing rights to the scholarly equivalent of a runaway best seller.[2]

I flew to New York a day later and visited Edward Kasinec at the New York Public Library. Chief of the Slavic and Baltic Division, he was one of the most respected Slavic librarians in the USA. As we walked through one of the reading rooms, he pointed at the hundreds of books on the Soviet

Union, telling me that they were now all out of date because their authors had not had access to the archives.

I then went on to stay in Palo Alto with Charles and Miriam Palm, whom I had met several years previously. Palm, who was now deputy director of the Hoover Institution, congratulated me on our project but said that he was planning something much bigger. Pikhoia had visited him at Hoover in May 1991 and they had met again in Moscow in November. He had proposed to Pikhoia that Hoover and the Russian government enter into an agreement to microfilm twenty-five million pages of the archives of the Central Committee of the Communist Party, with Hoover providing money, equipment, and materials and the Russians providing the facilities, the labor, and the archives themselves. He asked me if we would be interested in being the third partner, the enabler who would ensure that the microfilm was produced to international standards and who would make the microfilm copies for both the participants and any other libraries in Russia entitled to them. We would also be the sales agent, selling the microfilms to libraries throughout the world to help fund the project. It was an extraordinarily ambitious project that depended on full cooperation by the Russians and the provision of several million dollars of investment by Hoover, and I was immediately excited by it. Pikhoia had also met with James Billington, the Librarian of Congress, in London on December 17, 1991, the day that he signed our agreement. Billington was a noted Sovietologist and had been director of the Woodrow Wilson International Center for Scholars, where he had founded the Kennan Institute for Advanced Russian Studies. He regarded himself as a central figure in the opening up of the Soviet archives and had invited Pikhoia and his colleagues to meet in London for a private conference entitled "Archival Project: Discussion," attended by twelve people, including Howlett.

The discussion was characteristic of the approach of librarians and academics to any new project. All aspects were explored in theoretical and abstract ways. There were discussions on the organization of the archives and technical questions on preservation and access. There were the broad priorities of world scholarship and the prioritization of sixteen projects for rapid publication, with proposals for three archival projects and for nine longer-term projects. Billington himself proposed seven subjects, including Soviet high politics, Soviet foreign policy from 1939 to 1956, the demography of twentieth-century Russia, and the Soviet terror system. The seven subjects came to be known as the "seven sisters." There was a list of the institutions that already had agreements or were in discussions with Pikhoia. They included the American Enterprise Institute; the Hoover Institution; a project from the University of California–Riverside, headed by J. Arch Getty, who later was so critical of the Hoover project; the British Academic Committee for Liaison with Soviet Archives, headed by John Barber and Tony Cross at the University of Cambridge; the Fondazione Giangiacomo Feltrinelli in Italy; and the International Institute of Social History, Amsterdam. Our agreement was also listed but described as only including *opisi* (in this case, finding aids). In Russia, archives are divided into *fondy* or, to use the US term, record groups, and are further divided into *opisi*, which contain from one to several thousand *dela* or files. The average number of *dela* in an *opis* is 150. Confusingly, *opisi* is also the term for finding aids, which often contain enough information to satisfy a researcher's inquiry. Finally, there were three Jewish projects relating to the Holocaust and Jewish genealogy. But there was no mention in the minutes of the meeting as to how this huge mass of material would be published.

In contrast to Billington's, Palm's approach was urgent and direct. The doors to the Central Committee Archives were being opened for the first time; Hoover, whose mission has always included collecting the archives of left-wing and communist regimes, wanted to bring out as much material as possible before the doors were closed again. Professor John A. Armstrong, in a memo that was part of the papers of the Billington meeting, pointed out that in the Khrushchev era, Russian dissertations had been available to foreign researchers, but then access to them had suddenly been curtailed. Palm did not think that this unpredictability would change. The editorial decisions about what records to select, which so preoccupied Billington and his colleagues, could be made later once we had a binding agreement and a plan for the infrastructure that would allow large-scale microfilming to take place.

I flew to Moscow on February 23, 1992, for our first meeting. I was not prepared for the unnerving experience of arriving at Moscow's

Sheremetyevo Airport for the first time. Designed by the East Germans in time for the 1980 Olympic Games, the international terminal was a brutal concrete monstrosity. After leaving the plane, passengers descended into a huge, dimly lit space crowded with people. The oppressive nature of the scene was brought about by the lowness of the ceiling and the dim concealed lighting. In the middle distance were the immigration desks manned by men in military uniforms. New arrivals joined the milling crowd hoping that in some way they would be swept close to a desk and an exit. Strangely, it worked, while the time spent waiting for the bags was not much longer than in most third-world airports. On our next visit, Palm was escorted through a side door while I descended into the bowels. He had paid $100 for special clearance and from then on I did the same, both arriving and departing.

The next day we meet in the Rosarkhiv office in the old headquarters of the Central Committee, a building which had been a bank before the revolution and still had elegant, high-ceilinged halls on the ground floor that housed part of the Central Committee's archives. Palm is accompanied by Joseph Dwyer, Robert Shanks from the law firm Latham and Watkins, and Richard Kahn. Howlett is there to advise, and Volkova, who had shown us around Moscow a year earlier, is our translator. I am accompanied by Edward Lee-Smith, a lawyer from Norton Rose whom I have hired to advise us. Rosarkhiv, the ministry headed by Pikhoia, presides, among others, over three physically and organizationally separate archives, generally known by challenging acronyms because of their long names. They are RTsKhIDNI (now RGASPI), the former Central Party Archive in Pushkin Square; TsKhSD (now RGANI), the former CPSU Secretariat Archive in Old Square; and GARF, formerly TsGAOR, Central State Archives of the October Revolution. Each has its own director: Vladimir P. Kozlov at RTsKhIDNI, Rem A. Usikov at TsKhSD, and Sergei V. Mironenko at GARF. Pikhoia's relationship with them is a delicate one in that, although he has overall authority, they have considerable independence within their own archives.

Pikhoia hands round a draft agreement, saying that he would like to see a general definition of the material we are going to microfilm and that he wants the agreement to state that creating a microfilm copy will enhance the security of the documents. Kozlov then says that he wishes to make a personal statement:

> I look on this proposal as one of many proposals and it needs very careful analysis. The public reaction to the Chadwyck-Healey announcement [the press coverage that we got in response to our press release] makes me feel that I must be much more careful. I would prefer to see a gradual, stage-by-stage approach: first, filming of secondary material aimed at making the world understand the kind of life that the Communist Party was trying to make and to include material from local party archives. But I recognize that there is disagreement with this among my colleagues.

After further discussion Kozlov continues:

> There will be enormous technical problems, particularly in disbinding, and material that is being filmed being out of use for long periods of time. It could take one and a half years to find out if this exercise has value for Russians. I agree that it is important for the rest of the world.

Vladimir P. Tarasov, whom I had met with Pikhoia the year before and who is head of the Department of International Relations, asks why a target of twenty-five million pages has been chosen. Palm explains that it relates to the $2.5 million Hoover is investing in the project. It could be more if the project is successful, less if it is not. There is a further discussion on the supply of free copies of the microfilm to Russian libraries. We break for a typical Russian lunch with salads, fish and meats, wine, beer, and coffee, and in the afternoon in the falling snow we look at a building that might be suitable to house the project, a gaunt concrete shell called the Center for Cosmic Documentation. I can see that it will not be ready for at least a year, but we are later told that there will be space for microfilm cameras and for processing film in the three principal archives themselves.

Our meetings with Pikhoia are scheduled for Monday and Tuesday, but he has a meeting with the deputy prime minister on Tuesday morning and a press conference for the public opening of the archives in the afternoon.

So, at 6:15 p.m. on the same day, we start a new meeting to put together a letter of intent. Pikhoia proposes that the material to be microfilmed will be the archives of the most recent period, including the papers of the Central Committee of the Communist Party and the papers of the central, local, and party organs, chosen by a committee of American and Russian scholars.

Pikhoia then tells us that he has a fax from Billington requesting that the "seven sisters" be passed on to Research Publications. For the first time I become aware that Billington and a rival US microfilm publisher, Research Publications International (RPI), are working together. Palm suggests that he will offer Billington an invitation to join our group and drop RPI. Tarasov observes that the chief problem is the accusation that they are giving it all away. Palm replies that Hoover and the committee are both making a large commitment, while the sale and distribution of the film by Chadwyck-Healey is very much a secondary part. Both Pikhoia and Kozlov agree that they need to prepare for the response to what is being proposed from the "Russian Billingtons." As a further contribution, Palm offers to give Rosarkhiv all Russian materials at the Hoover Institution that have already been microfilmed, including the diplomatic files from embassies in Paris and the Okhrana files of the Tsarist Secret Police organization. Kozlov asks if the embassy files at Hoover are stolen property. Palm answers, "Possibly." Palm has already suggested that Chadwyck-Healey should pay a royalty of 40 percent on the sale of microfilm copies and Pikhoia thought that 27 percent should go to Rosarkhiv to emphasize that it was being properly compensated for making its archives available, while 13 percent would go to Hoover. Palm points out that "Hoover's contributions are really very substantial. . . . It is [the] expression of our desire to do something important for you." Kozlov replies, "The desire for a positive relationship is mutual, but Hoover will become the owner of the most valuable collection in Russian history. The increase that this will give to the moral authority and reputation of Hoover is a much greater gain than money."

Kozlov knows that we have published on microfiche Foreign Office Registers on Russia and Persia, and I offer to donate a set. As the meeting ends, Kozlov states, "It is very important that this agreement is seen as adding to our national pride which has been so damaged in this past two years. In ten to twenty years, Russian scholars will be able to use these materials." We go back to our hotel to draft a two-page protocol. After Pikhoia returns from his meeting with the deputy prime minister the next day, the meeting continues. Rosarkhiv's letter of intent states that a separate agreement will be signed within a month. They will be paid a royalty of 27 percent and Palm offers to pay an advance against royalties of $50,000 on signature of the agreement.

The opening of the archives in the afternoon is a symbolic event of extraordinary importance and I feel privileged to be there. The archives of the Central Committee have been among the most inaccessible archives on earth, available only to a few trusted members of the elite—and even they would be dependent on the archivists since they had no direct access to them. The archives were for the day-to-day running of the Communist Party. When action had to be taken against an individual, the record of some past error or miscalculation was there in the archives to be used against him. Now these archives were being thrown open to the world, and the hope in the faces of the young people present in the hall, with many smartly dressed men and women in army and navy uniforms, was very moving. There was such expectation in the air, which events of the next twenty-five years have so signally failed to fulfill.

After the press conference we return to the letter of intent. For every change that is made, Pikhoia's secretaries have to retype the complete page on their electric typewriters. Eventually a much reduced and somewhat general two-page letter of intent in Russian is signed by all three of us. The last hurdle is the farewell dinner. Even though Kozlov advises me to not mix beer and vodka, the endless toasts extract a heavy price and the last day of each visit to Moscow is always marred by a hangover that simply has to be endured.

A press release was issued in March announcing the forthcoming agreement and we met again in Moscow on April 14. Before the meeting I had been told by Palm that RPI had been in Moscow to discuss the publication of an electronic edition of the catalogs of the Central Committee Archives. He also told me that for some time Billington had been "badmouthing" Chadwyck-Healey both in Washington and in Moscow. RPI had also been running down Chadwyck-Healey in Moscow by saying that the company was just me and a few helpers (at the time we had over one hundred employees in Cambridge). Palm also told me that when the Hoover agreement had been announced, he had a call from someone at RPI to say how astonished they had been when they went to Moscow in February and had been refused a meeting with Pikhoia.

In the afternoon of April 15, Pikhoia, who has shown remarkable goodwill toward us, now seems distracted by the momentous events happening in congress at that time and by the possibility of an end to Yeltsin's government. Howlett is on vacation in Morocco and is due to arrive two days later, and Palm has brought his own translator, Dena Schoen, a Slavic cataloger and fluent Russian speaker. We discuss Palm's original proposal that Hoover provide all the equipment and materials and the Russians provide the labor and facilities, but we realize that it is not going to work because the Russian archives have so little money. Hoover then agrees to pay for the labor costs as well.

The next day we spend the morning drafting changes in English and then in Russian. Schoen incorporates the clauses on her laptop, but every time she tries to charge it, it blows the fuses, leaving the public areas of the hotel in semidarkness. Fortunately, I have the same model, a Toshiba CX2200, and am able to lend her a battery and recharge hers. We do not have a printer for the Cyrillic version, and Volkova and Schoen write out the Russian draft incorporating the changes. We arrive late for the meeting but find Pikhoia in a better mood and anxious to get on with it. He is expecting a party of US congressmen and senators, including Senator Bill Bradley, a basketball star and future presidential candidate. I ask Kozlov if I can see the microfilming they are doing in his archive for the *Leaders* project. He replies that he is no longer the archivist of RTsKhIDNI as he has been promoted to vice chairman of Rosarkhiv. He is clearly so unhappy that I change my congratulations to condolences. There is a look of surprise and consternation on Bradley's face when he meets Palm. We know that Bradley is a supporter of Billington, but as a senator in a foreign country he cannot show support for one American institution against another. Colin Kyte, who is the manager of RPI in the United Kingdom, is also in the group, but we do not speak. Pikhoia's assistant takes us in search of a printer. As we go through a door down a wood-paneled corridor with an embroidered carpet, she says, "You are now entering the archives of the Central Committee. You will realize by the change of atmosphere that you are now entering a 'holy place.'" We do not find a printer and Schoen and Volkova start typing the Russian draft so that it can be ready to print the next morning. At 10:30 p.m. I leave them exhausted but still working. The following day, April 17, we print out both versions at the Norton Rose office.

That afternoon, when we are all tired and dispirited, Howlett arrives from Morocco. She is wearing a white tunic and with her deep tan she brings the exoticism of the desert into the drab Moscow meeting room. The atmosphere improves. She acts as both mediator and translator, breaking her own rule that you cannot do both, and we finally sign the agreement. The main changes are that Hoover's investment is increased from $2.5 million to $3 million to cover the salaries of the Russian staff as well as paying for all the microfilming equipment and materials. The advance against royalties is doubled to $100,000, of which we are to pay half. Repayments of advances against royalties will not start until March 31, 1994. Our position has been strengthened in several ways. One of my fears had been that we would pay out money and then find that the project did not get underway because of arguments about what to microfilm. But now we will only pay our share of the advance when the list of *fondy* to be filmed is agreed.

After the signing of the agreement on April 17, there was immediate criticism of both the *Leaders* project and the Hoover project. Although the details were kept confidential, it was known that Hoover was promising large amounts of money, and suspicions ranged from it being too much, with some going into certain pockets, to that it was not enough, and the soul of Russia was being sold for a pittance. The criticism came from Russia, the United States, and the United Kingdom. A journalist, Natalya Davydova, published articles on "the sale of the 'Party's Paper Gold'" about the *Leaders* project and "the 'party cause' for sale" in response to the Hoover project, writing that "the top-secret venture is arousing serious opposition even . . . amongst Roskomarkhiv [Rosarkhiv] personnel." She suggested that Chadwyck-Healey's involvement was an important part of the arrangement:

> Wasn't a merchant required for the project precisely because it could peter out in the near future due to a shortage of money? And who will vouch that while Chadwyck-Healey is pocketing net earnings from the sale of our archives we will not be repaying our debt with interest from the sales?[3]

A more serious criticism came from Yuri N. Afanasiev, who wrote an article in *Izvestiia* calling into question both projects.[4] He had left the Communist Party in 1990 and helped found the Democratic Russia political movement. He was a liberal reformer who should have welcomed the dissemination of information in the archives but asked if such agreements "would serve to benefit individual researchers or a private company" and whether "such a transfer of copied materials" would "move the center for the study of Russian history to the USA—the Hoover Institution" when it might be better "to establish a similar international center here." He thought that documents transferred to Hoover might be accessible abroad even before they were accessible in Russia and that Russian historians were being given a raw deal. Pikhoia responded with an article in *Izvestiia* and also addressed the Russian Academy with Afanasiev present.[5] He was relieved when the agreement was applauded by all. In the English translation of an interview with Pikhoia entitled "Shameless Trade Goes On Around Archives," he is reported as saying:

> We had been conducting the most complicated negotiations with the firm Research Publications, but we didn't sign the agreement. And do you know how it was interpreted by our Western partners? "That you don't sign the agreement with us," a representative of the firm said to me, "it contradicts democratic principles!" So I'm often seen as a non-democrat in the eyes of my foreign colleagues just because I try to defend Russian interests.

A distinguished historian at Stanford, Terence Emmons, in an article in *Izvestiia,* wrote, "I don't quite understand you gentlemen; compare this to 'the bad old days' when foreign researchers in Soviet archives were systematically refused access to materials that had not been previously used by Soviet researchers."[6]

In the United States, Billington, who on the announcement of our project in January 1992 had said that "these archives are perhaps the most important, single untapped resource for understanding the history of the 20th century anywhere," by July was saying that "the bulk of it [the archives] is 'banal' bureaucratic paper work. Besides, the archives have been purged several times by Soviet leaders over the years."[7]

Patricia Kennedy "Pat" Grimsted, an expert on Soviet archives at Harvard, sent Palm and me a forty-eight-page prepublication review copy of an article, "More *Glasnost* than *Perestroika*: Russian Archives in a New World Setting." She approved the Library of Congress's exhibition of three hundred documents from Rosarkhiv but was critical of the Hoover project. She recited Afanasiev's criticisms in full and went on to list the direct benefits to Russian archives that "large Western supported archival filming projects" ought to provide, without pointing out that that was exactly what the Hoover project provided. She also stated that Pikhoia had turned down a project with RPI, which meant that "a major Western microform publisher . . . was turned away at the negotiating table in May with no adequate explanation." Palm responded to her draft with a five-page letter. Toward the end, he wrote:

> Your reference to Hoover as "a traditionally conservative, private research institute" and your lament at the absence of projects by "more neutral Western academic institutions" leaves the unmistakable suggestion that our motives are crassly ideological and political. You clearly defame our scholarly integrity. In my own 20-year career as an archivist, you are the first person ever to question my professional integrity. Indeed, to my knowledge, you are the only person, either in Russia or in the United States, to question the appropriateness of the Hoover Institution as a sponsor of the sort of project we have undertaken with Roskomarkhiv [Rosarkhiv].

Grimsted duly amended her article, but Palm's indignation was entirely justified: that year, *The Economist* had rated the Hoover Institution as the world's number-one think tank. There were Soviet historians in the United States who had left-wing leanings and saw Hoover as a right-wing Republican institution. They were infuriated that the Hoover Institution had brought off the largest and most important project to obtain copies of Soviet archives, overlooking the fact that the Hoover Library & Archives was a resource for scholarship and had no political bias.

In spite of her initially hostile attitude, we developed a good relationship with Grimsted. In January 1993, she sent us a preprint of an article entitled "Russian Archives 1992: Amidst the Politics and Economics of Transition." It made the point that Russian public opposition to large-scale Western microfilming was hard for foreigners to understand and had not been limited to the Hoover project alone. She told us that we could use her article as a "menu" to select any topics that we might want her to highlight in her talk at the American Library Association (ALA) midwinter conference in Denver in January 1993. In *The Guardian* David Hearst wrote in his "Moscow Diary," "Not a day seems to pass without another former Soviet institution succumbing to the predations of the free market. The *Moscow Times* recently gave a chilling account of how the body in charge of most of the state and federal historical archives in Russia was selling off publication rights to Western publishers."[8] He went on to mention Hoover and Chadwyck-Healey and other projects in other countries, adding, ". . . apart from the fact that none of these countries or institutions would allow the same thing to happen to their archives." This was not correct: the National Archives in the United States and the Public Record Office (since 2003, the National Archives) in the United Kingdom had had microfilming agreements with commercial publishers since the 1960s, and at the time we had cameras in the Archives Nationales in Paris. As sometimes happens in *The Guardian*, righteous indignation was undermined by a failure to check facts.

Another critique came from an acquaintance in Cambridge, the Russian dissident Vladimir Bukovsky. In a long letter to Christopher DeMuth, president of the American Enterprise Institute, Bukovsky wrote, "I have returned from Moscow a week ago from what may be described as a most useless trip in my life, only to discover a copy of the letter you received from the Hoover Institution." (This was a letter of March 9, 1992, from John Raisian, director of the Hoover Institution, to DeMuth.) He continued:

> I am convinced that Hoover is making a monumental mistake in signing their agreement with Pikhoia at this moment and in the form they indicated. This agreement will simply be used as a smokescreen by the KGB in the Russian leadership, as a result of which we might never see the true picture.

I admired Bukovsky, whom I had met in Cambridge through a mutual friend. His strong views about the Soviet Union and the inadequacies of its successor governments were hardly surprising, since he had spent twelve years in prisons, labor camps, and psychiatric prison hospitals, and had been tortured before being expelled from the Soviet Union in 1976. Bukovsky's "true picture" was different from ours. He was interested in the most recent archives because in 1992 he was called as an expert witness at the trial at the Constitutional Court where the Communist Party (CPSU) was suing Yeltsin for banning the party and seizing its assets. Bukovsky had gone back to Russia to help Yeltsin prove that the CPSU was an unconstitutional organization and he was given access to documents from the Central Committee Archives at TsKhSD. He secretly scanned many documents and smuggled them out to the West. Our approach was more historical, although Fond 89, the collection of 3,500 documents assembled from a wide range of archives for the trial, was later microfilmed and sold by us (see below). While it did include many of the key documents that excited Bukovsky, because it was selective it did not give the true insight into life under communism that was given by the *fondy* that we were microfilming in their entirety.

In May, three Russians responsible for microfilm production came to Cambridge and were entertained by Alastair Everitt, our managing director, at his home, which Valery I. Abramov, their chief, said "sealed the relationship." We took them to the photographic department of Cambridge University Library to show them that the Kodak MRD microfilm cameras that Hoover was about to give them were widely used. But, on their way home, they made a detour through Germany to look at another make of microfilm camera, as a way of asserting their independence by going through the motions of selecting a more "modern" design.

Meanwhile, the *Leaders* project was quietly making progress. Rosarkhiv had started by microfilming the personal papers of Julius Martov. Though Jewish and middle-class, Martov had been a close colleague of Lenin. He was one of the outstanding Menshevik leaders but was politically marginalized when the Bolsheviks came to power and he died in exile in 1923. I received a letter in English from a Tamara Popova, who said that she was Martov's granddaughter. She explained that his papers had been stolen from her family or had gone astray when Martov's brothers had been arrested. She was writing a book about her family and was trying to establish her rights of inheritance and complained that the authorities had negotiated with us without any reference to her family. She raised no objection to the microfiche project but hoped that it would not affect the sales of her book. I replied sympathetically without promising anything.

The first Editorial Board meeting took place in Moscow in June 1992 with Palm, Emmons, and John B. Dunlop, a leading Sovietologist, from Hoover, plus Pikhoia and Howlett. Dmitri Volkogonov, who was also at the meeting, was a Russian general who had headed the political and propaganda sections of the Soviet army but was forced to resign from the Communist Party in 1991 after he had published a biography of Stalin. He supported Pikhoia in the opening of the archives. At the meeting it was agreed to start microfilming the *opisi* of materials in the Central State Archives of the October Revolution. A second, more substantive Editorial Board meeting was held in Washington in September. Delegates from Hoover included the historian Robert Conquest, an Anglo-American Hoover fellow and eminent historian who, in his book *The Great Terror: Stalin's Purge of the Thirties*, had in 1968 revealed for the first time the full extent of Stalin's purges. At the time they were much disputed, but the archives to which we now had access would fully support Conquest's analysis. I did not attend these meetings as we had no direct responsibility for editorial decisions. They decided that they would microfilm the following:

> Materials from the archives of the Communist Party of the Soviet Union, and also from state archives, pertaining in the first place to the mechanisms

> of power, including documentation of political decision making of the central organs of the CPSU and of the most important political figures of the CPSU.

Led by Emmons, the board began to refine these to the following:

- Party congresses, conferences, protocols (to the 18th Congress)
- Central Committee plenums (to 1941)
- Politburo: protocols, transcripts, decisions, materials (to 1941)
- Secretariat CC CPSU
- CC CPSU Apparat
- NKVD RSFSR 1917–1930

We had chosen the microfilm medium because it was reliable and was a technology that was familiar to the Russians. Hoover agreed to ship fifteen microfilm cameras, costing $10,000 each, and other equipment including microfilm processors, a PC, a printer, a microfilm reader, and a fax machine. The project was divided into four parallel streams. The first was the high-level policy and editorial discussions between Rosarkhiv and Hoover, interspersed by board meetings in Moscow, Cambridge, and Washington that, at the beginning, took place every six months. The second was the day-to-day issues of microfilm production—the filming of the correct documents, the quality of the microfilm, and the rate at which it was being produced. These were well managed by Judith Fortson at Hoover, Everitt in Cambridge, and Dave Chapman, production director at our microfilm bureau in Bassingbourn, a village near Cambridge, together with their staffs. The third was the contractual and practical relationship between Hoover and Chadwyck-Healey and, to a lesser extent, between Rosarkhiv and Chadwyck-Healey. The fourth, which came later, was the sale of microfilm copies, handled by our sales staff in the United Kingdom and United States.

The Hoover schedule forecast production between May 1992 and July 1996 of 540 reels a month or 6,480 reels per year, with equipment to be installed by August 1. But none of this was achieved. In a letter to Palm on February 24, 1993, I wrote, "It is almost a year since we signed the agreement with Roskomarkhiv [Rosarkhiv] and five months since the three cameras were delivered to Moscow, and all we have to show for it today is six reels of film brought back last week." We arranged for Volkova to go to the archives every week, collect whatever film had been produced, and ship it to us. By May, film began to come through regularly. But because the shipments were so small, transport was costing us $5 per reel, which was more than Hoover had agreed to pay us. In May, Hoover delivered a further eight cameras together with film developers, splicers, densitometers, microfilm readers, water-mixing valves, and all the accessories needed for a fully functioning microfilm bureau. Chapman and one of his managers, Reuben Starling, spent two weeks in Moscow to help install the equipment and make sure that it was working.

When Emmons at Hoover received the first sales brochure on the *Leaders of the Russian Revolution,* he wrote to congratulate us: "I predict this series will be in use by scholars long after the Yale project will have been totally forgotten."[9] The "Yale project" was to publish a series of books containing selected documents with commentaries. The price for the *Leaders* project was £28,900, but it sold well, with libraries being able to buy the papers of individuals from Pavel Axelrod to Vera Zasulich, the only woman in the collection. Prices ranged from £270 for Axelrod to £12,100 for the papers of Mikhail Kalinin. The papers differed from much of the material in the Hoover project because they were so personal—diaries, family letters, photographs, and other ephemera—and they contained much information about the social history of Russia in the 1930s and 1940s. The core of the collection had come from the archives of Istpart, the Department for the History of the Party, formed in 1918 by the Bolsheviks. It was supplemented by personal papers, which were given—or seized, as in the case of Julius Martov.

The next Editorial Board meeting, held in Cambridge in January 1993, was hosted by us and was held at Jesus College, where Howlett was a fellow. Over the next few years, we held several meetings at Jesus, always in the Prioress's Room, which opens out on to the cloisters. The intimacy of those ancient spaces seemed to suit our meetings and the atmosphere was always better tempered than in Moscow. In the evening, a dinner was held in the college attended by the Master, Colin Renfrew, and by several

Soviet historians, including Orlando Figes and Robert Conquest. Dinners for subsequent Russian delegations were held in pubs around Cambridge. At the meeting, which included a visit to the microfilming bureau in Bassingbourn, the subjects chosen for microfilming ranged from agriculture, heavy industry, and schools to the NKVD administration of prisons and camps.

A further amendment made to the agreement on August 18, 1993, required Hoover to pay $60,000 to Rosarkhiv for labor costs. This was to be the first of five similar payments, each one of which would only be made when a further five thousand reels of film had been delivered. One of the reasons for the constant demands for more money was the deteriorating economic situation in Russia. In January 1992, just as we had our first meeting in Moscow, a collapse of the economy following the end of Gorbachev's tenure created enormous hardship, with a dramatic fall in GDP matched by runaway inflation. In the first half of 1992, a citizen's average income dropped by half. In September, Yeltsin tried to dissolve the legislature, which in turn declared his decision null and void. In early October 1993, demonstrators took over the mayor of Moscow's offices. The army stormed the Supreme Soviet building and arrested the leaders of the resistance. The ten-day conflict resulted in 187 people being killed—the unofficial figure was two thousand—with the deadliest street fighting in Moscow since the revolution. In December, Yeltsin pushed through his new constitution, giving the president sweeping powers. The result was that while Russia was now ruled by a dual presidential–parliamentary system, substantial power now lay in the president's hands, which Yeltsin and his successor, Vladimir Putin, have used to the full.

The positions of Rosarkhiv and Pikhoia were strengthened by the crisis. From February 1994, Rosarkhiv was made part of a formal structure of government, reporting directly to the Office of the President, along with defense, foreign affairs, and internal security, and Pikhoia himself had more direct control. This new status was surprising, as Howlett had once said that because archives were so unimportant compared to defense, security, and transport, they were a useful political football to be kicked around by politicians to score points off one another, knowing that none of it would do any real harm. But all archives that we filmed had to be declassified by archivists, who read through the files looking out for sensitive and confidential material, which they would remove or flag as not to be filmed.

We were still concerned about the amount of film being sent through—by then about two hundred reels a month, which was still not enough. Many of the *fondy* we wanted to microfilm had already been filmed by the Russians and copies of their film were available. But the quality was too variable and too much time was spent checking it and ordering refilms, which also had to be checked. In the end, the only existing microfilm we used had been produced at GARF on a German microfilm stock that was superior to Russian film. At an Editorial Board meeting in Moscow at the end of September 1994, we now noted that 1,837 reels of film had been produced by the three archives.

But, once again, the discussion was dominated by money. Between 1992 and 1994 the cost of living in US dollars had increased 16.2 times, but the monthly salary of a camera operator was still only $100 plus a further 50 percent for benefits. According to Pikhoia, electricity had increased in price from 30 kopeks per kwh in 1992 to 98 rubles in 1994, an increase of over three hundred times, which directly affected the cost of production in the archives. In response, Palm agreed to increase payments to the Russians and persuaded me to increase the royalty we paid to Hoover from 13 percent to 15 percent. At the end of the visit, Pikhoia and his wife entertained us and some of his friends in his large dacha outside Moscow in a fashionable neighborhood containing the dachas of other ministers and senior functionaries. The long journey back to our hotel gave us time to partially recover from the many vodka toasts.

In May 1994, IDC, a Dutch microfilm publisher, announced the publication on microfiche of the archives of Comintern, the international communist organization. The agreement was made with RTsKhIDNI and its director, Kyrill Anderson, not with Rosarkhiv. We now understood the limitations of Pikhoia's authority in respect to agreements made by the individual archives. In December 1994, he warned that he might be sacked and wanted an annex to the agreement to strengthen his position. But he also confirmed that we would be given the documents in Fond 89 (see above) and all *opisi* at RTsKhIDNI except the Trophy and Comintern *opisi* and the American Communist Party *opisi* and *fondy*. The Trophy Archive was primarily German archives removed from Germany at the end of the war.

The year 1995 passed quietly. A meeting took place in Cambridge in June when a "Third Annex to the Agreement of April 17, 1992" was signed. In it, there is a definition of the limits of the agreement and the circumstances by which it might be renewed or ended. Howlett kept us aware of how precarious our agreement was in the face of continuing hostility within the three archives and hostility to Rosarkhiv and Pikhoia from outside. It was like living with a frail relative who you know may die at any time—but when he does, it still comes as a shock. The success of the Communist Party in achieving 22.1 percent of the vote in the election further weakened Pikhoia's position, and the shock came on December 28, 1995, when we received a faxed letter in Russian signed by Pikhoia, followed by an English translation. It was headed, "Notification regarding extraordinary circumstances (conditions of 'force-majeure')." It started by praising what we had achieved but went on to note several shortcomings, including the absence of joint teamwork by Russian and foreign scholars and archivists and "insufficient financial incentives for the Russian archives." It also noted:

> The agreement contradicts current Russian laws—which forbid government institutions including Rosarkhiv, to conclude agreements involving the receipt of non-government funds, especially from non-government sources. It also contradicts a Federal law of the Russian Federation regarding "participation in international information exchange" passed by the Duma on December 8, 1995, and now under consideration by the Council of the Federal Assembly of the Russian Federation. . . . Rosarkhiv must inform you of its decision to abrogate the Agreement of April 17, 1992, citing extraordinary ("force-majeure") circumstances.

The letter invited us to meet in Moscow "to discuss new principles for the organization of collaborative scholarly work on the archival collections as well as the microfilming of documents." Immediately on receiving this, Pikhoia, Palm, and Howlett met in Prague, a meeting of which I was unaware until sometime later, and there was then a meeting in Moscow on January 11–12. Palm and Schoen were joined by Herbert "Pete" Hoover III, the grandson of the founder of the Hoover Institution and chairman of the Hoover Board of Overseers. His family foundation was a substantial donor to the project. Howlett and I were also present. Pikhoia, now main state archivist of Rosarkhiv, was accompanied by ten Russians, including the archivists of the three main archives, Vladimir A. Tiuneev, Pikhoia's first deputy, and Kozlov, who was now his second deputy. Pikhoia explained that there was a new civil code that prevented Rosarkhiv from participating in commercial activity, while the new law on international informational exchange, still to be adopted, limited the export of archival *fondy*. This was understood, but Palm objected to the use of clause 23, "force-majeure," as the reason for termination of the original agreement because it would mean that the Hoover Institution had entered into an agreement that was unlawful according to Russian law, which Palm regarded as harmful to Hoover's reputation.

He suggested that the agreement should be ended without cause as set out in clause 6(c) by one or both parties giving each other six months' notice of termination. To encourage Rosarkhiv to agree, Hoover offered to donate to the archives two-thirds of the equipment, together with half of the supplies and materials, which had an estimated value of $135,000. Hoover also offered to give to Rosarkhiv the same number of microfilm reels of archives in the United States as had been filmed in the Russian archives. Palm suggested that they reduce the number of reels to be filmed from the previously agreed 25,000 to 13,500 while agreeing to increase the amount paid for a reel of film from $27 to $40. This was a generous offer, considering that all materials and equipment were also being paid for by Hoover, and Palm hoped that it would encourage the Russians to continue the project. By the end of the second day, a memorandum of mutual understanding had been drafted. Shortly after, Pikhoia resigned as head of Rosarkhiv.

The termination of the agreement and Pikhoia's resignation were reported in the *Sunday Telegraph* as a "double blow," describing Pikhoia as "one of the many middle-ranking Kremlin officials hit by a purge of liberals by Mr. Yeltsin's administration."[10] *The Economist* published a long article, "The Battle for the Moscow Archives," stating that "access to the archives has been miraculously transformed since 1988. They are not yet as open as the British Public Record Office. . . . But Russian archives are now more fully open than those of Turkey or the Vatican—roughly comparable with those of France."[11] It goes on to say, "A vast private contract to microfilm the former party archives seems sound to Western historians, despite its cost. But it was bitterly resented by many Russian historians and archivists." The article ends, "To save the archivists from poverty and protect tens of millions of files for the 21st century requires a substantial injection of money from private charities or international agencies," which was exactly what Hoover had done, and for which it was being so widely criticized.

In the May/June 1996 issue of *Perspectives,* the newsletter of the prestigious American Historical Association, the Soviet historian J. Arch Getty, who had his own publishing agreement with Rosarkhiv, published an article, "Russian Archives: Is the Door Half Open or Half Closed?" with a well-informed description of the state of archives in Russia and this statement: "On its face, the Hoover Project(s) seemed to be good for everyone." It is followed by extraordinary mudslinging against Pikhoia:

> Pikhoia's reputation and a cloudy financial atmosphere surrounding the Hoover Project also led to trouble in Moscow. One archive official told me in December that his archive had received "not one kopek" from Pikhoia, Hoover, or Chadwyck-Healey. Meanwhile, the Americans were busy photographing his entire archive. . . . An archive official said at one point last year "Pikhoia and Company are touring Europe and America in high style, but the city is about to shut off our electricity because we cannot pay our bills."

On the day we had paid over $40,000 of royalties into the RTsKhIDNI's bank account in Moscow, the bank was closed by the government and its assets frozen. The archivists told us that they were sure that they would get their money eventually, but perhaps not in time to pay their electricity bills. Palm wrote a letter to the editor of *Perspectives,* which was published in the December 1996 issue. They also published Getty's reply, in which he asked whether there were "valid questions to be raised here about the privatization and commercialization of archives? (Hoover is not a public organization and Chadwyck-Healey is a private firm)." I had also written to the editor and she replied to say that their lawyer did not regard the quotation regarding "the archives not receiving one kopek from Pikhoia, Hoover, or Chadwyck-Healey" as libelous, but that "we are exploring whether our policy regarding quotations may need to be sharpened." It was an admission that the article was unreliable, and she also offered to publish my letter, but Palm and I decided that this would give more air to Getty and it was best to let the issue die.

While these articles were creating background noise, Palm was trying to reach a new agreement with either all three of the archives or whichever archive was prepared to cooperate. In a letter to me of May 1, 1996, he wrote, "Dealing with people who lack the capacity to know their own self-interest is the most difficult part of our relationship with the Russians. If we are going to continue this project, we will have to try to do a better job of educating them."

In a letter signed by Tiuneev, who was now acting chairman, and Mironenko, the director of GARF, they agreed to continue the microfilming of archives at GARF while they finished work on the draft of the new agreement, which they admitted was taking a long time. Mironenko understood how important it was to get as much of the archives microfilmed as possible, both for security and to generate revenues to help keep GARF, his large archive, going at a time when he was getting no financial support from the government. The new agreement consisted of a detailed agreement with GARF supported by a "Framework Agreement" with Rosarkhiv. The other two archives did not wish to make new agreements with Hoover.

GARF agreed to microfilm

- the remaining parts of Fond r-393: the NKVD in the 1920s;
- Fond r-9401: the NKVD-USSR c. 1930–46; and
- the most important *opisi* relating to the Gulag.

Palm was concerned that his donors and our customers might not be sufficiently interested in the Gulag, while Tiuneev was nervous about filming complete sets of *opisi* on sensitive subjects such as the NKVD. There was no longer a need for an Editorial Board because the selection of material for filming was incorporated into the agreement. An interim agreement with GARF came through in December 1996 in the form of an order from Hoover listing the *opisi* and *dela* from Fond r-393 to be filmed: six hundred thousand frames, equivalent to 660 nominal reels. The film was declared to be for scholarly research, not for resale (by Chadwyck-Healey), to avoid having to pay substantial export duty. Palm regarded this as a stopgap until a further agreement could be negotiated with GARF.

In the summer of 1997 Hoover ended its consultancy agreement with Howlett and its employment of Volkova. By now there was only one archive to deal with, and Hoover was employing another agent in Moscow to work on other projects. I was deeply concerned. Without Howlett, the Hoover project would never have got off the ground. Her fluent Russian and her personality, which was so Russian, enabled her to fit in at all levels of Russian society. She had a good relationship with Pikhoia—as fellow historians, they shared many of the same interests. She got on well with the archivists, even the difficult ones, and she knew by name all the camera operators, the doormen, and the security staff in each of the archives. When one of the camera operators lost her husband, Howlett knew that it was customary to give her some money toward the funeral and did so. We were now trying to organize a large-scale microfilming project in Moscow without anyone there to represent our interests and with no one in the office in Cambridge who spoke Russian. But Hoover had no objection to us directly employing Howlett, which we did.

It had now become GARF's responsibility to ship film back to the United Kingdom. Palm sent GARF a new, longer-term proposal in January 1997. This included an agreement to copublish a documentary work on the Gulag with Hoover.[12] Hoover also wanted a five-year exclusive agreement with Rosarkhiv and GARF to microfilm the remaining records in Fond r-393 so that Palm could raise the money to pay for it. In September, Palm asked for some minor changes to a new draft agreement submitted by Mironenko. Clearance by customs in Russia was becoming increasingly difficult. Some camera operators had been laid off because replacement parts for cameras were held up in customs, and one of our staff, Inga Markan, went to Moscow to bring out as much film as possible as excess baggage. Yet, a few weeks later, Palm complained that GARF had exceeded Hoover's order of December 1996 and had filmed more than the five million pages in Fond r-393 and Fond r-9414.[13]

At a meeting in Cambridge in October 1996, we had confirmed that we were due to pay Rosarkhiv £140,000 in royalties, some of which would go to GARF, but we were having our own frustrations with the Inland Revenue in the United Kingdom, which wanted us to withhold a portion of royalties due to Rosarkhiv and GARF as neither could demonstrate that it was a recognized part of the Russian government and therefore exempt from withholding taxes.[14] This was eventually resolved.

By the end of 1997, Tiuneev, the acting chairman, had been replaced by Kozlov. We were sorry to see him go. He was different from Kozlov, who was angular in every way. Both men were typical ex-communist functionaries: very cautious, concerned about having support from above, but determined to see the project continue, if only because it was such an important source of funds for the archives. We paid Rosarkhiv royalties of $333,949 for the year 1996–97.

In March 1998, Gordon Hahn, who had been appointed coordinator of Russian archival special research programs at the Hoover Institution, met with Mironenko in Moscow to discuss the signing of the new agreement, which had kept on being delayed. Mironenko wrote to Palm on May 27, 1998, "The situation with our contract is so complicated that making any changes to the draft Agreement approved by Rosarkhiv will take considerable time. . . . I suggest . . . we sign a Letter of Understanding and include all amendments in it."

The agreement and the letter of understanding were both signed on June 11, two and a half years after the last agreement had been terminated. The new agreement included the microfilming of 1.5 million frames, and the productivity at GARF was now creating a large volume of film duplication work for CHMPS (later renamed International Imaging). The processed camera film, which was the original master negative, was sent to International Imaging for checking and for duplication. Second-generation printing master negatives were made, and we also made two positive copies for Rosarkhiv and the Novosibirsk Regional Archives.

This was a political gesture to demonstrate that archives outside Moscow were benefiting from the project. Two further positive copies were made for Hoover and the Library of Congress (though the latter only received the first five thousand reels as a donation from Hoover and did not buy any more). Five of the negative and positive copies that were made were paid for by Hoover, and the sixth, our own printing master, was part of the cost of making copies for customers. We made a profit on every reel we duplicated. While in the first three years only five thousand reels were produced, in later years the annual output was around five thousand, and International Imaging was producing thirty thousand reels of film a year just for the partners, excluding the additional copies made to fulfill sales. By the mid-1990s, when microfilm publishing using archival silver film was in decline, International Imaging was probably the largest producer of silver microfilm copies outside the United States.

Under Mironenko's management, GARF had become a highly efficient producer of quality microfilm and there was a good relationship between it and Rosarkhiv. A memorandum from E. L. Lunacharskii, acting director of GARF, to Kozlov set out in positive terms the work that had been done since the agreement was signed in June 1998 and stated that the addition of further *fondy* would "raise the quality of the editions."[15] In his program of microfilming for 1999 he suggested the following:

- MVD (Ministry of Internal Affairs): main administration of camps for the metal-mining industry, 1941–53
- MVD USSR: camps for railway construction, 1934–53
- NKVD: child and labor educative colonies, 1943–56

He proposed to film documents from Fond r-1055, the VTsIK supreme revolutionary tribunal of 1921–22, "because in preparing a documentary history of the Gulags we must look at directives on the development of the camp system from the supreme organs of power." He ended by stating that the net income of the last two years ($141,000 in 1997 and $100,000 expected in 1998) "will allow us to resolve the hugely acute economic problem of the archival establishment in 1999–2000 on B. Pirogovskaia Street [at GARF], at least in part."[16]

Problems between Hoover and GARF did not entirely disappear. After I sold the Chadwyck-Healey group of publishing companies in October 1999, the project continued for another few years. In a letter to Mironenko of August 11, 2000, Palm expressed surprise that GARF had produced 1.3 million frames of microfilm (about 1,200 reels) in anticipation of a third agreement. He was concerned that this preemption limited his ability to choose material for filming under the third agreement. In a letter to Steven Hall, who was now chief executive of Bell & Howell Information and Learning in the United Kingdom (now ProQuest), Palm observed, "You will note that GARF has continued to produce a substantial amount of microfilm beyond what has been authorized. After seven years of partnership, the Russians still do not follow basic business practices!"[17]

For Palm, GARF's overproduction was a headache because he was responsible for raising the money to pay for the film and was directly responsible to his board if Hoover's liabilities exceeded allotted funds. Somehow, for over ten years, he raised the money, kept his donors onside, tried to control both the Russians and his British partner, and in the end completed what was one of the largest and most important microfilm publications ever undertaken. But he could not have done it without Pikhoia's remarkable vision and straight-dealing pragmatism.

The fourth strand of the Hoover project was sales. There were few libraries in the world that could consider an open-ended commitment to buy around twelve thousand reels of microfilm at a price (in 1995) of $95 per reel. This would be an outlay of $1,140,000 plus shipping costs, plus VAT (value-added tax) at 15 percent in the case of UK libraries. But the first indications of a sale came as early as November 1992, when I was in Japan and was told by Kinokuniya (Japanese bookstore chain) that the National Diet Library, Japan's national library, was likely to buy. In January 1993 the British Library was the first library to place an order, for $160,000 of microfilm. In the same month, at the ALA midwinter meeting in Denver, I introduced a short film, *The Russia House*, that had been made by a British filmmaker, John Quick, on behalf of the UK Foreign and Commonwealth Office, followed by presentations by Dwyer from Hoover and by Grimsted, who was now our ally. A few days later, Howlett, Cheryl Crosby (one of our best salespeople), and I made a presentation at Yale University to twenty-one historians and librarians who were in the East Coast Consortium of Slavic Library Collections. We expected to make a sale to the consortium, but it was not until 1999 that Harvard ordered the complete collection, the first library in the United States to do so. As an example of the extent of our sales activity, in one week in 1995 we were exhibiting the Hoover and the *Leaders* projects at events in Birmingham in the United Kingdom; Göttingen, Germany; Pretoria; and Montreal, and in August at the International Congress of Slavists. In November, the Bayerische Staatsbibliothek in Munich ordered a further 2,991 reels, and sales for 1995 totaled $945,054. Hall was concerned by how difficult we were finding it to make sales because the material being filmed was so extensive and so difficult to describe. But in 1996 sales increased slightly to $1,120,762.

We marketed separately from the rest of the archives Fond 89, the 3,500 selected documents assembled for the trial of the Communist Party, and it sold well on its own. The documents ranged from Politburo agendas recording the setting up of labor camps in the first years of the party to the money paid to foreign communist parties known as "Moscow gold." The twenty-five reels of microfilm cost $3,500, a price that was affordable even by smaller libraries.

In late October, after the sale of Chadwyck-Healey to Bell & Howell, I returned to the United States at the invitation of the Harvard College Library to speak at a celebration of the acquisition of ten thousand reels of microfilm of the *Archives of the Central Committee of the Soviet Communist Party* through a gift by Harvard alumnus George O'Neill and his wife, Abby. I enjoyed the occasion, and the sale, worth $600,000, was a valuable contribution to our total sales in such an important year. But the ceremony was marred by an ill-informed press comment made earlier in the month. The *Boston Globe*, reporting on the "Harvard archives deal," stated that the Davis Center for Russian Studies at Harvard had responded to our offer to reduce the price from $1 million if ordered before April 15, 1999, thinking that they would be the only library in the United States to have a set of the microfilms.[18] Presumably, the donors had also been told this. Harvard had now discovered that there was a set at the Hoover Institution, leading the *Globe* to describe the microfilm as "old" rather than "new." Palm was unhappy, not only through the disclosure of the price, which concerned us, too, but because the Harvard press release suggested that I had negotiated the microfilming of the archives and Hoover's only role had been to finance the project. I shared Palm's annoyance, and in my address at the ceremony I gave a full account of the Hoover project.

It remains the only large-scale project to make important archives of the Soviet state available to scholars outside Russia. It has been constantly misreported by the world's press and misunderstood by many of the scholars who would most benefit from it. Much of what has been written about it is little more than speculation, and in 1998 the British best-selling author Robert Harris published *Archangel*, a "fast-paced thriller" in which the hero, an American academic, attends a conference in Moscow to discuss a large-scale microfilming project by Rosarkhiv.[19] At the conference, Adelman, a delegate from Yale, exclaims, "He's talking about how the Hoover Institution tried to buy the Party archive for five million bucks." This time it does not pretend to be fact. But, in the end, the only facts that matter are those recorded on the almost twelve thousand reels of microfilm that the three partners have made available to scholars throughout the world.

My penultimate meeting in Moscow was in April 1999 with Mironenko, Kozlov, and Howlett, but without Palm. I could not tell them about the forthcoming sale of Chadwyck-Healey, but it was almost as if Mironenko knew that it might be my last visit. At GARF, he took me to a room where, inside a box on a table, there was a square Perspex box purportedly containing Hitler's skull, pierced by a jagged hole where the bullet had entered. It was only shown to important visitors, and I felt that it was a gesture of appreciation for all that we had done together in the previous seven years. We met once more, in 2003, when I was passing through Moscow on my way back from a bird-watching trip in eastern Siberia. We had lunch and talked about the old days, and he told me of the dinner held to celebrate the end of the project where there were many toasts, including one to me. I thought then that it was better to be toasted than to toast.

All photographs are by or courtesy of Charles Chadwyck-Healey unless otherwise credited.

Rudolf G. Pikhoia announces the opening of the Soviet Communist Party archives at a press conference at former party headquarters, Moscow, February 25, 1992. Standing left to right are Pikhoia and Rem A. Usikov.

Press conference on the opening of the Soviet Communist Party archives, Moscow, February 25, 1992.

Sergei Mironenko addresses the press conference, Moscow, February 25, 1992.

Guests attend a luncheon following the press conference at which Pikhoia announced the opening of the Soviet Communist Party archives, Moscow, February 25, 1992. Clockwise around the table, starting at front left: Robert Shanks, Joseph Dwyer, Charles Palm, Rudolf G. Pikhoia, Natalia Volkova, Valery I. Abramov, Richard Kahn, Jana Howlett, Vladimir P. Kozlov, Edward Lee-Smith, and Vladimir P. Tarasov. (Not shown is Charles Chadwyck-Healey, who took the photo.)

Negotiating the agreement with Pikhoia in his office, February 1992. Jana Howlett, left, served as both translator and mediator.

Signing the historic agreement between Rosarkhiv, the Hoover Institution, and Chadwyck-Healey Ltd. to microfilm the archives of the Soviet Communist Party and Soviet State, at former party headquarters, Moscow, April 17, 1992. Left to right: Charles Palm, Rudolf G. Pikhoia, and Charles Chadwyck-Healey.

A handshake concludes the historic agreement between Rosarkhiv, the Hoover Institution, and Chadwyck-Healey Ltd. to microfilm the archives of the Soviet Communist Party and Soviet State, at former party headquarters, Moscow, April 17, 1992. Left to right: Charles Chadwyck-Healey, Charles Palm, Vladimir N. Bondarev, and Rudolf G. Pikhoia.

In exchange for the right to copy the Soviet Communist Party archives, the Hoover Institution gave Rosarkhiv microfilm of its entire collection of Russian archives. Here, Hoover deputy director Charles Palm presents the microfilm to Rudolf G. Pikhoia, Stauffer Auditorium, Hoover Institution, Stanford, California, March 23, 1993. In the background are boxes of microfilm to be shipped to Russia. Photo: Hoover Institution Public Affairs.

Examining a shipment of microfilm received at the Hoover Institution, Stanford, California, 1995, are Charles Palm and Judith Fortson. Photo: Hoover Institution Public Affairs.

Meeting with the Rosarkhiv Collegium that terminated the 1992 agreement, Moscow, January 12, 1996. Clockwise around the table: Natalia Volkova (back to camera), Herbert Hoover III, Dena Schoen, Charles Palm, unidentified person, Natalia G. Tomilina (facing camera), unidentified person, Andrei N. Artizov, Vladimir P. Tarasov, Rudolf G. Pikhoia, Vladimir A. Tiuneev, Vladimir P. Kozlov, and L. S. Shatenshtein. (Not shown is Charles Chadwyck-Healey, who took the photo.)

Storage cabinets used in the Russian State Archives (TsKhSD). The hall housing the cabinets is in a building that formerly had been the headquarters of the Central Committee of the Soviet Communist Party. Before the Revolution, this building had been a bank.

Storage cabinets used in the Russian State Archives (TsKhSD).

Document folders in archives storage cabinets.

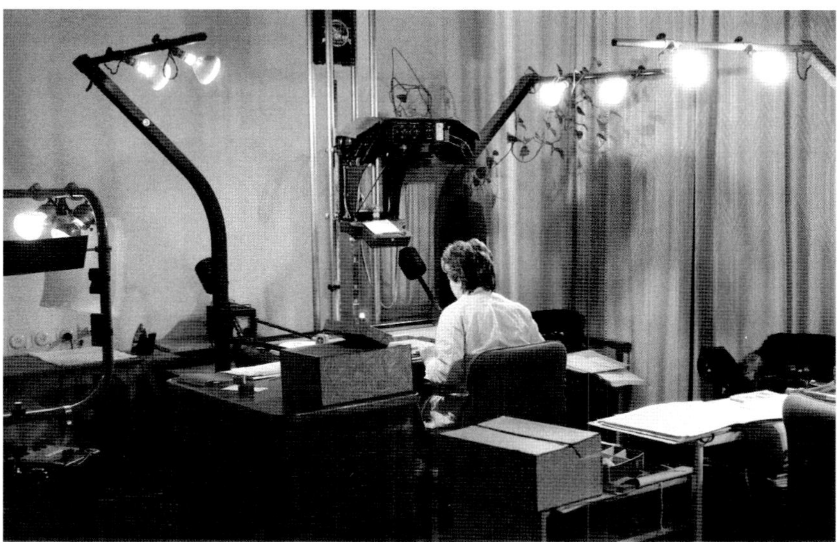

Old microfilm camera used in the Russian State Archives before the start of the Hoover project, manufactured by André Debrie, an established French manufacturer of 35mm motion picture cameras.

Kodak MRD microfilm camera supplied by Hoover.

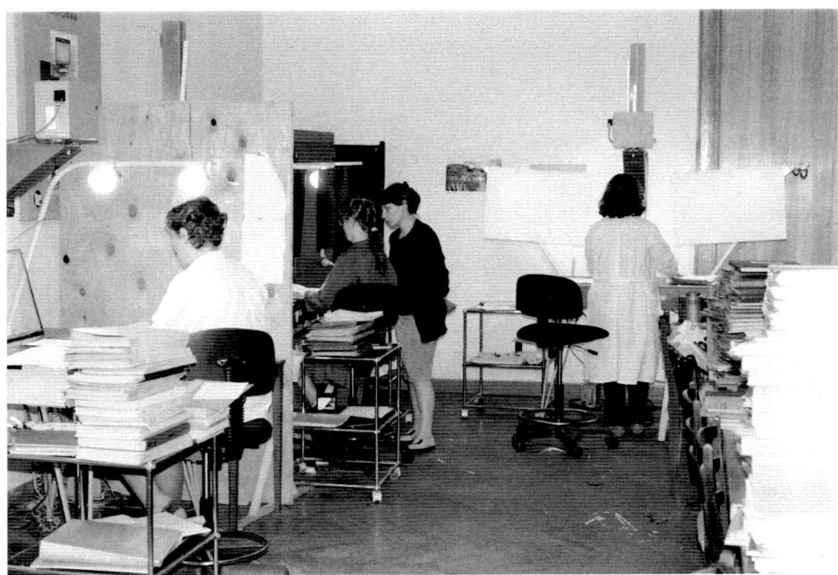

In the microfilm workroom housing camera workstations, Natalia Volkova watches the camera operator at work. Volkova was responsible for collecting the finished film from the archives and shipping it to the Chadwyck-Healey plant near Cambridge, England.

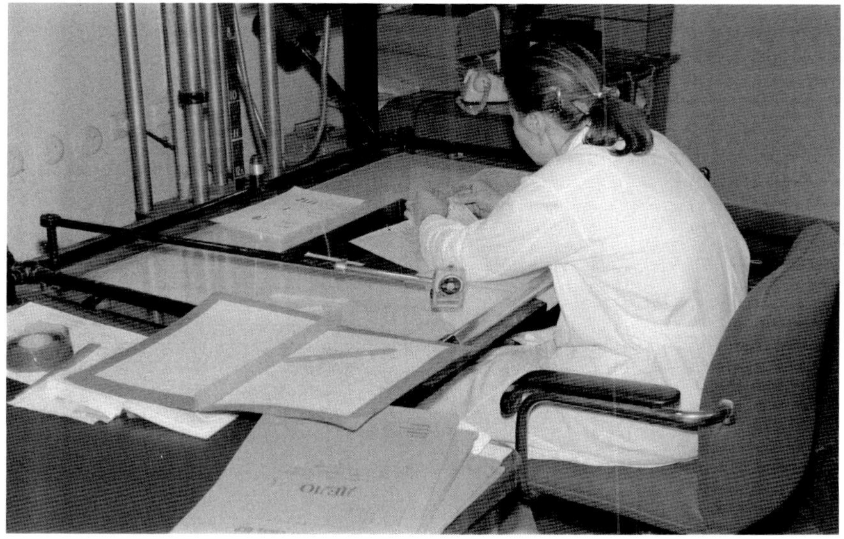

A camera operator prepares documents for filming.

An archivist checks microfilm on a microfilm reader for errors such as missing or out-of-focus pages or other problems.

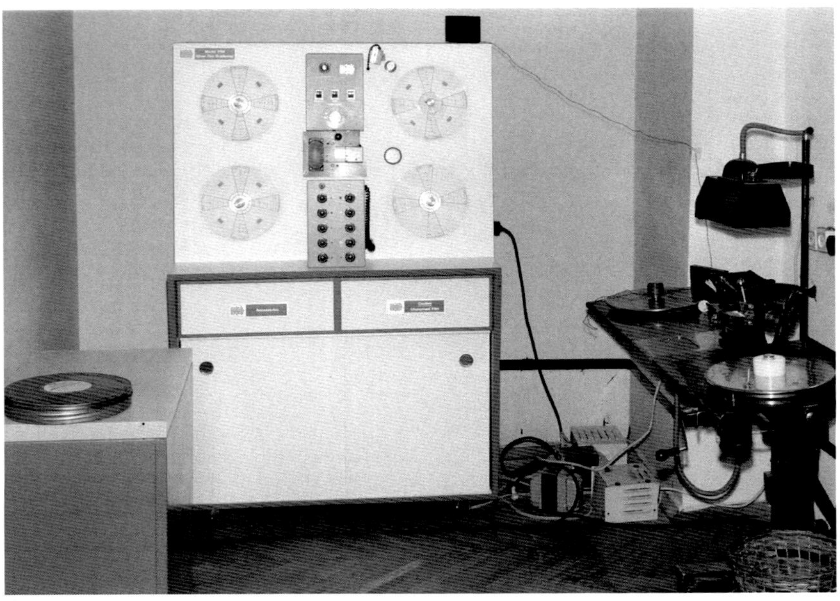

An Extek silver film duplicator supplied by Hoover for making copies of microfilms stands next to a microfilm splicer for joining lengths of film.

An Allen Products microfilm processor was supplied by Hoover for developing silver microfilm.

Archival documents have been photographed by the Hoover Institution Library & Archives from its Archives of the Soviet Communist Party and Soviet State microfilm collection.

Document showing Soviet support of agents of the Comintern (Communist International) in the United States and other countries amounting to millions of rubles, 1919–20. Fond 89, opis 52, delo 6, leaf 1, reel 11006.

~49

39

дллежит возврату в течение 24 часов во 2-ю часть Особого Сектора ЦК

(Пост. ПБ ЦК от 5.V.27г., пр. № 100, п. 5)

1

СТРОГО СЕКРЕТНО
(Из О. П.)

есоюзная Коммунистическая Партия (большевиков) ЦЕНТРАЛЬНЫЙ КОМИТЕТ

№ П51/206

10.УП 1937г.

тов. Ежову.- все;
указанным организациям - соответствующее.

Выписка из протокола № 51 заседания Политбюро ЦК от 193 г.

Решение от 10.УП.37г.

206.- Об антисоветских элементах.
(ПБ от 2.УП.37г., пр.№ 51,п.94).

Утвердить тройки по проверке антисоветских элементов:

1)По Куйбышевской области в составе т.т.Попашенко, Нельке и Полякова.

Утвердить намеченных к расстрелу 1881 чел. и высылке 4259 чел.

2)По Дагестанской АССР в составе т.т.Самурского, Леонссова и Гипсрова.

Утвердить намеченных к расстрелу 600 чел. и высылке 2485 чел.

3)По Дальне-Восточному краю в составе т.т.Дерибаса (с заменой Западным), Птуха и Федина.

Утвердить намеченных к расстрелу 2017 чел. и высылке 2681 чел.

Распространить действие директивы ЦК также на находящиеся на Дальнем Востоке спецпоселки.

Разрешить тройке рассматривать дела лагерников, проявляющих враждебную деятельность, с применением к ним расстрела.

4)По Мордовской АССР в составе т.т.Вейзагера, Михайлова и Путнина (с заменой Котелевым).

Утвердить намеченных к расстрелу кулаков 920, уголовников 320 чел. и высылке кулаков 1883, уголовников 780 чел.

(см.н/др.стр.).

Politburo resolution confirming 23,000 citizens shot and 51,000 sent to the Gulag in just two days. July 10, 1937. Fond 89, opis 73, delo 49, leaf 1, reel 11011.

СССР
НАРОДНЫЙ КОМИССАРИАТ
ВНУТРЕННИХ ДЕЛ

" " марта 1940 г.
№ 794/Б
г. Москва

СОВ. СЕКРЕТНО

ЦК ВКП(б)

товарищу СТАЛИНУ

В лагерях для военнопленных НКВД СССР и в тюрьмах западных областей Украины и Белоруссии в настоящее время содержится большое количество бывших офицеров польской армии, бывших работников польской полиции и разведывательных органов, членов польских националистических к-р партий, участников вскрытых к-р повстанческих организаций, перебежчиков и др. Все они являются заклятыми врагами советской власти, преисполненными ненависти к советскому строю.

Военнопленные офицеры и полицейские, находясь в лагерях, пытаются продолжать к-р работу, ведут антисоветскую агитацию. Каждый из них только и ждет освобождения, чтобы иметь возможность активно включиться в борьбу против советской власти.

Органами НКВД в западных областях Украины и Белоруссии вскрыт ряд к-р повстанческих организаций. Во всех этих к-р организациях активную руководящую роль играли бывшие офицеры бывшей польской армии, бывшие полицейские и жандармы.

Среди задержанных перебежчиков и нарушителей гос-

т. Калинин - за
т. Каганович - за

Resolution of the Central Committee of the Soviet Communist Party on the execution of 14,700 captured Polish officers and others at Katyn and other camps, original draft by Lavrentiy Beria (chief of NKVD, 1938–53) with signatures of Joseph Stalin and Kliment Voroshilov (Soviet minister of defense, 1925–40) indicating approval. March 5, 1940. Fond 89, opis 14, dela 1–20, leaf 9, reel 1993.

Подлежит возврату в течение 24 часов
в ЦК КПСС (Общий отдел, 1-й сектор)

Пролетарии всех стран, соединяйтесь!

Коммунистическая Партия Советского Союза. ЦЕНТРАЛЬНЫЙ КОМИТЕТ

№ П73/1

СТРОГО СЕКРЕТНО
ОСОБАЯ ПАПКА

Т.т.Пономареву, Андропову.

Выписка из протокола № 73 заседания Политбюро ЦК от 4 марта 1968г.

Вопрос Международного отдела ЦК КПСС.

1. Оказать финансовую помощь:

Компартии Испании	в размере	120.000	долларов
Компартии Дании	"	30.000	"
Гватемальской партии Труда	"	65.000	"
Ливанской компартии	"	50.000	"
Союзу народов Кении	"	50.000	"
Народному движению за освобождение Анголы	"	25.000	"
Социалистической рабоче-крестьянской партии Нигерии	"	45.000	"
Всенародному Конгрессу Сьерра-Леоне	"	15.000	ф.ст.

2. Передачу средств поручить Комитету госбезопасности.

СЕКРЕТАРЬ ЦК

2477

Minutes of a Politburo meeting showing large sums of money transferred to communist parties in Spain, Denmark, Guatemala, Kenya, Sierra Leone, and other countries. March 4, 1968. Fond 89, opis 51, delo 27, leaf 1, reel 11006.

СССР
КОМИТЕТ
ГОСУДАРСТВЕННОЙ БЕЗОПАСНОСТИ
при СОВЕТЕ МИНИСТРОВ СССР

„25" июля 1962 г.
№ 1900-с
гор. Москва

Совершенно секретно

ЦК КПСС

Докладываю, что за последнее время значительно возросло количество враждебных проявлений, связанных с распространением антисоветских анонимных документов. В первом полугодии текущего года на территории страны было распространено 7705 антисоветских листовок и анонимных писем, изготовленных 3522 авторами, что в два раза больше, чем за тот же период 1961 года.

Наибольшее число антисоветских документов обнаружено на Украине, в Азербайджане, Грузии, Латвии, Ставропольском и Красноярском краях, Ростовской, Ленинградской и Московской областях.

В листовках и анонимных письмах содержатся призывы к активной борьбе против существующего в СССР строя, злобные клеветнические измышления в отношении отдельных руководителей Советского государства, националистические настроения, неверие в построение коммунистического общества в нашей стране, клевета на советскую демократию. В ряде анонимных документов высказывается ненависть к КПСС и коммунистам, угрозы по адресу местного партийного и советского актива.

После длительного перерыва вновь начали рассылаться анонимные документы с восхвалением участников антипартийной группы. Значительно больше стало поступать писем, содержащих террористические намерения в отношении руководителей коммунистической партии и правительства.

После опубликования решения ЦК КПСС и Совета Министров СССР о повышении цен на продукты животноводства увеличился

2554

KGB report recording the extent of internal resistance to the government: 7,705 discrete pieces of opposition literature circulated clandestinely both internally and abroad during the first six months of 1962. July 25, 1962. Fond 89, opis 51, delo 1, leaf 1, reel 11006.

ЛИГАЧЕВ. Третий Съезд мы провели, ничего не принимаем.

ГОРБАЧЕВ. Ну, будут здесь, считаю, встречи, беседы, увещевания.

ЛИГАЧЕВ. Ну, это я считаю...

ГОРБАЧЕВ. Ну, это другое дело.

ЛИГАЧЕВ. Пришел к выводу и твердо уверен.

ГОРБАЧЕВ. Я не исключаю, что у тебя другая позиция, Егор Кузьмич. Я ее вижу...

Ну что, не так что ли? Я это вижу и я вынужден считаться. Если даже я веду Пленум, говорю, а ты встаешь и заявляешь, возражаешь. Я тем не менее вынужден считаться с фактами. Значит, ты имеешь право. Что-то тебя не держит. Ну, что же я тут буду делать? Я же тоже не "царь" партии. И тем более ты же для меня не просто кто-то случайный человек. Значит, это уж твое дело. Я свою позицию выражаю. Я не думаю, что тут нам разгоны или что-то подобное нужно устраивать, но если потребуется кое-где с коммунистов спросить, то надо спрашивать. А решение принимать сейчас... Ну, что мы по "Известиям" примем? Вот пусть товарищ Лукьянов на Верховном Совете рассматривает "Известия". А у т.Медведева надо приглашать коммунистов, беседовать, как мы это делаем. И вновь надо их пригласить на индивидуальную беседу уже.

МЕДВЕДЕВ. Это делается.

ГОРБАЧЕВ. Ну, ладно, это следующий вопрос.

РЫЖКОВ. Михаил Сергеевич, надо обязательно альтернативы. Мы этому научились теперь. Единственное, что мы тех людей, кто подставил себя, мы должны морально поддержать, а не дискредитировать.

ГОРБАЧЕВ. Безусловно.

Когда я был на Украине, Владимир Антонович Ивашко мне шепнул: "Михаил Сергеевич, ради бога, поддержите Гуренко". И я публично это сделал. Сегодня Гуренко - второй секретарь и работает.

Кстати, что тут плохого, если человека двигают конкурентом на эту роль. Это же хорошо, значит, базу какую-то имеет. Люди же выдвигают.

218

Minutes of a Politburo meeting revealing the factional struggle between hard-liners, led by Yegor Ligachev (second secretary of the Soviet Communist Party, 1985–90) and Vladimir Kryuchkov (chief of KGB, 1988–91), and reformers, led by Mikhail Gorbachev. March 22, 1990. Fond 89, opis 42, delo 26, leaf 127, reel 11003.

МЕДВЕДЕВ. Это хороший способ.

ИВАШКО. Если бы так не сделали, а Гуренко на второй день "уничтожили", то кто после этого пойдет альтернатом специально подставлять свою шею. Это надо тоже учитывать.

ГОРБАЧЕВ. Это, вообще пакостные выступления.

В России мы должны продумать это. И действительно иметь основную фигуру, основное предложение, как мы и говорили. Если начнут там "двигаться", то надо пойти на то, чтобы выдвинуть альтернативную кандидатуру для подстраховки. Должна выиграть наша позиция.

Особенно меня смущает то, что времени в распоряжении москвичей и ленинградцев мало - всего 20 дней. Вот где нужна работа. Одно, товарищ Прокофьев, ясно: есть люди, которые уже определили позиции, а другие - колеблются. Вот с ними надо работать в первую очередь. И индивидуально, с кем надо. Секретари - один с двумя-тремя поговорил, второй-с другими. С кем-то Сайкин побеседует, понимаете? А где-то и группу людей собрать. Потому что Попов уже провел в аудитории в МГУ заседание. Кстати, вот вы считаете, что за ним идет 246 человек, а собралось у него только 58 депутатов. Я хочу сказать, что наверное за ними не побежат люди, как им хотелось бы. Это открывает возможности, для того чтобы работать с ними, а не смотреть на это дело пораженчески. Тем более, основная масса среди депутатов - коммунисты.

ВОРОТНИКОВ. Российские депутаты из Москвы хотят собираться у нас в нашем здании. Я думаю, что это будет неплохо. Пусть у нас собираются и мы там можем принять участие. Они, видимо, хотят основные силы немножко в стороне держать, там Бочарова, Ельцина, а вот Травкин просит вот такие собрания проводить у нас в Совете.

ГОРБАЧЕВ. Ельцин попросил путевку: плохо себя чувствует, жалуется на сердце, на нервные срывы и припадки. О путевке он звонил Анатолию Ивановичу Лукьянову.

Короче говоря, даже в таких тяжелых регионах как Москва и Ленинград реальные возможности для борьбы остались. И надо все сделать, чтобы эти возможности были превращены в действительности. Как говорят, не нужно паниковать. Но из всего этого очень большие выводы вытекают и для того, как вести дело выборов делегатов съезда.

219

Appendix B

PROJECT PARTICIPANTS

Hoover Institution on War, Revolution and Peace, Stanford University

Charles G. Palm, Deputy Director
Judith Fortson, Head Librarian
Anne Van Camp, Archivist
Elena Danielson, Archivist from 1996
Joseph Dwyer, Deputy Curator, Russian Collection
Dena Schoen, Librarian and Russian Specialist
Cathy Aster, Preservation Officer
Gordon Hahn, Research Fellow
Semion Lyandres, Research Fellow
Lora Soroka, Archival Specialist
Kathleen Power, Administrative Assistant
Lois Christopherson, Administrative Assistant from 1994
Natalia Volkova, Assistant in Moscow
Nina Ivanovskaia, Assistant in Moscow

State Archival Service of Russia (Rosarkhiv)

[After August 1996, it was renamed the Federal Archival Service of Russia, retaining the acronym Rosarkhiv.]

Rudolf G. Pikhoia, Chairman and Chief Archivist of Russia
Vladimir A. Tiuneev, First Deputy Chairman; Chairman from January 1996
Vladimir P. Kozlov, Deputy Chairman; Chairman from November 1996
Valery I. Abramov, Deputy Chairman

Vladimir P. Tarasov, Director, Department of International Relations
Vladimir Bondarev, Deputy Director, Department of International Relations
L. S. Shatenshtein, Director of the Department of Acquisitions, Government Agencies, and Record Keeping
Andrei N. Artizov, Adviser to the Administration of the President of the Russian Federation from 1997

Center for the Preservation of Contemporary Documentation (TsKhSD)

[Before 1992, it was named the Current Archive of the Soviet Communist Party Central Committee; it is now named the Russian State Archives of Recent History (RGANI).]

Rem A. Usikov, Director
A. S. Prokopenko, Director from April 1993
Natalia G. Tomilina, Director from September 1993

Center for the Preservation and Study of Records of Modern History (RTsKhIDNI)

[Before 1992, it was named the Central Party Archive and Marx-Engels-Lenin Institute; it is now named the Russian State Archives of Socio-Political History (RGASPI).]

Vladimir P. Kozlov, Director
Kyrill M. Anderson, Director from March 1992

State Archive of the Russian Federation (GARF)

[Before 1992, it was named the Central State Archives of the October Revolution and Russian Soviet Federative Socialist Republic (RSFSR).]

Sergei V. Mironenko, Director

Chadwyck-Healey Ltd.

Charles Chadwyck-Healey, Chairman
Alastair Everitt, Managing Director
Steven Hall, Sales and Marketing Director; Managing Director from 1994; Senior Vice President and General Manager at Bell & Howell

Information and Learning from 1999; and Senior Vice President at ProQuest Information and Learning from 2001

Don McCrae, Group Finance Director

Alison Maynard, Financial Controller

Dave Chapman, CEO, CHMPS

Reuben Starling, Assistant Manager, CHMPS

Inga Huld Markan, Administrative Assistant

Editorial Board

Robert Conquest, Senior Research Fellow, Hoover Institution

John B. Dunlop, Senior Fellow, Hoover Institution

Terence Emmons, Professor of History, Stanford University

Jana Howlett, Fellow, Jesus College, Cambridge University

Rudolf G. Pikhoia, Chairman, Rosarkhiv

Nikolai N. Pokrovskii, Deputy Director for Research, Siberian Section, Russian Academy of Sciences

Dmitri Volkogonov, Special Assistant to President Boris Yeltsin

Appendix C

CHECKLIST OF MICROFILMED RECORDS

The following checklist describes the *fondy* (record groups) and *opisi* (record series) that constitute the microfilmed document collection, entitled *Archives of the Soviet Communist Party and Soviet State,* that was produced and published by the State Archival Service of Russia (Rosarkhiv) and the Hoover Institution and distributed by Chadwyck-Healey Ltd. More detailed descriptions, prepared by Lora Soroka, are available at the Online Archive of California website. Entry titles beginning "Selected Records" describe *opisi* that were not filmed in their entirety; however, the *dela* (folders) selected from these *opisi* were filmed in their entirety. Dates are beginning and end dates of the records, not of the party and state entities.

1. TsKhSD (RGANI)—1,012 reels

Finding aids—15 reels

Records—997 reels:

Fond 6 — Records of the Party Control Commission of the Central Committee of the All-Russian Communist Party (Bolsheviks), 1934–52; the Party Control Committee of the Central Committee of the Communist Party of the Soviet Union, 1952–62; the Party Commission of the Central Committee of the Communist Party of the Soviet Union, 1962–66—973 reels

- Opis 1 — Minutes of the Party Control Commission, 1934–39—159 reels
- Opis 2 — Minutes of the Committee for Party Control, 1939–52—335 reels

Opis 3 Minutes of the Committee for Party Control, 1952–56—121 reels

Opis 4 Minutes of the Committee for Party Control, 1956–61—137 reels

Opis 5 Minutes of the Commission for Party Control, 1961–66—49 reels

Opis 6 Reports, References, Verbatim Accounts, Protocols—172 reels

Fond 89 Records of the Constitutional Court of the Russian Federation relating to the 1992 Trial of the Communist Party of the Soviet Union, 1918–92—24 reels

Opisi 1–76 The Communist Party of the Soviet Union on Trial, 1918–92—24 reels

2. RTsKhIDNI (RGASPI)—2,775 reels

Finding aids—55 reels

Records—2,720 reels:

Fond 17 Records of the Central Committee of the Communist Party of the Soviet Union, 1903–71—2,460 reels

Opis 1 Records of the Central Committee of the Russian Social Democratic Labor Party, 1903–05—5 reels

Opis 2 Records of the Plenums of the All-Russian Communist Party (Bolsheviks) Central Committee, 1918–41—88 reels

Opis 7 Records of the Statistics Department of the Central Committee, All-Russian Communist Party (Bolsheviks), 1920–41—79 reels

Opis 8 Materials of the 1922 All-Union Party Census and Data on the People Who Were Admitted to or Resigned from the Russian Communist Party (Bolsheviks), 1922–24—282 reels

Opis 9 Records of the Department of Registration and Statistics, 1926–27—1,422 reels

Opis 75 Records of the Administration of Affairs of the Central Committee, Communist Party of the Soviet Union, Department of Finance and Budget Department, 1939–65—10 reels

Opis 76 Records of the Administration of Affairs of the Central Committee, Communist Party of the Soviet Union, Department of Budget and Finance, 1939–55—262 reels

Opis 77 Records of the Administration of Affairs of the Central Committee, Communist Party of the Soviet Union, Department of Budget and Finance, 1939–63—56 reels

Opis 79 Records of the Administration of Affairs of the Central Committee, Communist Party of the Soviet Union, Instructions, 1935–56—5 reels

Opis 86 Records of the Bureau of the Secretariat of the Central Committee of the Russian Communist Party (Bolsheviks), 1918–34—17 reels

Opis 109 Documents Related to the Defense of the Soviet Republic and to the Building of the Red Army, 1917–24—24 reels

Opis 139 Records of the Department of Organizational and Party Work Information Sector, 1971—210 reels

Fond 34 Records of the Second Congress of the Russian Social Democratic Workers Party, 1903—4 reels

Fond 35 Records of the Third Congress of the Russian Social Democratic Workers Party, 1905—4 reels

Fond 36 Records of the Fifth Congress of the Russian Social Democratic Workers Party, 1907—1 reel

Fond 37 Records of the Sixth (Prague) Conference of the Russian Social Democratic Workers Party, 1912—1 reel

Fond 38	Records of the Sixth Congress of the Russian Social Democratic Workers Party, 1917—1 reel
Fond 39	Records of the Seventh (April) All-Russian Conference of the Russian Social Democratic Workers Party, 1917–24—2 reels
Fond 40	Records of the Seventh Congress of the Russian Communist Party (Bolsheviks), 1917–18—1 reel
Fond 41	Records of the Eighth Congress of the Russian Communist Party (Bolsheviks), 1918–19—4 reels
Fond 42	Records of the Eighth All-Russian Conference of the Russian Communist Party (Bolsheviks), 1919—1 reel
Fond 43	Records of the Ninth Congress of the Russian Communist Party (Bolsheviks), 1919–20—2 reels
Fond 44	Records of the Ninth All-Russian Conference of the Russian Communist Party (Bolsheviks), 1920—2 reels
Fond 45	Records of the Tenth Congress of the Russian Communist Party (Bolsheviks), 1921–22—7 reels
Fond 46	Records of the Tenth All-Russian Conference of the Russian Communist Party (Bolsheviks), 1921—1 reel
Fond 47	Records of the Eleventh All-Russian Conference of the Russian Communist Party (Bolsheviks), 1921–22—2 reels
Fond 48	Records of the Eleventh Congress of the Russian Communist Party (Bolsheviks), 1921–22—4 reels
Fond 49	Records of the Twelfth Conference of the Russian Communist Party (Bolsheviks), 1922—1 reel
Fond 50	Records of the Twelfth Congress of the Russian Communist Party (Bolsheviks), 1922–23—12 reels
Fond 51	Records of the Thirteenth Conference of the Russian Communist Party (Bolsheviks), 1923–24—3 reels
Fond 52	Records of the Thirteenth Congress of the Russian Communist Party (Bolsheviks), 1924—13 reels

Fond 53 Records of the Fourteenth Conference of the All-Russian Communist Party (Bolsheviks), 1924–25—5 reels

Fond 54 Records of the Fourteenth Congress of the All-Russian Communist Party (Bolsheviks), 1925—20 reels

Fond 55 Records of the Fifteenth Conference of the All-Russian Communist Party (Bolsheviks), 1926–29—15 reels

Fond 56 Records of the Fifteenth Congress of the All-Russian Communist Party (Bolsheviks), 1927—15 reels

Fond 57 Records of the Sixteenth Conference of the All-Russian Communist Party (Bolsheviks), 1928–29—6 reels

Fond 58 Records of the Sixteenth Congress of the All-Russian Communist Party (Bolsheviks), 1930—20 reels

Fond 59 Records of the Seventeenth Congress of the All-Russian Communist Party (Bolsheviks), 1933–34—19 reels

Fond 337 Records of the Fifth (London) Congress of the Russian Social Democratic Workers Party, 1907—3 reels

Fond 447 Records of the Fourth (Unifying) Congress of the Russian Social Democratic Workers Party, 1906—2 reels

Fond 477 Records of the Eighteenth Congress of the All-Russian Communist Party (Bolsheviks), 1938–39—26 reels

Fond 572 Records of the Central Auditing Commission of the Russian Communist Party (Bolsheviks), 1921–25, 1944–50—4 reels

Fond 582 Records of the Twenty-fourth Congress of the Communist Party of the Soviet Union, 1971—2 reels

Fond 586 Preparatory Materials for Third Program of the Communist Party of the Soviet Union, 1958–61—33 reels

Fond 592 Records of the Nineteenth Congress of the Communist Party of the Soviet Union, 1951–52—13 reels

Fond 593 Records of the Twenty-third Congress of the Communist Party of the Soviet Union, 1966—1 reel

Fond 604 Records of the Twenty-fifth Congress of the Communist Party of the Soviet Union, 1976—4 reels

Fond 620 Records of the Twenty-sixth Congress of the Communist Party of the Soviet Union, 1981—3 reels

Fond 628 Records of the Twenty-seventh Congress of the Communist Party of the Soviet Union, 1986—1 reel

Fond 646 Records of the Twenty-eighth Congress of the Communist Party of the Soviet Union, 1990—2 reels

3. GARF—8,032 reels

Finding aids—399 reels

Records—7,633 reels:

Fond 393 Records of the People's Commissariat of Internal Affairs (NKVD) of the Russian Soviet Federative Socialist Republic (RSFSR), 1917–31—4,205 reels

Opis 1 Records of the Chancellery of the Commissar of Internal Affairs, 1917–19—31 reels

Opis 1A Records of the Administration of Affairs, 1918–30—63 microfilm reels

Opis 2 Records of the Administrative Sub-department, 1917–19—35 reels

Opis 3 Records of the Department of Local Administration, 1917–19—233 reels

Opis 4 Records of the Press Bureau, 1917–20—26 reels

Opis 5 Records of the Local Economy Department, 1917–19—105 reels

Opis 6 Records of the Main Directorate of the Militia (Police) and the Central Administration of Criminal Investigation, 1917–22—14 reels

Opis 7 Records of the Foreign Department, 1918–19—38 reels

Opis 8	Records of the Central Veterinary Department, 1918–20—5 reels
Opis 9	Records of the Department of Finance, 1918–19—2 reels
Opis 10	Records of the Secretariat of the Collegium and General Chancellery, 1919–21—13 reels
Opis 11	Records of the Directorate of Administration and Management, 1919–20—46 reels
Opis 12	Records of the Department of Instructions, Press Department, and Department of Statistics, 1918–20—12 reels
Opis 13	Records of the Department of Information and Statistics, 1919–21—313 reels
Opis 14	Records of the Department of Local Economy, 1918–19—6 reels
Opis 15	Records of the Main Militia (Police) Directorate, 1918–20—5 reels
Opis 16	Records of the Central Directorate of Criminal Investigation, 1919—10 reels
Opis 17	Records of the Central Veterinary Department, 1918–19—6 reels
Opis 18	Records of the Department of Finance, 1919—7 reels
Opis 18A	Records of the Department of Finance, 1918–22—118 reels
Opis 19	Records of the Secretariat of the Collegium; Records of the General Chancellery of the Administration of Affairs, 1920–22—4 reels
Opis 20	Records of the Secretariat and Administrative Sub-department, Complaints Bureau, Sub-department of Administrative Units, and Sub-department of Vital Statistics, Department of Management, 1920—21 reels

Opis 21	Records of the Foreign Sub-department of the Department of Management, 1920–22—152 reels
Opis 22	Records of the Department of Information and Statistics, Department of Management and Instructions, and Municipal Department, 1920–21—153 reels
Opis 23	Records of the Main Directorate of the Workers' and Peasants' Militia and Central Directorate of Criminal Investigation, 1920–23—16 reels
Opis 23A	Records of the Main Militia (Police) Directorate, 1920–23—88 reels
Opis 24	Records of the Statistics Department, 1920–21—18 reels
Opis 25	Records of the Department of Finance and Department of General Services, 1919–22—11 reels
Opis 26	Records of the Administration of Affairs and the Secretariat of the Collegium, 1920–22—14 reels
Opis 27	Records of the Directorate of Administration and Management, 1921–23—236 reels
Opis 28	Records of the Organizational Department of the Directorate of Administration and Management, 1921—135 reels
Opis 29	Records of the Statistic Department of the Directorate of Administration and Management, 1921–22—5 reels
Opis 30	Records of the Department of Vital Statistics of the Directorate of Administration and Management, 1920–22—2 reels
Opis 31	Records of the Main Militia (Police) Directorate, 1920–22—37 reels
Opis 32	Records of the Administration of Affairs, 1922–25—12 reels

Opis 33	Records of the Administrative Department and Consulting Bureau of the Directorate of Administration and Management, 1919–24—46 reels
Opis 34	Selected Records of the Department of Vital Statistics of the Directorate of Administration and Management, 1921–23—21 reels
Opis 35	Selected Records of the Organizational Department of the Directorate of Administration and Management, 1922–23—134 reels
Opis 36	Selected Records of the Department of Statistics of the Directorate of Administration and Management, 1922–23—17 reels
Opis 37	Selected Records of the Main Directorate of the Workers' and Peasants' Militia (Police), 1921–25—61 reels
Opis 38	Selected Records of the Directorate of Criminal Investigation, 1922–23—23 reels
Opis 39	Selected Records of the Administration of Affairs, 1923–26—30 reels
Opis 40	Selected Records of the Department of Statistics of the Administration of Affairs, 1922–26—14 reels
Opis 41	Selected Records of the Directorate of Administration and Management, 1919–23—12 reels
Opis 42	Selected Records of the Main Directorate of the Soviet Workers' and Peasants' Militia (Police) and the Central Directorate of Criminal Investigation, 1919–23—14 reels
Opis 43	Selected Records of the Secretariat and Administrative Department of the Central Administrative Directorate, 1921–30—185 reels
Opis 43A	Records of the Central Administrative Directorate, 1919–30—261 reels

Opis 44	Selected Records of the Militia (Police) Department of the Central Administrative Directorate, 1923–25—14 reels
Opis 45	Selected Records of the Department of Criminal Investigation of the Central Administrative Directorate, 1923–26—22 reels
Opis 46	Selected Records of the Organizational Directorate, 1923—129 reels
Opis 47	Selected Records of the Secretariat of the Collegium and the General Department of the Administration of Affairs, 1923–30—36 reels
Opis 48	Selected Records of the Department of Statistics of the Administration of Affairs, 1923–27—26 reels
Opis 49	Records of the Organizational Directorate and the Department of Registration and Assignment, 1922–25—57 reels
Opis 50	Selected Records of the Secretariat, Inspectorate, and Administrative Department of the Central Administrative Directorate, 1921–29—128 reels
Opis 51	Records of the Militia Department of the Central Administrative Directorate, 1922–26—34 reels
Opis 52	Records of the Department of Criminal Investigation of the Central Administrative Directorate, 1924–25—19 reels
Opis 53	Selected Records of the Secretariat of the Collegium and the General Department of the General Directorate, 1923–29—42 reels
Opis 54	Selected Records of the Organizational Department and Department of Registration and Assignments, 1925–26—56 reels
Opis 55	Selected Records of the Department of Statistics and Department of Finance of the General Directorate, 1924–27—46 reels

Opis 56	Selected Records of the Inspectorate and Secretariat of the General Administrative Directorate, 1925–27—18 reels
Opis 57	Selected Records of the Administrative Department of the General Administrative Directorate, 1922–28—51 reels
Opis 58	Selected Records of the Militia Department of the General Administrative Directorate, 1925–28—16 reels
Opis 59	Selected Records of the Criminal Investigation Department of the General Administrative Directorate, 1925–26—16 reels
Opis 60	Selected Records of the Secretariat of the Collegium and of the General Department of the General Directorate, 1926–27—39 reels
Opis 61	Selected Records of the Organizational Directorate and Department of Registration and Distribution of the Central Administrative Directorate, 1926–27—47 reels
Opis 62	Selected Records of the Department of Statistics and Department of Finance of the General Directorate, 1925–27—48 reels
Opis 63	Selected Records of the Inspectorate and Secretariat of the Central Administrative Directorate, 1926–27—11 reels
Opis 64	Selected Records of the Administrative Department of the Central Administrative Directorate, 1926–27—39 reels
Opis 65	Selected Records of the Militia Department of the Central Administrative Directorate, 1926—11 reels
Opis 66	Selected Records of the Criminal Investigation Department of the Central Administrative Directorate, 1926–27—37 reels

Opis 67 Selected Records of the Secretariat of the Collegium, General Department of the General Directorate, 1927–28—46 reels

Opis 68 Selected Records of the Department of Registration and Assignment and Organizational Department of the General Directorate, 1927—33 reels

Opis 69 Selected Records of the Department of Statistics and Department of Finance of the General Directorate, 1926–27—20 reels

Opis 70 Selected Records of the Secretariat and Inspectorate of the Central Administrative Directorate, 1927–28—5 reels

Opis 71 Selected Records of the Administrative Department of the Central Administrative Directorate, 1921–28—16 reels

Opis 72 Selected Records of the Militia Department of the Central Administrative Directorate, 1926–27—12 reels

Opis 73 Selected Records of the Criminal Investigation Department of the Central Administrative Directorate, 1926–28—13 reels

Opis 74 Selected Records of the Secretariat of the Collegium and the General Department, 1924–29—33 reels

Opis 75 Selected Records of the Department of Registration and Assignment and Department of Management, 1927–28—16 reels

Opis 76 Selected Records of the Department of Finance, 1927–29—14 reels

Opis 77 Selected Records of the Department of Administrative Supervision, 1923–30—34 reels

Opis 78 Selected Records of the Militia Directorate and Department of Criminal Investigation, 1925–29—26 reels

Opis 79 Selected Records of the Secretariat of the Collegium and the General Department of the Directorate of Administration and Management, 1928–30—18 reels

Opis 80 Selected Records of the Department of Organization and Information of the Directorate of Administration and Management, 1928–30—13 reels

Opis 81 Selected Records of the Administrative Department of the Directorate of Administration and Management, 1923–29—21 reels

Opis 82 Selected Records of the Department of Finance of the Directorate of Administration and Management, 1927–31—16 reels

Opis 83 Selected Records of the Criminal Investigation Department, 1928–29—8 reels

Opis 84 Records of the Administration of Affairs, Directorate of Administration and Management, and Department of Finance, 1921–31—21 reels

Opis 87 Selected Records of the Secretariat, 1927–30—4 reels

Opis 88 Selected Records of the Directorate for Personnel Management, 1929–31—1 reel

Opis 89 Selected Records of the Main Directorate of Forced Labor, 1918–25—47 reels

Opis 90 Selected Records of the Local Trade Union Committee of the Employees, 1918–30—34 reels

Opis 91 Selected Records of the All-Union Young Communists League Cell of the People's Commissariat of Internal Affairs, 1920–27—2 reels

Fond 1005 Records of the Supreme Tribunal of the All-Russian Executive Committee and the RSFSR Supreme Court, 1917–67 (Revolutionary Tribunal of the All-Russian Central Executive Committee, 1918–19; Supreme Revolutionary Tribunal of the All-Russian Central Executive

Committee, 1919–21; Tribunal of Appeal of the All-Russian Central Executive Committee, 1919–21; Supreme Tribunal of the All-Russian Central Executive Committee, 1921–22)—288 reels

Opis 1	Records of the Military Collegium, 1921–23—28 reels
Opis 1A	Selected Investigatory Files, 1918–40—52 reels
Opis 2	Records of the Appellate Collegium, 1918–23—36 reels
Opis 3	Records of the Directorate of Court Supervision, 1919–23—25 reels
Opis 4	Records of the Department of Finance and General Service, 1921–23—5 reels
Opis 7	Selected Appeals, Filed by Convicts, 1918–23—67 reels
Opis 8	Investigatory Materials of the Revolutionary Military Council of the All-Russian Central Executive Committee, 1917–67—3 reels
Opis 67	Copies of the Minutes of the Executive Sessions of the Court and Sentences Rendered by the Revolutionary Tribunals in Guberniias, 1918–26—72 reels

Fond 4042 Records of the Main Directorate of Places of Confinement (GULAG) of the People's Commissariat of Internal Affairs (NKVD) of the Russian Socialist Federative Soviet Republic (RSFSR), 1919–30—325 reels

Opis 1	Records of the Secretariat, 1922–29—11 reels
Opis 1A	Records of the Moscow Directorate of Forced Labor, 1920–22—7 reels
Opis 2	Records of the Administrative and Penitentiary Department, 1922–29—104 reels
Opis 3	Records of the Department of Labor, 1922–29—121 reels

	Opis 4	Records of the Department of Culture and Education, 1920–29—34 reels
	Opis 5	Records of the Department of General Service and Supply, 1919–28—12 reels
	Opis 6	Records of the Finance Department, 1924–28—1 reel
	Opis 7	Records of the Assignment Commission, 1924–28—16 reels
	Opis 9	Records of the Main Directorate of Places of Confinement, 1922–24—1 reel
	Opis 10	Records of the Moscow Division, 1922–28—15 reels
	Opis 11	Records of the All-Russian Society for Aid to Released Prisoners, 1925–30—2 reels
	Opis 13	Records of the Main Directorate of Places of Confinement, 1924–25—1 reel
Fond 5446	Records of the Council of People's Commissars (Sovnarkom) of the USSR, 1921–53—81 reels	
	Opis 5	Selected Records of the Administration of Affairs, 1924—1 reel
	Opis 5A	Selected Records of the Administration of Affairs, 1924—1 reel
	Opis 6	Selected Records of the Administration of Affairs, 1925—1 reel
	Opis 7	Selected Records of the Administration of Affairs, 1926—1 reel
	Opis 7A	Selected Records of the Administration of Affairs, 1925–26—1 reel
	Opis 8	Selected Records of the Administration of Affairs, 1927—1 reel
	Opis 8A	Selected Records of the Administration of Affairs, 1927—1 reel

Opis 9	Selected Records of the Administration of Affairs, 1928—1 reel
Opis 9A	Selected Records of the Administration of Affairs, 1928—1 reel
Opis 10	Selected Records of the Administration of Affairs, 1929—1 reel
Opis 10A	Selected Records of the Administration of Affairs, 1929—1 reel
Opis 11	Selected Records of the Administration of Affairs, 1930—1 reel
Opis 11A	Selected Records of the Administration of Affairs, 1930—1 reel
Opis 12A	Selected Records of the Administration of Affairs, 1931—1 reel
Opis 13	Selected Records of the Administration of Affairs, 1932—1 reel
Opis 13A	Selected Records of the Administration of Affairs, 1932—1 reel
Opis 14	Selected Records of the Administration of Affairs, 1932—1 reel
Opis 14A	Selected Records of the Administration of Affairs, 1933—1 reel
Opis 15	Selected Records of the Administration of Affairs, 1934—1 reel
Opis 15A	Selected Records of the Administration of Affairs, 1934—1 reel
Opis 16	Selected Records of the Administration of Affairs, 1935—1 reel
Opis 16A	Selected Records of the Administration of Affairs, 1935—1 reel
Opis 17	Selected Records of the Secretariat of the Administration of Affairs, 1936—1 reel

Opis 18	Selected Records of the Administration of Affairs, 1936—1 reel
Opis 18A	Selected Records of the Administration of Affairs, 1936—2 reels
Opis 20	Selected Records of the Administration of Affairs, 1937—2 reels
Opis 20A	Selected Records of the Administration of Affairs, 1937—2 reels
Opis 22	Selected Records of the Administration of Affairs, 1938—2 reels
Opis 22A	Selected Records of the Administration of Affairs, 1938—2 reels
Opis 23	Selected Records of the Administration of Affairs, 1939—3 reels
Opis 23A	Selected Records of the Administration of Affairs, 1939—4 reels
Opis 24	Selected Records of the Administration of Affairs, 1940—1 reel
Opis 24A	Selected Records of the Administration of Affairs, 1940—5 reels
Opis 25	Selected Records of the Administration of Affairs, 1941—1 reel
Opis 43	Selected Records of the Administration of Affairs, 1942—1 reel
Opis 44	Selected Records of the Administration of Affairs, 1943—1 reel
Opis 46	Selected Records of the Administration of Affairs, 1944—1 reel
Opis 47	Selected Records of the Administration of Affairs, 1945—1 reel
Opis 48	Selected Records of the Administration of Affairs, 1946—1 reel

Opis 49 Selected Records of the Administration of Affairs, 1947—1 reel

Opis 50 Selected Records of the Administration of Affairs, 1948—1 reel

Opis 51 Selected Records of the Administration of Affairs, 1949—1 reel

Opis 80 Selected Records of the Administration of Affairs, 1950—2 reels

Opis 81 Selected Records of the Administration of Affairs, 1951—4 reels

Opis 81A Selected Records of the Secretariat of A. Ya. Vyshinsky, Deputy Chairman of the USSR Sovnarkom, 1939–44—12 reels

Opis 86 Selected Records of the Administration of Affairs, 1952—5 reels

Opis 87 Selected Records of the Administration of Affairs, 1953—2 reels

Fond 7521 Records of the Commission for Private Amnesty of the Presidium of the USSR Central Executive Committee, 1926–37—43 reels

Opis 1 Records of the Commission for Private Amnesty of the Presidium of the USSR Central Executive Committee, 1926–37—43 reels

Fond 7863 Records of the Commission for Grievances and Requests for Pardon of the Presidium of the USSR Supreme Soviet, 1937–48—38 reels

Opis 1 Records of the Commission for Grievances and Requests for Pardon of the Presidium of the USSR Supreme Soviet, 1937–48—1 reel

Opis 2 Minutes of the Presidium of the USSR Supreme Soviet and the Commission for Grievances and Requests for Pardon of the Presidium of the USSR Supreme Soviet, 1938–47—37 reels

Fond 8131 Records of the USSR Procurator's Office, 1924–55 (Procurator's Office of the USSR Supreme Court, 1923–33; USSR Procurator's Office, 1933–55)—372 reels

Opis 1 Selected Records of the USSR Procurator's Office, 1924–25—3 reels

Opis 2 Selected Records of the USSR Procurator's Office, 1925—3 reels

Opis 3 Selected Records of the USSR Procurator's Office, 1925–27—4 reels

Opis 4 Selected Records of the USSR Procurator's Office, 1926–28—4 reels

Opis 5 Selected Records of the USSR Procurator's Office, 1926–29—12 reels

Opis 6 Selected Records of the USSR Procurator's Office, 1927–30—4 reels

Opis 7 Selected Records of the USSR Procurator's Office, 1929–30—2 reels

Opis 8 Selected Records of the USSR Procurator's Office, 1930–32—3 reels

Opis 9 Selected Records of the USSR Procurator's Office, 1931–32—4 reels

Opis 10 Selected Records of the USSR Procurator's Office, 1932–35—11 reels

Opis 11 Selected Records of the USSR Procurator's Office, 1933–35—14 reels

Opis 12 Selected Records of the USSR Procurator's Office, 1933–37—13 reels

Opis 13 Records of the USSR Procurator's Office, 1934–37—11 reels

Opis 14 Selected Records of the USSR Procurator's Office, 1936–38—10 reels

	Opis 15	Selected Records of the USSR Procurator's Office, 1936–38—11 reels
	Opis 16	Selected Records of the USSR Procurator's Office, 1937–40—19 reels
	Opis 17	Selected Records of the USSR Procurator's Office, 1938–40—12 reels
	Opis 18	Selected Records of the USSR Procurator's Office, 1938–41—8 reels
	Opis 19	Selected Records of the USSR Procurator's Office, 1937–42—6 reels
	Opis 20	Selected Records of the USSR Procurator's Office, 1942–44—7 reels
	Opis 21	Selected Records of the USSR Procurator's Office, 1942–44—8 reels
	Opis 22	Selected Records of the USSR Procurator's Office, 1943–46—20 reels
	Opis 23	Selected Records of the USSR Procurator's Office, 1941–47—19 reels
	Opis 24	Selected Records of the USSR Procurator's Office, 1944–48—25 reels
	Opis 25	Selected Records of the USSR Procurator's Office, 1946–49—26 reels
	Opis 26	Selected Records of the USSR Procurator's Office, 1946–50—30 reels
	Opis 27	Selected Records of the USSR Procurator's Office, 1936–50—18 reels
	Opis 28	Selected Records of the USSR Procurator's Office, 1949–55—52 reels
	Opis 29	Selected Records of the USSR Procurator's Office, 1948–52—13 reels
Fond 8409	Records of the E. P. Peshkova Society: Committee for Aid to Political Prisoners, 1921–38—465 reels	

Opis 1 — Records of the E. P. Peshkova Society: Aid to Political Prisoners, 1921–38—465 reels

Fond 8419 — Records of the Political Red Cross Society (Moscow), 1918–24—58 reels

Opis 1 — Records of the Political Red Cross Society (Moscow), 1918–24—58 reels

Fond 9412 — Records of the Department of Children's Labor and Educational Colonies of the USSR Ministry of Internal Affairs, 1941–60—275 reels

Opis 1 — Selected Records of the Department of Children's Labor and Educational Colonies of the USSR Ministry of Internal Affairs, 1941–60—242 reels

Opis 2 — Selected Records of the Department of Children's Labor and Educational Colonies of the USSR Ministry of Internal Affairs, 1954–60—33 reels

Fond 9414 — Records of the Main Administration of Places of Confinement of the USSR Ministry of Internal Affairs, 1930–60—900 reels

Opis 1 — Records of the Main Directorate of Places of Confinement of the USSR Ministry of Internal Affairs, 1930–60—564 reels

Opis 1A — Records of the Main Directorate of Places of Confinement of the USSR Ministry of Internal Affairs, 1934–60—227 reels

Opis 2 — Records of the Main Directorate of Places of Confinement of the USSR Ministry of Internal Affairs, 1930–57—23 reels

Opis 3 — Records of the Political Department, 1940–60—30 reels

Opis 3A — Records of the Political Department, 1939–60—8 reels

Opis 4 — Records of the Political Department, 1932–60—48 reels

Fond 9474 Records of the USSR Supreme Court, 1924–57—48 reels

Opis 16 Selected Records of the Secret Division of the USSR Supreme Court, 1924–57—48 reels

Fond 9479 Records of the Fourth Special Department of the USSR Ministry of Internal Affairs, 1930–59—123 reels

Opis 1 Records of the Fourth Special Department of the USSR Ministry of Internal Affairs, 1930–59—123 reels

Fond 9492 Records of the USSR Ministry of Justice, 1936–57; the People's Commissariat of Justice, 1936–46; the USSR Ministry of Justice, 1946–56—412 reels

Opis 1A Selected Records of the USSR Ministry of Justice, 1936–56—133 reels

Opis 2 Selected Records of the USSR Ministry of Justice, 1936–56—23 reels

Opis 3 Selected Records of the USSR Ministry of Justice, 1937–57—66 reels

Opis 4 Selected Records of the USSR Ministry of Justice, 1939–57—148 reels

Opis 5 Selected Records of the Administration of Camp Courts, 1945–55—42 reels

NOTES

During the first eleven years of the Russian Archives Project—from 1991 to the end of 2001—I was the deputy director of the Hoover Institution with administrative responsibility for the Hoover Institution Library & Archives. All my records as deputy director, including the Russian project files, are part of the records of the Institution, which are held in the Hoover Institution Archives. The most important records relating to the Russian project are minutes of the project directors' meetings, minutes of the Editorial Board meetings, reports to donors, agreements with the State Archival Service of Russia (Rosarkhiv) and with the State Archive of the Russian Federation (GARF), memoranda of conversations, and correspondence files. The Russian project files of Elena Danielson, who administered the Library & Archives after I retired, are also held in the Hoover Institution Archives. In the notes below I have identified my Russian project files with the abbreviation CPHIR (Charles Palm, Hoover Institution Records) and Danielson's files as EDHIR (Elena Danielson, Hoover Institution Records).

Chapter I

1. The microfilm collection was published by Rosarkhiv and the Hoover Institution and distributed by Chadwyck-Healey Ltd. under the title *Archives of the Soviet Communist Party and Soviet State, A Joint Publication on Microfilm of the State Archival Service of Russia and the Hoover Institution on War, Revolution and Peace*. A guide to the collection, edited by Jana Howlett, was published under the same title (Cambridge: Chadwyck-Healey, 1995), with *Supplement* (Cambridge: Chadwyck-Healey, 1996). The collection was distributed by Bell & Howell Information and Learning from 1999 to 2001 and by ProQuest Information and Learning after 2001.

2. The Committee on Archival Affairs of the Council of Ministers of the Russian Soviet Federative Socialist Republic (Roskomarkhiv) was established

in 1990. By presidential decree of September 20, 1992, it was renamed the State Archival Service of Russia (Rosarkhiv). The single acronym, Rosarkhiv, is used throughout this memoir for both.

3. The Russian Soviet Federative Socialist Republic (RSFSR), also known as the Russian Soviet Republic, was one of fifteen Soviet socialist republics that comprised the Soviet Union (USSR) from 1922 to 1991. On May 29, 1990, Boris Yeltsin was elected chairman of the Supreme Soviet of the RSFSR, a legislative body elected by the Congress of People's Deputies to govern between congressional sessions. As chairman, Yeltsin was the head of state of the RSFSR until the creation of the post of president of Russia. On June 12, 1991, Yeltsin was elected the first and only president of the RSFSR. On December 25, 1991, with the dissolution of the Soviet Union, the RSFSR was renamed the Russian Federation.

4. "Letter of Cooperation between the Hoover Institution and the Committee on Archival Affairs of the RSFSR Council of Ministers, Stanford, California," May 29, 1991, CPHIR.

5. Charles G. Palm, "Talk to the Hoover Institution Board of Overseers," July 23, 1992, CPHIR.

6. Theodore W. Karasik, *The Post-Soviet Archives, Organization, Access, and Declassification* (Santa Monica, CA: RAND Corporation, 1993), 3. See also Patricia Kennedy Grimsted, "Russian Archives in Transition: Caught Between Political Crossfire and Economic Crisis," *American Archivist* 56, no. 4 (Fall 1993): 614–62; and Robert W. Davies, *Soviet History in the Yeltsin Era* (New York and London: St. Martin's Press, 1997), 90–95.

7. *Making Things Work: Russian-American Economic Relations, 1900–1930: An Exhibition Catalog for a Joint Historical Exhibit of Documents and Photographs Organized by the Hoover Institution on War, Revolution and Peace and the Committee on Archival Affairs of the Russian Federation* (Stanford, CA: Hoover Institution Press, 1992). Exhibit described as "benign" in Grimsted, "Russian Archives in Transition," 619.

8. In a statement on the purpose of the Hoover Institution, Herbert Hoover wrote, "The purpose of the Institution must be, by its research and publications, to demonstrate the evils of the doctrines of Karl Marx—whether Communism, Socialism, economic materialism, or atheism—thus to protect the American way of life from such ideologies, their conspiracies, and to reaffirm the validity of the American system." See Minutes of the Special Committee on the Hoover Institution, Stanford University Board of Trustees, May 20, 1959.

9. Patricia Kennedy Grimsted, *A Handbook for Archival Research in the USSR* (Washington, DC: International Research and Exchanges Board and the Kennan Institute for Advanced Russian Studies, 1989), 132.

10. In 1991, the Russian government renamed the repositories holding the archives of the Soviet Communist Party. The records for the period October 1952 through August 1991 were held at the Center for the Preservation of Contemporary Documentation (TsKhSD), located at Il'inka (formerly Kuibysheva), 12, Moscow. Its previous name was the Current Archive of the CPSU Central Committee. In 1999, the name changed to Russian State Archives of Recent History (RGANI). In 2016, both Rosarkhiv and RGANI moved to a new location across the Moskva River on Sofiiskaya naberezhnaya. Its directors during the Hoover project were, successively, Rem A. Usikov, A. S. Prokopenko, and Natalia G. Tomilina.

11. The Soviet Communist Party records from the party origins through October 1952 were held at the Center for the Preservation and Study of Records of Modern History (RTsKhIDNI), located at Bol'shaia Dmitrovka (formerly Pushkinskaia), 15, Moscow. Its previous name was the Central Party Archive and Marx-Engels-Lenin Institute. It is now named the Russian State Archives of Socio-Political History (RGASPI). Its director during the Hoover project was Kyrill M. Anderson. Vladimir P. Kozlov served as director of RTsKhIDNI for a brief period between August 1991 and March 1992, when he was appointed vice chairman of Rosarkhiv.

12. For instances of destruction of records, see Mark Kramer, "Archival Research in Moscow: Progress and Pitfalls," Cold War International History Project *Bulletin* 3 (Fall 1993): 1, 18–39; see especially 19–20.

13. Bertram D. Wolfe, *A Life in Two Centuries: An Autobiography* (New York: Stein and Day, 1981), 321.

14. Charles Chadwyck-Healey, Notes on Discussion with the Committee, Moscow, February 24–25, 1992.

15. Charles Chadwyck-Healey, *Publishing for Libraries at the Dawn of the Digital Age* (London: Bloomsbury Academic, 2020), 280. Before 1991, the name of the State Archive of the Russian Federation (GARF) was the Central State Archives of the October Revolution and RSFSR. It is located at Bol'shaia Pirogovskaia, 17, Moscow. Its director during the Hoover project was Sergei V. Mironenko.

16. Mironenko's mother-in-law, Sarra Vladimrovna, was the former director of the Manuscript Division of the Lenin Library.

17. Bertrand M. Patenaude, *Defining Moments: The First One Hundred Years of the Hoover Institution* (Stanford, CA: Hoover Institution Press, 2019), 106; Edward Lazear, ed., *Economic Transition in Eastern Europe and Russia: Realities of Reform* (Stanford, CA: Hoover Institution Press, 1995).

18. Rudolf G. Pikhoia, "The State Archival Service of Russia and the Hoover Institution on War, Revolution and Peace: Perspectives for Cooperation," Washington, DC, February 5, 1992, CPHIR.

19. Palm, notes for meeting of the Executive Committee, Board of Overseers, Washington, DC, February 4, 1992, CPHIR.

20. Vladimir Bukovsky, *Judgment in Moscow: Soviet Crimes and Western Complicity* (Westlake Village, CA: Ninth of November Press, 2019), 74–75.

21. Draft letter, Palm to DeMuth, December 11, 1991, CPHIR. This unsent letter was the basis for my telephone conversation with DeMuth on December 12. Palm, notes of conversation with DeMuth, December 12, 1991, CPHIR.

22. Solzhenitsyn to Raisian, April 30, 1992, CPHIR; Raisian to Solzhenitsyn, May 19, 1992, CPHIR; Raisian to Bukovsky, May 22, 1992, CPHIR.

23. The agreement and attached budget were approved by both Stanford University's Office of the General Counsel and by the University Controller. The Controller's approval authorized expenditures in the amounts and purposes indicated in the agreement and attachments. Subsequently, Hoover project expenditures, as did all Hoover Institution expenditures, went through the Controller's Office. Within Hoover, the agreement and budget were reviewed by Associate Director Richard Sousa, who oversaw Hoover's finances and budget, and approved by Director John Raisian.

24. Michael Binyon, "Stalin's Secret Archives to Be Published," *London Times*, January 22, 1992; William E. Schmidt, "Lenin to Stalin to Gorbachev! Read All About Them Here!" *New York Times*, January 22, 1992. For more on Chadwyck-Healey Ltd., see Charles Chadwyck-Healey, *Publishing for Libraries: At the Dawn of the Digital Age* (London: Bloomsbury Academic, 2020). See also *Leaders of the Russian Revolution* (Cambridge: Chadwyck-Healey Ltd., n.d.). This printed brochure announced a microfilm publication of an estimated 355 reels of materials at RTsKhIDNI, including papers of nine Communist Party leaders: Pavel B. Axelrod, Mikhail Kalinin, Sergei Kirov, Julius Martov, Viacheslav Molotov, Grigori K. Ordzhonikidze, Lev D. Trotsky, Vera I. Zasulich, and Andrei A. Zhdanov.

25. Chadwyck-Healey, notes on discussions with the committee in Moscow, Monday, February 24, and Tuesday, February 25, 1992, CPHIR; Chadwyck-Healey, *Publishing for Libraries*, 275–78.

26. "Filming and Publishing Agreement," February 21, 1992, CPHIR.

27. "Statement of Intention," February 25, 1992, CPHIR.

28. In an article published in 2003, Vladimir P. Kozlov, Pikhoia's deputy and an early opponent of the Hoover project, stated that it was he who suggested that Hoover provide Rosarkhiv with microfilm of Hoover's Russian collections. If he made this suggestion, it was never made in my presence. When I made the offer to Pikhoia at the February 1992 meeting, Pikhoia gave no indication that he or any of his deputies had contemplated such an offer. After I made the offer, Kozlov claimed rather sourly that some of the documents in Hoover's collection—namely, the Paris and Washington, DC, embassies and Okhrana records—were "stolen" and

were the property of the Russian government. See Kozlov, "Problems of Archival Access and Use," *Novaia I Noveishaia Istoria,* no. 6 (2003): 88. For Kozlov's comment on "stolen" records, see Chadwyck-Healey, *Publishing for Libraries,* 281.

29. "News on Opening Up CPSU Archives," *RFE/RL Daily Report,* February 11, 1992; "Depth of Soviet Repression Comes to Surface at Archives," *Washington Times,* July 15, 1992; Judith Fortson, "Access to History: Microfilming the Archives of the Communist Party," *Conservation Administration News,* January 1995: 1.

30. "Agreement on Collaboration in the Areas of Exchange of Archival Information and Microfilms, and of the Organization of Microfilming," signed by Pikhoia, Palm, and Chadwyck-Healey, April 17, 1992, CPHIR.

31. "Annex to Agreement Dated 17 April 1992 on Collaboration in the Areas of Exchange of Archival Information and Microfilms, and of the Organization of Microfilming," signed by Pikhoia and Palm, July 20, 1992, CPHIR. Chadwyck-Healey signed the annex on July 23, 1992.

32. "Second Annex to Agreement Dated 17 April 1992 on Collaboration in the Areas of Exchange of Archival Information and Microfilms, and of the Organization of Microfilming," signed by Pikhoia, August 18, 1993, CPHIR. Palm signed on July 23, 1993, and Chadwyck-Healey on October 25, 1993.

33. "Third Annex to Agreement of April 17, 1992, on Cooperation in the Exchange of Archival Information, Microcopies, and Microfilming," signed by Pikhoia, Palm, and Chadwyck-Healey, June 9, 1995, CPHIR.

34. Patricia Kennedy Grimsted, *Archives of Russia Five Years After: 'Purveyors of Sensations' or 'Shadows Cast to the Past'?* (Amsterdam: International Institute of Social History, 1997), 14.

35. Chadwyck-Healey, Notes on Discussion with the Committee, Moscow, February 24–25, 1992.

36. See Wilson Center, https://www.wilsoncenter.org/.

37. The Thomson Corporation is now Thomson Reuters Corporation. Research Publications International is now Primary Source Media, a part of the Gale Group, a subsidiary of the Thomson Reuters Corporation.

38. Palm, notes for International Committee of Scholarly Advisers Meeting, December 2, 1991, CPHIR; Palm, memorandum of conversation, February 21, 1992, CPHIR; Palm, memorandum of conversation, February 28, 1992, CPHIR; Palm, memorandum of conversation, March 4, 1992, CPHIR.

39. "Protocol between Research Publications International and the Committee on Archival Affairs of the RSFSR Council of Ministers and the Library of Congress," February 4, 1992, CPHIR. The first paragraph of this document stated the following: "On February 4, 1992, a meeting was held among representatives of the Committee on Archival Affairs of the RSFSR Council of Ministers ('Committee'), the Library of Congress on its own behalf and on behalf of the

International Committee of Scholarly Advisers ('LC'), and Research Publications International ('RPI')." The document was signed by James H. Billington and dated February 21, 1992.

40. Palm, memorandum of conversation, February 21, 1992, CPHIR.

41. Palm, memorandum of conversation, February 28, 1992, CPHIR.

42. The so-called seven sisters consisted of the following: (1) the mechanisms of power in the USSR; (2) the end of the NEP (New Economic Policy) and the emergence of the Stalinist system; (3) demography of Russia in the twentieth century; (4) religion in the USSR; (5) the administration of the Soviets, particularly as relates to industry, agriculture, and trade unions; (6) public expectations and state response; and (7) international activity of the USSR.

43. Palm, memorandum of conversation, March 4, 1992, CPHIR.

44. "Joint Release from Committee on Archival Affairs Attached to the Government of the Russian Federation, Moscow, and the Hoover Institution on War, Revolution and Peace, Stanford University: Major Archival Program Announced by Hoover Institution and Roskomarkhiv," March 10, 1992, CPHIR.

45. Palm to Billington, March 9, 1992, CPHIR.

46. Irvin Molotsky, "Russians Get US Help on Baring Soviet Files," *New York Times*, March 11, 1992.

47. *Archives of the Soviet Communist Party and Soviet State, A Joint Publication on Microfilm of the State Archival Service of Russia and the Hoover Institution on War, Revolution and Peace* (Cambridge: Chadwyck-Healey, 1995), xv.

48. "Instrument of Gift," signed by Pikhoia, Billington, and Palm, September 9, 1995, CPHIR; Judith Fortson to Irene Steckler, April 17, 1996, CPHIR; "The Hoover Institution and the Russian State Archives Deposit Microfilms of Soviet Communist Party Archives at the Library of Congress," Library of Congress Public Affairs Office, July 5, 1996, CPHIR.

49. Billington to Palm, November 4, 1996, CPHIR.

50. Pikhoia briefed me on his dealings with RPI when we met in Washington in June 1992. See also Pikhoia, deposition, September 24, 1992, CPHIR.

51. Palm to Pikhoia, June 5, 1992, CPHIR; Palm, memorandum of conversation, June 29, 1992, CPHIR. I do not know the extent to which Meg Bellinger was involved with RPI's Russian initiative. I believe it was led by others. She left RPI in 1993 and had a long and distinguished career at the Online Computer Library Center Inc. and at Yale University.

Chapter 2

1. Russian Archives Project Account, March 31, 1999, CPHIR.

2. Stephen Langlois to Elena Danielson, September 26, 2002, CPHIR; Steven Hall to Danielson, May 10, 2004, EDHIR.

3. Statement of Herbert Hoover on the purpose of the Hoover Institution, Stanford University Board of Trustees, minutes, May 21, 1959, Stanford University Archives.

4. Minutes of Editorial Board meetings were prepared variously by Jana Howlett, Terence Emmons, and Palm, as follows: June 14, 1992 (Howlett); September 17–18, 1992 (Howlett and Emmons); January 28–29, 1993 (Howlett and Palm); and February 3, 1994 (Howlett and Palm), CPHIR. See appendix C for a list of all record groups (*fondy*) and record series (*opisi*) that were filmed by the project and that comprise the microfilm collection.

5. The page counts referenced in the following pages are based on an estimate of 850 frames per reel.

6. Some records were transferred. A batch of Stalin's papers was transferred from APRF to RGASPI in 1998–99. See Stephen Kotkin, *Stalin: Waiting for Hitler, 1929–1941* (New York: Penguin Press, 2017), xvi.

7. The finding aids for all three repositories are now available in digital form on the websites of the three repositories: http://рграни.рф/, http://rgaspi.org, and https://statearchive.ru (all sites accessed March 15, 2023).

8. The records of the First Congress in 1898 do not exist. The records of the Twentieth Congress (1956), Twenty-First Congress (1959), and Twenty-Second Congress (1961) were not filmed before the 1992 agreement ended.

9. My two paragraphs on the Central Committee draw on Mark Kramer's work: Mark Kramer, "Declassified Materials from CPSU Central Committee Plenums," *Cahiers du Monde russe* 40, nos. 1–2 (January–June 1999): 271–306.

10. Cheka was the common name for the All-Russian Extraordinary Commission, or AREOC. The other abbreviations translate as follows: GPU = State Political Directorate; OGPU = Unified State Political Directorate; and NKVD = People's Commissariat of Internal Affairs. See Wikipedia, s.v. "NKVD," last modified January 10, 2024, 09:38, https://en.wikipedia.org/wiki/NKVD.

11. In Russian archival practice, *opisi* has two different meanings: one means record series and the second means finding aids. The context informs the reader which meaning applies.

12. Especially noteworthy studies that validated our approach are Paul R. Gregory, *The Political Economy of Stalinism, Evidence from the Soviet Secret Archives* (Cambridge: Cambridge University Press, 2004), which won the 2004 Hewett Book Prize; Anne Applebaum, *Gulag: A History* (New York: Doubleday, 2003), which won the Pulitzer Prize in 2004; Paul R. Gregory, ed., *Behind the Façade of Stalin's Command Economy: Evidence from the Soviet State and Party Archives* (Stanford, CA: Hoover Institution Press, 2001); and Paul R. Gregory, *Lenin's Brain and Other Tales from the Secret Soviet Archives* (Stanford, CA: Hoover Institution Press, 2008).

13. See Merle Fainsod, *How Russia Is Ruled* (Cambridge, MA: Harvard University Press, 1953, revised 1963). See also Jerry F. Hough and Merle Fainsod, *How the*

Soviet Union Is Governed (Cambridge, MA: Harvard University Press, 1979). Two book reviews on Fainsod's place in Russian historiography are one on Fainsod's 1963 revision by Robert Legvold in *Foreign Affairs*, September–October 1997: 229–30, and a second on Hough's revision by Richard Pipes in *Commentary*, October 1979: 86–88.

14. The Constitutional Court upheld Yeltsin's decrees but permitted individual Communists to form a new party. See Timothy J. Colton, *Yeltsin: A Life* (New York: Basic Books, 2008), 251.

15. Grimsted, *Archives of Russia*, 166.

16. Arnold Beichman, "Moscow's Secret Gold," *Hoover Digest*, no. 1, 1996: 103–6; Gordon M. Hahn, "Fond 89 and the Fall of the Soviet Union," *Hoover Digest*, no. 1, 1998: 140–44; Gordon M. Hahn, "The Unknown Opposition to Soviet Rule," *Hoover Digest*, no. 2, 1998: 183–88; and Gordon M. Hahn, "Documents from the Terror," *Hoover Digest*, no. 3, 1998: 140–45. See also the facsimiles in the photo section.

17. In 1994, RTsKhIDNI concluded an agreement with Inter Documentation Company to publish microfilm of the records of seven Comintern congresses and thirteen plenums, 1919–35, as well as the finding aids to the Comintern archives. The US Communist Party records, also at RTsKhIDNI, were microfilmed by the Library of Congress.

18. Bukovsky, *Judgment*, 78.

19. For discussion of the Russian laws on government records, see Grimsted, *Archives of Russia*, 19–25.

20. Grimsted, 168. See also Kramer, "Archival Research in Moscow," 28–31.

21. Lora Soroka, *Fond 89: Communist Party of the Soviet Union on Trial: Archives of the Communist Party and Soviet State: Guide to the Microfilm Collection in the Hoover Institution Archives* (Stanford, CA: Hoover Institution Press, 2001).

22. When Everitt retired in 1994, Hall was appointed managing director. When the Chadwyck-Healey publishing companies were sold to Bell & Howell Information and Learning in 1999, Hall was appointed senior vice president and general manager and remained senior vice president after Bell & Howell changed its name to ProQuest Information and Learning.

23. Chadwyck-Healey to Palm, January 26, 1995, CPHIR.

24. Fortson, "Access to History," 2.

25. Chadwyck-Healey to Palm, May 19, 1993, CPHIR.

26. Hall to Palm, November 3, 1995, CPHIR.

27. Fortson, "Access to History," 3.

28. Palm, memorandum of conversation, August 12, 1992, CPHIR; Alastair Everitt, report, January 28, 1993, CPHIR; Inga Huld Markan to Palm, March 11, 1993, CPHIR; V. I. Abramov, statement, April 12, 1993, CPHIR; V. P. Tarasov to Palm, December 6, 1994, CPHIR.

29. Fortson, "Access to History," 1–4.

30. Fortson, 2.

31. Minutes, Editorial Board meeting, Cambridge, January 28–29, 1993, CPHIR; Palm to Pikhoia, April 12, 1993, CPHIR; Howlett to Palm, June 26, 1993, CPHIR; Palm, notes of meeting with Rudolf G. Pikhoia, Moscow, September 26–29, 1994, CPHIR; "Rosarkhiv/Hoover Project, Payment Obligations to Rosarkhiv," June 12, 1997, CPHIR; "Additional Contract to the Agreement on Scholarly Collaboration between the State Archives of the Russian Federation and the Hoover Institution," June 11, 1998, CPHIR; "Russian Archives Special Project Account," December 31, 2001, CPHIR.

32. Howlett to Palm, June 26, 1993, CPHIR; Howlett to Palm, September 19, 1993, CPHIR.

33. Howlett to Palm, September 19, 1993, CPHIR; Rosarkhiv report on results of Rosarkhiv, Hoover Institution, and Chadwyck-Healey Project, February 3, 1994, CPHIR; Pikhoia to Palm, May 13, 1994, CPHIR.

34. Alastair Everitt, general report, January 1, 1993, CPHIR; Howlett to Palm, January 6, 1993, CPHIR; Howlett, report, January 22, 1993, CPHIR; Howlett to Palm, January 22, 1993, CPHIR; Howlett to Palm, June 26, 1993, CPHIR; Judith Fortson, report, July 7, 1993, CPHIR; Fortson, "Access to History," 2.

35. Judith Fortson to Palm, September 21, 1995, CPHIR; Palm to Howlett, November 27, 1996, CPHIR; Chadwyck-Healey to Sergei V. Mironenko, January 10, 1997, CPHIR; Chadwyck-Healey to Palm, April 14, 1997, CPHIR; Palm to Chadwyck-Healey, April 14, 1997, CPHIR; Palm to Mironenko, April 14, 1997, CPHIR; Markan to Mironenko, May 16, 1997, CPHIR; Mironenko to Palm, May 16, 1997, CPHIR; Markan to Fortson, May 20, 1997, CPHIR.

36. Chadwyck-Healey to Palm, November 4, 1992, CPHIR; Howlett to Palm, January 22, 1993, CPHIR; Palm to Howlett, May 10, 1993, CPHIR; Howlett to Palm, June 26, 1993, CPHIR; Fortson, memorandum of conversation with Jana Howlett, August 10, 1993, CPHIR; Palm, notes on meeting with Rudolf G. Pikhoia, Moscow, September 26–29, 1994, CPHIR; Fortson, report on meeting with Pikhoia, November 16–18, 1994, CPHIR; Howlett to Palm, January 23, 1995, CPHIR; Howlett to Pikhoia, January 29, 1995, CPHIR; Pikhoia to Palm, February 14, 1995, CPHIR; Palm, minutes of project directors' meeting, Cambridge, June 8–9, 1995, CPHIR; Howlett to Pikhoia, August 18, 1995, CPHIR; Howlett to Pikhoia, October 20, 1995, CPHIR.

37. Palm to Howlett, May 10, 1993, CPHIR; Alastair Everitt to Fortson, May 11, 1993, CPHIR; Palm to Chadwyck-Healey, May 13, 1993, CPHIR; Fortson, report on meeting with Pikhoia, Moscow, November 16–18, 1994, CPHIR.

38. Howlett, report, May 13, 1993, CPHIR; Howlett to Palm, June 26, 1993, CPHIR; Howlett to Palm, June 6, 1994, CPHIR; Palm, minutes of project directors'

meeting, Moscow, October 3, 1994, CPHIR; Fortson, report on meeting with Pikhoia, Moscow, November 16–18, 1994, CPHIR; Chadwyck-Healey, *Publishing for Libraries*, 293.

39. Howlett to Palm, June 26, 1993, CPHIR.

40. Fortson to Palm, March 22, 1993, CPHIR; Palm to Chadwyck-Healey, April 2, 1993, CPHIR; Pikhoia to Palm, April 22, 1993, CPHIR.

41. Howlett to Palm, January 22, 1993, CPHIR; Fortson, "Access to History," 3.

42. Howlett to Palm, June 26, 1993, CPHIR; Palm, notes on meeting with Pikhoia, Moscow, September 26–29, 1994, CPHIR; Kramer, "Archival Research in Moscow," 28–31.

43. Fortson, report on meeting with Pikhoia, Moscow, November 16–18, 1994, CPHIR.

44. Colton, *Yeltsin*, 282, 349; "Communist Comeback," *New York Times*, December 19, 1995; Michael McFaul, *Russia's Unfinished Revolution: Political Change from Gorbachev to Putin* (Ithaca, NY: Cornell University Press, 2001), 286.

Chapter 3

1. Colton, *Yeltsin*, 291, 312, 315, 351, 397.

2. Howlett to Palm, September 13, 1995, CPHIR; Palm to Howlett, December 12, 1995, CPHIR; Pikhoia to Palm and Chadwyck-Healey, December 28, 1995, CPHIR.

3. Paragraph 23 in its entirety stated the following: "Force Majeure. The parties shall not be liable for delay in performance under this Agreement when solely resulting from acts of God, wars, revolutions, civil disturbances, strikes, floods, fire, perils of the sea or other interruption of transportation, or any decisions of the highest organs of power in Russia, the United States or the United Kingdom, which would make it impossible to carry out this Agreement. Notice to this effect ('Notice of Force Majeure') shall be given in writing or by facsimile confirmed in writing at once to the other parties. The existence of such causes of delay shall justify the suspension of performance for a period equal to the period of delay attributable to the event of force majeure."

4. "Law on the Archival Fond of the Russian Federation and Archives," signed into law, July 7, 1993, promulgated on August 14, 1993. This law replaced earlier decrees of June 24, 1992, September 30, 1992, and December 22, 1992. It reaffirmed the right of Rosarkhiv to conclude agreements for commercial use and publication of archival holdings and set restrictions protecting national security classified documents and privacy of individuals.

5. Paragraph 6(c) in its entirety stated the following: "Either Roskomarkhiv or Hoover may elect to terminate this Agreement upon six months' written notice

to the other parties. Chadwyck-Healey may elect to withdraw from the Agreement upon six months' written notice to the other parties."

6. Howlett to Palm, January 4, 1996, CPHIR.

7. Palm, minutes of project directors' meeting, Moscow, January 11–12, 1996, CPHIR; V. N. Kovalev, "Minutes of Negotiations between Rosarkhiv, Hoover Institution, and Chadwyck-Healey on the Termination of the April 17, 1992 Agreement," January 19, 1996, CPHIR.

8. Robert Shanks to Palm, January 9, 1996, CPHIR.

9. "Memorandum of Mutual Understanding," January 12, 1996, CPHIR; Vladimir P. Kozlov, "Draft Agreement" (not accepted), January 12, 1996, CPHIR.

10. Howlett to Palm, January 4, 1996, CPHIR. On the effect of the election on the Yeltsin insiders, see McFaul, *Russia's Unfinished Revolution*, 287–88. Robert W. Davies attributes the termination of the Hoover agreement to "the increasing general hostility to 'Western interference' in internal Russian affairs." See Davies, *Yeltsin Era*, 102.

11. Grimsted, *Archives of Russia*, 14–15, 110.

12. Ella Maksimova, "How Much Is Our History Worth?" *Izvestiia*, January 17, 1996; Charles Hecker, "Hoover Deal for Archives in Jeopardy," *Moscow Times*, January 25, 1996; Grimsted, *Archives of Russia*, 110.

13. Hecker, "Hoover Deal for Archives in Jeopardy."

14. Grimsted, *Archives of Russia*, 14.

15. Grimsted, 102. Grimsted was coeditor with Vladimir Kozlov of ArcheoBiblioBase, an online Russian archival directory database.

16. Grimsted, 16–18.

17. Pikhoia to Palm, January 18, 1996, CPHIR; Colton, *Yeltsin*, 249. Robert W. Davies summed up the achievement of these years: "The story of the archives is a success story. Improvements before August 1991 were transformed into a revolution thereafter." See Davies, *Yeltsin Era*, 95.

18. Vladimir A. Tiuneev to Palm, February 23, 1996, CPHIR; Howlett to Palm and Chadwyck-Healey, June 11, 1996, CPHIR; Tiuneev to Palm, July 16, 1996, CPHIR.

19. Report from Chadwyck-Healey Ltd., March 1, 1996, CPHIR; Fortson to Palm, January 22, 1996, CPHIR; Palm, report to donors, April 1, 1996, CPHIR; Tiuneev to Palm, July 16, 1996, CPHIR.

20. Palm, minutes of project directors' meeting, Stanford University, April 10, 1996, CPHIR; "Agreement on Co-operation between the Federal Archival Service of Russia, the Hoover Institution on War, Revolution and Peace, and Chadwyck-Healey Ltd., Great Britain," signed by Tiuneev, Palm, and Chadwyck-Healey, October 10, 1996, CPHIR.

21. Tiuneev to Palm, July 16, 1996, CPHIR; Palm to Tiuneev, September 19, 1996, CPHIR; Palm, minutes of project directors' meeting, Cambridge, October 9–10, 1996, CPHIR; Palm to Mironenko, December 16, 1996, CPHIR.

22. Colton, *Yeltsin*, 372.

23. Amy Knight, "Russian Archives: Opportunities and Obstacles," *International Journal of Intelligence and Counterintelligence* 12, no. 3 (Fall 1999): 331–32.

24. Chadwyck-Healey report, January 17, 2000.

25. Chadwyck-Healey to Palm, December 19, 1996, CPHIR.

26. Fortson to Palm, October 4, 1996, CPHIR; Palm to Chadwyck-Healey, December 19, 1996, CPHIR; Chadwyck-Healey to Mironenko, January 10, 1997, CPHIR; Chadwyck-Healey to Mironenko, February 3, 1997, CPHIR; Palm to Mironenko, April 14, 1997, CPHIR; Mironenko to Palm, May 16, 1997, CPHIR; Markan to Mironenko, May 16, 1997, CPHIR; Chadwyck-Healey to Palm, August 14, 1997, CPHIR; Chadwyck-Healey to Palm, December 2, 1997, CPHIR; Gordon Hahn, notes on meeting with Sergei Mironenko, March 26, 1998, CPHIR.

27. Hahn, notes on meeting with Sergei Mironenko.

28. Colton, *Yeltsin*, 411–19.

29. Applebaum, *Gulag*, xvi–xvii, xxix, 580–84.

30. "Agreement on Scholarly Collaboration between the State Archives of the Russian Federation and the Hoover Institution on War, Revolution and Peace," signed by Mironenko, Palm, and Chadwyck-Healey, June 11, 1998, CPHIR.

31. "Letter of Understanding Amending Agreement of 11 June 1998 between the State Archives of the Russian Federation, the Hoover Institution on War, Revolution and Peace, and Chadwyck-Healey Ltd.," signed by Mironenko, Palm, and Chadwyck-Healey, June 11, 1998, CPHIR; "Annex to the Agreement of Scholarly Collaboration between the State Archives of the Russian Federation and the Hoover Institution on War, Revolution and Peace," signed by Mironenko, Palm, and Hall, October 3, 1998, CPHIR.

32. Mironenko to Palm, May 25, 1998, CPHIR; Palm, trip report, June 8–12, 1998, CPHIR; Chadwyck-Healey to Palm, March 19, 1999, CPHIR.

33. "Russian Federation Law on Participation in International Exchange Information," passed on June 5, 1996, and signed by President Boris Yeltsin on July 9, 1996; Howlett, report, August 24, 1996, CPHIR.

34. Palm, memorandum of conversation with Jonathan Brent, July 8, 1997, CPHIR; Oleg V. Khlevniuk, *The History of the Gulag: From Collectivization to the Great Terror* (New Haven, CT: Yale University Press, 2004).

35. T. V. Tsarevskaya, "Protocol, A Meeting of the Editorial Council for the Documentary Publication, 'History of the Gulag,' in Six Volumes," Moscow, December 29, 1998, CPHIR; Hahn, notes on January 27, 1998, meeting of Russian

Archives Group of Advisers, January 29, 1999, CPHIR; Palm to Robert Conquest et al., August 16, 2000, CPHIR; Emmons to Palm, December 12, 2020, and January 1, 2021.

36. Vladimir A. Kozlov to Lois Christopherson, August 31, 1998, CPHIR. (Note: Two persons named Vladimir Kozlov figure in this story. The Kozlov referenced in this endnote was a deputy to Sergei V. Mironenko at GARF, where among other duties he assisted Mironenko in directing the seven-volume Gulag documentary publication. The Kozlov referenced elsewhere in this memoir—Vladimir P. Kozlov—was Pikhoia's deputy and later chairman of Rosarkhiv.) Chadwyck-Healey to Palm, September 25, 1998, CPHIR; Howlett to Alison Maynard, January 12, 1999, CPHIR; Howlett to Maynard, January 12, 2000, CPHIR; Palm to Mironenko, February 23, 2000, CPHIR; Palm to Mironenko, April 12, 2000, CPHIR.

37. Palm to Mironenko, August 5, 1999, CPHIR; Mironenko to Palm, July 23, 2000, CPHIR; Hall to Howlett, April 4, 2001, CPHIR.

38. *The History of the Gulag, 1918–1953* (Moscow: Russian Political Encyclopedia Publishing House, 2004 and 2005), 7 vols., including the following: vol. 1: *Mass Repressions in the USSR, 1930 to the Beginning of the 1950s,* edited by S. N. Mironenko and N. Werth; vol. 2: *The Penal System, Structure and Personnel, 1918–1954,* edited by N. V. Petrov; vol. 3: *The Economics of the Gulag, 1930s–1950s,* edited by Oleg V. Khlevniuk; vol. 4: *Gulag Population, Structure, Numbers, and Living Conditions, 1930–1950s,* edited by A. B. Bezborodov and V. M. Khrustalev; vol. 5: *Special Deportees in the USSR, 1930–1954,* edited by Tsarevskaya-Diakina; vol. 6: *Prison Uprising, Riots, and Strikes,* edited by Vladimir A. Kozlov; vol. 7: *The History of Soviet Repressive-Punitive Policy and Penal System in the Holdings of the State Archives of the Russian Federation, Annotated Guide to the Files,* edited by Vladimir A. Kozlov and S. V. Mironenko.

39. On December 28, 2021, the Supreme Court of Russia closed the Memorial Society and its branches. It was liquidated on April 5, 2022.

Chapter 4

1. Ella Maksimova, "Archival Piracy," *Izvestiia,* February 22, 1992; Roy Medvedev, "Goats in the Garden," *Levaya Gazeta,* April 9, 1993; Ella Maksimova, "How Much Is Our History Worth?" *Izvestiia,* January 17, 1996.

2. *Den',* no. 14, April 11–17, 1993. English translation cited in Grimsted, *Archives of Russia,* 108.

3. Yuri Afanasiev, "Arbitrariness in the Treatment of Our Collective Memory Is Impermissible," *Izvestiia,* March 9, 1992; Yuri Afanasiev, "Archival 'Berezka,'" *Komsomolskaya Pravda,* May 23, 1992; Yuri Afanasiev, "The 'Deal of the Century'

on Documents?" *Frankfurter Allgemeine Zeitung,* March 13, 1992; Rudolf G. Pikhoia, "Fakty: vymysly o 'Rasprodazhe istoricheskoi pamiati,'" *Rossiiske vesti,* June 19, 1992; Irina Karpenko, "Vokrug arkhivov idet bessovestnaia torgovlia, schitaet predsedatel' Komiteta po delam arkhivov pri Pravitel'stve Rossiiskoi Federatsii Rudolf Pikhoia," *Rossiiske vesti,* June 19, 1992.

4. Robert Conquest, "The Archival Bonanza," *AAASS Newsletter* 32, no. 3 (May 1992): 1–2; Terence Emmons, "I Don't Understand You, Gentlemen," *Moscow News,* August 16, 1992; Davies, *Yeltsin Era,* 101–2.

5. J. Arch Getty, "Russian Archives: Is the Door Half Open or Half Closed?" *Perspectives,* May/June 1996: 19–23; Charles Palm, "Hoover Institution Takes Issue with Getty Interpretation of Russian Archive Situation," *Perspectives,* December 1996: 33–34.

6. Grimsted, *Archives of Russia,* 107.

7. Chadwyck-Healey to Palm, April 15, 1999, CPHIR.

8. List of collections sent to the Russian archives, September 2002, EDHIR; Mironenko to Danielson, July 15, 2003, EDHIR.

9. Dale Reed to Anne Van Camp, May 12, 1995, CPHIR.

10. Palm, report to donors, April 1, 1996, CPHIR; Don McCrae to Mironenko, October 10, 1997, CPHIR; Chadwyck-Healey to Robert Brent Toplin [editor of *Perspectives*], November 11, 1996, CPHIR; Rosarkhiv/Hoover Project, payment obligations to Rosarkhiv, June 12, 1997, CPHIR. For the false statements of Anderson and others, see Grimsted, *Archives of Russia,* 110.

11. Russian Archives Special Project Account, December 21, 2001, CPHIR; Hall to Danielson, May 10, 2004, EDHIR. For the average monthly salaries, see State Commission of the Russian Federation on Statistics, Russian Statistical Yearbook (Moscow: 1997), 146–47. See the Russian Central Bank website for the June 1996 exchange rates.

12. "Memorandum of Mutual Understanding," January 12, 1996, CPHIR.

13. See also J. Arch Getty, "Commercialization of Scholarship: Do We Need a Code of Behavior," *Slavic Review* (Spring 1993): 101–4).

14. "Final Report of the Joint Task Force on Archives American Association for the Advancement of Slavic Studies and The American Historical Association 1 April 1995," *Slavic Review* 54, no. 2 (Summer 1995): 407–26. Members of the task force were Norman Naimark (AAASS coordinator), William G. Rosenberg (AHA coordinator), William Taubman, Kathryn Weathersby, Donald J. Raleigh, Gregory Freeze, and David Ransel.

15. Stephen Kotkin, *Armageddon Averted: The Soviet Collapse, 1970–2000* (Oxford: Oxford University Press, 2008), 124, 128.

16. "Final Report of the Joint Task Force on Archives," 419.

17. Michael McFaul is the Peter and Helen Bing Senior Fellow at the Hoover Institution as well as the Ken Olivier and Angela Nomellini Professor of

International Studies, director and senior fellow at the Freeman Spogli Institute for International Studies, and a senior fellow at the Woods Institute at Stanford University. In 2012–14, he was the US ambassador to the Russian Federation. The oral histories McFaul collected were source material for his book *The Troubled Birth of Russian Democracy: Parties, Personalities, and Programs* (Stanford, CA: Hoover Institution Press, 1993).

18. Robert Conquest et al. to Pikhoia, December 15, 1995, CPHIR.

Chapter 5

1. Chadwyck-Healey, *Publishing for Libraries*, 40, 340.
2. Hall to Palm, October 5, 2001, CPHIR.
3. Hall to Kozlov, July 10, 2001, CPHIR; Hall to Kozlov, September 5, 2001, CPHIR; Hall to Palm, October 3, 2001, CPHIR.
4. Kozlov to Palm and Hall, August 22, 2001, CPHIR. Hall declared the microfilming project at an end in his email to Danielson, May 10, 2004, EDHIR.
5. Palm to Danielson, December 31, 2001, CPHIR.
6. Martin Sieff, "Soviet Repression Comes to Surface at Archives," *Washington Times*, July 15, 1992.
7. "Hoover Institution Archives Use Statistics, 1997–2018," Hoover Institution Archives.
8. Fortson, RAPP costs breakdown, March 28, 1994, CPHIR; ProQuest report, "Sale of Soviet Archive reels," September 2002, EDHIR; "Summary of Sales and Royalties," May 10, 2004, EDHIR.
9. See Kozlov's statement in *Deloproizvodstvo*, 2012, no. 1. See also Vladimir P. Kozlov, "Problemy dostupa v arkhvi i ikh ispol'zovaniia" [Problems of archival access and use], *Novaia i noveishais istoria* (December 2003), an account at variance with my account in almost every respect.

Appendix A: Red Archives, by Charles Chadwyck-Healey

1. When produced over the next few years, some of the nine archives were on microfiche and the others were on microfilm.
2. William E. Schmidt, "Files to Be Opened, from Lenin to Gorbachev," *New York Times*, January 22, 1992.
3. Natalya Davydova, "Bumazhnoe zoloto partii," *Moskovsii novosti*, no. 8 (February 23, 1992); *Moscow News*, no. 19 (1992).
4. *Izvestiia*, March 10, 1992.
5. *Izvestiia*, March 17, 1992, and April 30, 1992.
6. *Izvestiia*, June 26, 1992.
7. *Financial Times*, January 22, 1992, but widely quoted elsewhere, including *Library Journal*, March 1, 1992; *Wall Street Journal*, July 7, 1992, in a front-page

article, "Information Flow Is Freer in Russia, But It Is Not Free," commenting on Afanasiev's criticism.

8. David Hearst, "A Heritage in Hock to Keep the Lights On," Moscow Diary, *The Guardian*, July 27, 1992.

9. Letter from Professor Terence Emmons to Charles Chadwyck-Healey, May 26, 1993.

10. *Sunday Telegraph*, February 4, 1996.

11. *The Economist*, March 2, 1996.

12. *The History of the Gulag, 1918–1953* (Moscow: Russian Political Encyclopedia Publishing House, 2004 and 2005), 7 volumes.

13. Letter from Palm to Mironenko, December 9, 1997.

14. The UK tax authority, the Inland Revenue, was renamed Her Majesty's Revenue & Customs in 2005.

15. March 16, 1999.

16. VTsIK is the All-Russian Central Executive Committee, which was the highest legislative and administrative body from 1917 to 1937.

17. August 11, 2000.

18. *Boston Globe*, October 6, 1999.

19. Robert Harris, *Archangel* (London: Hutchinson, 1998).

ABOUT THE AUTHOR

Charles G. Palm is the deputy director emeritus of the Hoover Institution. Before retiring in 2002, he completed thirty-one years at Hoover, including eighteen years directing, variously, the Hoover Institution Library & Archives. His positions included deputy director of the Hoover Institution (1990–2002), associate director (1987–90), head librarian (1986–87), archivist (1984–87), deputy archivist (1974–84), and assistant archivist (1971–74).

In 1992 Palm negotiated an agreement with the State Archival Service of Russia (Rosarkhiv) to microfilm archives of the Soviet Communist Party and Soviet State. In addition to directing this project, he initiated and led a multifaceted program to document communism after the fall of the Berlin Wall. It included the acquisition of papers on communism and the transition to democracy in Eastern Europe, a project in collaboration with the Gorbachev Foundation to conduct oral histories with members of the Reagan and Gorbachev presidencies on the end of the Cold War, the publication with the International Democracy Foundation of documentary collections on Soviet history, and the acquisition of the archives of Radio Free Europe/Radio Liberty. His published works include *Milton Friedman on Freedom* (coeditor) and *Guide to the Hoover Institution Archives* (coeditor).

He was appointed by President George H. W. Bush to the National Historical Publications and Records Commission in 1990 and by Governor George Deukmejian to the California Heritage Preservation Commission in 1983, serving as chairman from 1997 to 2004. Palm is a fellow of the Society of American Archivists, past president of the Society of California Archivists, and a trustee of the Herbert Hoover Foundation.

INDEX